# ENGLISH ONE-ACT PLAYS
## OF TODAY

4
62

# ENGLISH
# ONE-ACT PLAYS
# OF TODAY

*Selected and Introduced*
*by*
DONALD FITZJOHN

*Published for the*
*English Association by the*
OXFORD UNIVERSITY PRESS
LONDON NEW YORK TORONTO
1962

*Oxford University Press, Amen House, London* E.C.4

GLASGOW  NEW YORK  TORONTO  MELBOURNE  WELLINGTON
BOMBAY  CALCUTTA  MADRAS  KARACHI  LAHORE  DACCA
CAPE TOWN  SALISBURY  NAIROBI  IBADAN  ACCRA
KUALA LUMPUR  HONG KONG

*Printed in Great Britain*

# INTRODUCTION

Between the wars the popularity of the one-act play in the professional theatre in England steadily declined, with the result that many established professional writers abandoned this most difficult form. On the other hand there was a steady growth in the number of amateur societies, and with it an increase in the number of amateur drama festivals and the number of new dramatists who wrote, and still write, more or less exclusively for this market. Even in the amateur little theatres a proposed double or triple bill was regarded with apprehension by finance committees and the phrase 'box office poison' was bandied around. There were of course exceptions to this. Noël Coward's *Tonight at 8.30* between the wars, and Terence Rattigan's *Playbill* in 1948, were successful exceptions, but these were firmly established authors whose names could draw the public. A season of verse plays under the direction of E. Martin Browne at the tiny Mercury Theatre in 1946 had given us, amongst others, Christopher Fry's *A Phoenix Too Frequent*, but on the whole serious writers tended to stick to the three-act form.

Today the situation has changed considerably; television has helped. Several writers, after their plays have been successfully televised, have brought out stage versions of them. These plays, owing to television time restrictions, are short enough to come into the category of the one-act play. Then too the progressive policy of certain theatres, such as the Royal Court, coupled with foreign influences, have stimulated young writers to try this form. The strongest of these foreign influences in the field of the one-act play is probably Ionesco, a Rumanian living in Paris, writing in French, whose one-act plays caught the public fancy. Much of our surrealist drama of non-communication and obsession has been directly influenced by Ionesco, and much of our present 'comedy of menace' springs from the same source. The writings of Brecht and Beckett have also had a great deal of influence. Today more and more gifted dramatists are writing short plays which look like becoming once more a form of theatre acceptable to the general public.

No anthology is without its regretted omissions, and this is no exception. In this volume are eight one-act plays of varying styles, but all have quality, and all are 'theatre' in the best sense of the word.

No producer, however brilliant, or student, however intelligent, can realize the potentials of a play by reading it. A play in script form is incomplete, because it is something that needs to be seen and heard in action—that action which a good dramatist implies in his dialogue. The plays contained in this volume all make absorbing reading, but it is in action that they should finally be judged.

*The Browning Version*, by Terence Rattigan, has already become a classic. It combines great skill of construction with a compassion which never lapses into sentimentality. Its theme is loneliness, a theme which Rattigan again used in the two plays which comprised *Separate Tables*. It calls for sincerity and sensitivity of playing. Attention should be paid to the dramatic development of the characters, and care taken in performance not to outpace the intentions of the author. This particularly applies to the character of Millie Crocker-Harris, the depth of whose unpleasantness is gradually revealed. She is not a stage villainess, but a physically passionate woman whose heart is dead. Her husband's physical coldness on the other hand, disguises, in spite of his words, a heart which has remained alive.

In Christopher Fry's *A Phoenix Too Frequent* we have a

successful example of that most difficult of all dramatic forms, a comedy in verse. The story of this delightfully witty, paradoxical play, based on the theme of life and death, 'was got from Jeremy Taylor who had it from Petronius'. It was also used by Dibden for his charming operetta *The Ephesian Matron*. The play is simple to stage, but by no means easy to act. It demands a sense of comedy and the ability to speak verse, but above all it demands an understanding of its style of comedy, and the ability to interpret that style. Often the comedy arises from the dramatic contrast between the fantastic situation, the fantastic lyrical verse, and the sudden delightful drops into colloquially expressed practicalities. It would be a mistake to think of the play only as a jeu d'esprit. What it has to say is summed up in Dynamene's penultimate speech which begins:

'How little you can understand. I love
His life not his death. And now we can give his death
The power of life. Not horrible: wonderful!'

Wolf Mankowitz has described his play, *The Bespoke Overcoat*, as 'a sustained, typically over-long Jewish joke—than which there is no sadder and no funnier story'. He also says it is a play about love. Fender, in spite of his poverty, would prefer to go on living. He accepts his life with humour and humility because he can share these with his friend. 'To prefer to go on living,' writes Mr. Mankowitz, 'is to love in the context of this story, and because this is loving at its most deprived the story is a sad one.' *The Bespoke Overcoat*, with its vivid characters and idiom, offers great opportunities to actors, and its unforced mixture of the comic and the sad has rarely been surpassed in our time. In the original production, sets were dispensed with, properties cut to a minimum, and darkness broken by constantly moving areas of light used to define the different locations. Some notes have been added to the text in this volume, to explain a few of the words.

A great many plays have been written about resistance movements during the last war. Many of these suffer from the excessive nobility of their protagonists and the exploitation of situation at the expense of character. The late Gordon Daviot, whose best known play is *Richard of Bordeaux*, certainly did not fall into these traps. She was a quiet dramatist, and it is the calmness of her central character that makes *The Pen of My Aunt* so effective. It is altogether a well characterized play, and its domestic setting and atmosphere throw into relief the life and death struggle that is going on. The play contains several dramatic surprises which spring naturally from character and situation, and help to make it effective theatre. The chief problem in the production and acting of this play is that of reaching its successive climaxes without letting them become overstressed and melodramatic.

J. B. Priestley's *Mother's Day* is in the tradition of English broad comedy. The unfailing theme of the underdog getting the upper hand is given a new and amusing twist. The dialogue is pungent, and as they speak it the characters come warmly to life. A production of the play should concentrate on the reality of its characters. The comedy should be kept in hand and never be overplayed to an extent when it becomes farce.

*Trifles* is the oldest play in this volume, but it is by no means dated. It is not simply a play of detection, in which the two women discover the missing motive for a murder and decide to suppress the evidence. That is the plot on the surface level only. Fundamentally it is a play about compassion; although this is never mentioned specifically. In fact one of the most interesting things about *Trifles* is the use made of implicit rather than explicit dialogue. By this means a vivid picture is created for the audience of the lives of two people who never appear. The significance of what is left unspoken must be realized in a production of this play. The atmosphere of desolation should be carefully created and it is interesting to note that two of the main climaxes of the play—the finding of the bird and the pocketing of the box—depend upon something seen rather than something spoken.

John Mortimer is one of the most interesting of the authors who have sprung suddenly into prominence during the last few years. In his world, fantasy and actuality are never far apart, and are certainly interchangeable. His characters in the main are what are known as 'failures'— humble misfits in a world which bewilders them, but against which they bear no grudge. *The Dock Brief* is a tour-de-force sustained by two characters, both of whom have only a tenuous grasp of reality, and who escape, willingly and together, into a world of fantasy, preserving always an off-beat integrity of their own, and a looney logic which is often wildly funny. John Mortimer's dialogue has a very definite pattern and style, which give a remarkable impression of snatches of conversation overheard in buses; in the street; in saloon bars. Apart from this, what helps to sustain the play is its dramatic progression. We know a great deal about these people when the curtain finally drops, and in a good production, we care what will happen to them.

One of the American writers who has made a great impact on audiences, and who has influenced contemporary writing, is undoubtedly Tennessee Williams. *Lord Byron's Love Letter* is an early play of his, which already contains some of those elements which distinguish his later plays—a feeling for mood and atmosphere, strong dramatic contrast, evocative dialogue, and a firm grasp of climax. This play is concerned with one of life's backwaters. The darkened room, the old woman living in the past, the spinster resigned to a grey and poverty-stricken present, are all thrown into sharp relief against the crude, vigorous life which surges in the streets outside. It is the brief impact of this heedless vitality of the present upon the deadness of the past which provides the play's chief conflict, and leads through desperation to the final climax.

DONALD FITZJOHN

1961.

# CONTENTS

## ACKNOWLEDGEMENTS

The English Association is indebted to the following for permission to reprint the undermentioned plays:

For *The Browning Version* (published in 1949) to Mr. Terence Rattigan and Messrs. Samuel French; for *A Phoenix Too Frequent* (published in 1946) to Mr. Christopher Fry and Messrs. Actac (Theatrical & Cinematic) Ltd.; for *The Bespoke Overcoat* (published in 1953) to Mr. Wolf Mankowitz and Messrs. Evans Bros.; for *The Pen of My Aunt* by the late Miss Gordon Daviot to Messrs. David Higham Associates Ltd., Literary Executors, and to Messrs. Peter Davies Ltd. publishers of the Gordon Daviot Plays, Vol. II (1954), from which this play is taken; for *Mother's Day* (published in 1953) to Mr. J. B. Priestley and Messrs. Samuel French; for *Trifles* by the late Mrs. Susan Glaspell to Messrs. Dodd, Mead & Co. Inc. publishers of *Plays* (1924) from which this play is taken, and to Messrs. Ernest Benn Ltd. and Messrs. Samuel French; for *The Dock Brief* (published in 1958) to Mr. John Mortimer; and for *Lord Byron's Love Letter* to Mr. Tennessee Williams, to Messrs. Secker & Warburg, publishers of *Twenty-Seven Wagons Full of Cotton* (1949) from which this play is taken, and to Messrs. New Directions of New York. In the case of this last play all inquiries should be addressed to Miss Audrey Wood, the author's representative, c/o Music Corporation of America, 598 Madison Avenue, New York 22. The Music Corporation of America state 'It must be clear that the usage of *Lord Byron's Love Letter* is strictly for schools and universities and not for stage productions of any kind'.

# THE BROWNING VERSION

By Terence Rattigan

# CHARACTERS

JOHN TAPLOW

FRANK HUNTER

MILLIE CROCKER-HARRIS

ANDREW CROCKER-HARRIS

DR. FROBISHER

PETER GILBERT

MRS. GILBERT

## *Scene*

The sitting-room of the Crocker-Harris's flat at
a Public School in the South of England

Time: About 6.30 p.m. of a day in July

# THE BROWNING VERSION

SCENE—*The sitting-room in the Crocker-Harris's flat in a public school in the south of England. About 6.30 p.m. of a day in July.*

*The building in which the flat is situated is large and Victorian, and at some fairly recent time has been converted into flats of varying size for masters, married and unmarried. The Crocker-Harris have the ground floor and their sitting-room is probably the biggest—and gloomiest—room in the house. It boasts, however, access (through a stained glass door L.) to a small garden, and is furnished with chintzy and genteel cheerfulness. Another door, up R., leads into the hall and a third, up C., to the rest of the flat. The hall door is partially concealed by a screen. There is a large bay-window in the L. wall below the garden door. Near the window is a flat-topped desk with a swivel chair behind it and an upright chair on the other side. The fireplace is down R. Below it is an easy chair and a small table with a telephone. A settee stands in front of the fire place at R.C. There is an oval dining-table with two chairs up C. R. of the door up C. is a sideboard; and against the wall L. of the door up R. is a hall-stand, in which some walking-sticks are kept. A small cupboard stands against the wall down R.*

*When the* CURTAIN *rises the room is empty. There are copies of 'The Times' and the 'Tatler' on the settee. We hear the front door opening and closing and immediately after there is a timorous knock on the door up R. After a pause the knock is repeated. The door opens and* JOHN TAPLOW *makes his appearance. He is a plain moon-faced boy of about sixteen, with glasses. He carries a book and an exercise-book. He is dressed in grey flannels, a dark blue coat and white scarf. He stands in doubt at the door for a moment, then goes back into the hall.*

TAPLOW (*off; calling*). Sir! Sir!

[*After a pause he comes back into the room, crosses to the garden door up* L. *and opens it.*

(*He calls.*) Sir!

[*There is no reply.* TAPLOW, *standing in the bright sunshine at the door, emits a plaintive sigh, then closes it firmly and comes down* R. *of the desk on which he places the book, the notebook and a pen. He sits in the chair* R. *of the desk. He looks round the room. On the table* C. *is a small box of chocolates, probably the Crocker-Harris's ration for the month.* TAPLOW *rises, moves above the table and opens the box. He counts the number inside, and removes two. One of these he eats and the other, after a second's struggle, either with his conscience or his judgement of what he might be able to get away with, virtuously replaces in the box. He puts back the box on the table, and moves up* R. *to the hall-stand. He selects a walking-stick with a crooked handle, comes down* C., *and makes a couple of golf-swings, with an air of great concentration.* FRANK HUNTER *enters up* R. *and appears from behind the screen covering the door. He is a rugged young man—not perhaps quite as rugged as his deliberately-cultivated manner of ruthless honesty makes him appear, but wrapped in all the self-confidence of the popular master. He watches* TAPLOW, *whose back is to the door, making his swing.*

FRANK (*coming down behind* TAPLOW). Roll the wrists away from the ball. Don't break them like that.

[*He puts his large hands over the abashed* TAPLOW'S.

Now swing.

[TAPLOW, *guided by* FRANK'S *evidently expert hands, succeeds in hitting the carpet with more effect than before.*

(*He breaks away* R. *of* TAPLOW.) Too quick. Slow back and stiff left arm. It's no good just whacking the ball as if you were the headmaster and the ball was you. It'll never go more than fifty yards if you do. Get a rhythm. A good golf swing is a matter of aesthetics, not of brute strength.

[TAPLOW, *only half listening, is gazing at the carpet.*

FRANK. What's the matter?
TAPLOW. I think we've made a tear in the carpet, sir.

[FRANK *examines the spot perfunctorily.*

FRANK (*taking the stick from* TAPLOW). Nonsense. That was there already. (*He crosses up* R. *and puts the stick in the hallstand.*) Do I know you? (*He comes down* L. *of the settee to* R. *of* TAPLOW.)
TAPLOW. No, sir.
FRANK. What's your name?
TAPLOW. Taplow.
FRANK. Taplow? No, I don't. You're not a scientist, I gather.
TAPLOW. No, sir. I'm still in the lower fifth. I can't specialize until next term—that's to say if I've got my remove all right.
FRANK. Don't you know yet if you've got your remove?
TAPLOW. No, sir. Mr. Crocker-Harris doesn't tell us the results like the other masters.
FRANK. Why not?
TAPLOW. Well, you know what he's like, sir.
FRANK (*moving away to the fireplace*). I believe there *is* a rule that form results should only be announced by the headmaster on the last day of term.

TAPLOW. Yes; but who else pays any attention to it—except Mr. Crocker-Harris?

FRANK. I don't, I admit—but that's no criterion. So you've got to wait until tomorrow to know your fate, have you?

TAPLOW. Yes, sir.

FRANK. Supposing the answer is favourable—what then?

TAPLOW. Oh—science sir, of course.

FRANK (*sadly*). Yes. We get all the slackers.

TAPLOW (*protestingly*). I'm extremely interested in science, sir.

FRANK. Are you? I'm not. Not at least in the science I have to teach.

TAPLOW (*moving above the desk*). Well, anyway, sir, it's a good deal more exciting than this muck. (*He indicates the book he put on the desk.*)

FRANK. What is this muck?

TAPLOW. Aeschylus, sir. *The Agamemnon.*

FRANK (*moving to the* L. *end of the couch*). And your considered view is that *The Agamemnon* of Aeschylus is muck, is it?

TAPLOW. Well, no, sir. I don't think the play is muck—exactly. I suppose, in a way, it's rather a good plot, really; a wife murdering her husband and having a lover and all that. I only meant the way it's taught to us—just a lot of Greek words strung together and fifty lines if you get them wrong.

FRANK. You sound a little bitter, Taplow.

TAPLOW. I am rather, sir.

FRANK. Kept in, eh?

TAPLOW. No, sir. Extra work.

FRANK. Extra work—on the last day of school?

TAPLOW. Yes, sir—and I might be playing golf. (*He moves into the window, upstage end.*) You'd think *he'd* have enough to do anyway himself, considering he's leaving tomorrow for good—but oh no. I missed a day last week when I had 'flu—so here I am—and look at the weather, sir.

FRANK. Bad luck. Still there's one consolation. You're pretty well bound to get your remove tomorrow for being a good boy in taking extra work.

TAPLOW (*crossing to* C.). Well, I'm not so sure, sir. That would be true of the ordinary masters all right. They just wouldn't dare not give a chap a remove after his taking extra work—it would be such a bad advertisement for them. But those sort of rules don't apply to the Crock— Mr. Crocker-Harris. I asked him yesterday outright if he'd given me a remove and do you know what he said, sir?

FRANK. No. What?

TAPLOW (*mimicking a very gentle, rather throaty voice*). 'My dear Taplow, I have given you exactly what you deserve. No less; and certainly no more.' Do you know, sir, I think he may have marked me down, rather than up, for taking extra work. I mean, the man's barely human. (*He breaks off quickly.*) Sorry, sir. Have I gone too far?

FRANK (*sitting on the settee*, L. *end, and picking up 'The Times'*). Yes. Much too far.

TAPLOW. Sorry, sir. I got sort of carried away.

FRANK. Evidently. (*He opens 'The Times' and reads.*)

[TAPLOW *moves to the chair* R. *of the desk and sits.*

Er—Taplow.

TAPLOW. Yes. sir?

FRANK. What was that Mr. Crocker-Harris said to you? Just—er—repeat it, would you?

TAPLOW (*mimicking*). 'My dear Taplow, I have given you exactly what you deserve. No less; and certainly on more.'

[FRANK *snorts, then looks stern.*

FRANK. Not in the least like him. Read your nice Aeschylus and be quiet.

TAPLOW (*with weary disgust*). Aeschylus.

FRANK. Look, what time did Mr. Crocker-Harris tell you to be here?

TAPLOW. Six-thirty, sir.

FRANK. Well, he's ten minutes late. Why don't you cut? You could still get nine holes in before lock-up.

TAPLOW (*genuinely shocked*). Oh, no, I couldn't cut. Cut the Crock—Mr. Crocker-Harris? I shouldn't think it's ever been done in the whole time he's been here. God knows what would happen if I did. He'd probably follow me home, or something.

FRANK. I must admit I envy him the effect he seems to have on you boys in his form. You all seem scared to death of him. What does he do—beat you all, or something?

TAPLOW (*rising and moving to the* L. *end of the settee*). Good Lord, no. He's not a sadist, like one or two of the others.

FRANK. I beg your pardon?

TAPLOW. A sadist, sir, is someone who gets pleasure out of giving pain.

FRANK. Indeed? But I think you went on to say that some other masters . . .

TAPLOW. Well, of course they are, sir. I won't mention names, but you know them as well as I do. Of course I know most masters think we boys don't understand a thing—but dash it, sir, you're different. You're young—well comparatively anyway—and you're science and you canvassed for Labour in the last election. You must know what sadism is.

[FRANK *stares for a moment at* TAPLOW, *then turns away.*

FRANK. Good Lord! What are public schools coming to?

TAPLOW (*crossing to* R. *of the desk, below the chair, and leaning against it*). Anyway, the Crock isn't a sadist. That's what I'm saying. He wouldn't be so frightening if he were—because at least it would show he had some feelings. But he hasn't. He's all shrivelled up inside like a nut and he seems to hate people to like him. It's funny, that. I don't know any other master who doesn't like being liked.

FRANK. And I don't know any boy who doesn't trade on that very foible.

TAPLOW. Well, it's natural, sir. But not with the Crock.

FRANK (*making a feeble attempt at re-establishing the correct relationship*). Mr. Crocker-Harris.

TAPLOW. Mr. Crocker-Harris. The funny thing is that in spite of everything, I do rather like him. I can't help it. And sometimes I think he sees it and that seems to shrivel him up even more.

FRANK. I'm sure you're exaggerating.

TAPLOW. No, sir. I'm not. In form the other day he made one of his little classical jokes. Of course nobody laughed because nobody understood it, myself included. Still, I knew he'd meant it as funny, so I laughed. Not out of sucking-up, sir, I swear, but ordinary common politeness, and feeling a bit sorry for him having made a dud joke. (*He moves round below the desk to* L. *of it.*) Now I can't remember what the joke was—but let's say it was—(*mimicking*) Benedictus, benedicatur, benedictine . . . Now, you laugh, sir.

[FRANK *laughs formally.* TAPLOW *looks at him over an imaginary pair of spectacles, and then, very gently crooks his fore-finger to him in indication to approach the table.* FRANK *rises. He is genuinely interested in the incident.*

(*In a gentle, throaty voice.*) Taplow—you laughed at my little pun, I noticed. I must confess I am flattered at the evident advance your Latinity has made that you should so readily have understood what the rest of the form did not. Perhaps, now, you would be good enough to explain it to them, so that they too can share your pleasure.

[*The door up* R. *is pushed open and* MILLIE CROCKER-HARRIS *enters. She is a thin woman in the late thirties, rather more smartly dressed than the general run of school-masters' wives. She is wearing a cape and carries a shopping basket. She closes the door and then stands by the screen watching* TAPLOW *and* FRANK. *It is a few seconds before they notice her.*

Come along, Taplow.

[FRANK *moves slowly above the desk.*

Do not be so selfish as to keep a good joke to yourself. Tell the others . . . (*He breaks off suddenly, noticing* MILLIE.) Oh Lord!

[FRANK *turns quickly, and seems infinitely relieved at seeing* MILLIE.

FRANK. Oh, hullo.

MILLIE (*without expression*). Hullo. (*She comes down to the sideboard and puts her basket on it.*)

TAPLOW (*moving up to* L. *of* FRANK; *whispering frantically*). Do you think she heard?

[FRANK *shakes his head comfortingly.* MILLIE *takes off her cape and hangs it on the hall-stand.*

I think she did. She was standing there quite a time. If she did and she tells him, there goes my remove.

FRANK. Nonsense. (*He crosses to the fireplace.*)

[MILLIE *takes the basket from the sideboard, moves above the table* C. *and puts the basket on it.*

MILLIE (*to* TAPLOW). Waiting for my husband?

TAPLOW (*moving down* L. *of the table* C.). Er—yes.

MILLIE. He's at the Bursar's and might be there quite a time. If I were you I'd go.

TAPLOW (*doubtfully*). He said most particularly I was to come.

MILLIE. Well, why don't you run away for a quarter of an hour and come back? (*She unpacks some things from the basket.*)

TAPLOW. Supposing he gets here before me?

MILLIE (*smiling*). I'll take the blame. (*She takes a prescription out of the basket.*) I tell you what—you can do a job for him. Take this prescription to the chemist and get it made up.

TAPLOW. All right, Mrs. Crocker-Harris. (*He crosses towards the door up* R.)

MILLIE. And while you're there you might as well slip into Stewart's and have an ice. Here. Catch. (*She takes a shilling from her bag and throws it to him.*)

TAPLOW (*turning and catching it*). Thanks awfully. (*He signals to* FRANK *not to tell, and moves to the door up* R.)

MILLIE. Oh, Taplow. (*She crosses to him.*)

TAPLOW (*turning on the step*). Yes, Mrs. Crocker-Harris.

MILLIE. I had a letter from my father today in which he says he once had the pleasure of meeting your mother.

TAPLOW (*uninterested but polite*). Oh, really?

MILLIE. Yes. It was at some fête or other in Bradford. My uncle—that's Sir William Bartop, you know—made a speech and so did your mother. My father met her afterwards at tea.

TAPLOW. Oh really?

MILLIE. He said he found her quite charming.

TAPLOW. Yes, she's jolly good at those sort of functions. (*Becoming aware of his lack of tact.*) I mean—I'm sure she found him charming, too. So long.

[*He goes out up* R.

MILLIE (*coming down to the* L. *end of the settee*). Thank you for coming round.

FRANK. That's all right.

MILLIE. You're staying for dinner?

FRANK. If I may.

MILLIE. If you may! (*She crosses below the settee to him.*) Give me a cigarette.

[FRANK *takes out his case and extends it to her.* MILLIE *takes a cigarette.*

(*Indicating the case.*) You haven't given it away yet, I see.

FRANK. Do you think I would?

MILLIE. Frankly, yes. Luckily it's a man's case. I don't suppose any of your girl friends would want it.

FRANK. Don't be silly.

MILLIE. Where have you been all this week?

FRANK (*sitting in the easy chair*). Correcting exam papers— making reports. You know what end of term is like.

MILLIE (*crossing below the settee and moving above the table* C.). I do know what end of term is like. But even Andrew has managed this last week to take a few hours off to say good-bye to people. (*She takes some packages out of the shopping basket.*)

FRANK. I really have been appallingly busy. Besides, I'm coming to stay with you in Bradford.

MILLIE. Not for over a month. Andrew doesn't start his new job until September first. That's one of the things I had to tell you.

FRANK. Oh. I had meant to be in Devonshire in September.

MILLIE (*quickly*). Who with?

FRANK. My family.

MILLIE. Surely you can go earlier, can't you? Go in August.

FRANK. It'll be difficult.

MILLIE. Then you'd better come to me in August.

FRANK. But Andrew will still be there.

[*There is a pause.* MILLIE *crosses to* L. *of the desk, opens a drawer and takes out some scissors.*

FRANK. I think I can manage September.

MILLIE (*shutting the drawer*). That'd be better—from every point of view. (*She moves below the table* C. *and puts down the scissors.*) Except that it means I shan't see you for six weeks.

FRANK (*lightly*). You'll survive that, all right.

MILLIE. Yes, I'll survive it—(*she moves to the* L. *end of the settee*) but not as easily as you will.

[FRANK *says nothing.*

I haven't much pride, have I? (*She crosses to* FRANK *and stands above the easy chair.*) Frank, darling—(*she sits on the arm of the chair and kisses him*) I love you so much.

[FRANK *kisses her on the mouth, but a trifle perfunctorily and then rises and breaks quickly away, as if afraid someone had come into the room. He moves below the settee.*

(*She laughs.*) You're very nervous.

FRANK. I'm afraid of that screen arrangement. You can't see people coming in.

MILLIE. Oh yes. (*She rises and stands by the fireplace.*) That reminds me. What were you and Taplow up to when I came in just now? Making fun of my husband?

FRANK. Afraid so. Yes.

MILLIE. It sounded rather a good imitation. I must get him to do it for me sometime. It was very naughty of you to encourage him.

FRANK. I know. It was.

MILLIE (*ironically*). Bad for discipline.

FRANK (*sitting on the settee*). Exactly. Currying favour with the boys, too. My God, how easy it is to be popular. I've only been a master three years, but I've already slipped into an act and a vernacular that I just can't get out of. Why can't anyone ever be natural with the little blighters?

MILLIE. They probably wouldn't like it if you were. (*She crosses below the settee and moves above the table* C. *She picks up the scissors and a packet of luggage labels and cuts the latter one by one from the packet.*)

FRANK. I don't see why not. No one seems to have tried it yet, anyway. I suppose the trouble is—we're all too scared of them. Either one gets forced into an attitude of false and hearty and jocular bonhomie like myself, or into the sort of petty, soulless tyranny which your husband uses to protect himself against the lower fifth.

MILLIE (*rather bored with this*). He'd never be popular—whatever he did.

FRANK. Possibly not. He ought never to have become a schoolmaster really. Why did he?

MILLIE. It was his vocation, he said. He was sure he'd make a big success of it, especially when he got his job here first go off. (*Bitterly.*) Fine success he's made, hasn't he?

FRANK. You should have stopped him.

MILLIE. How was I to know? He talked about getting a house, then a headmastership.

FRANK (*rising*). The Crock a headmaster! That's a pretty thought.

MILLIE. Yes, it's funny to think of now, all right. Still, he wasn't always the Crock, you know. He had a bit more gumption once. At least I thought he had. Don't let's talk any more about him—(*she comes* R. *round the table to* C.) it's too depressing. (*She starts to move* L.)

FRANK. I'm sorry for him.

MILLIE (*stopping and turning; indifferently*). He's not sorry for himself, so why should you be? It's me you should be sorry for.

FRANK. I am.

MILLIE (*moving in a few steps towards* FRANK; *smiling*). Then show me. (*She stretches out her arms to him.*)

[FRANK *moves to her and kisses her again quickly and lightly. She holds him hungrily. He has to free himself almost roughly.*

FRANK (*crossing to the fireplace*). What have you been doing all day?

MILLIE. Calling on the other masters' wives—saying fond farewells. I've worked off twelve. I've another seven to do tomorrow.

FRANK. You poor thing! I don't envy you.

MILLIE (*moving above the desk to* L. *of it with some labels*). It's the housemasters' wives that are the worst. (*She picks up a pen and writes on the labels.*) They're all so damn patronizing. You should have heard Betty Carstairs. 'My dear—it's such terrible bad luck on you both—that your husband should get this heart trouble just when, if only he'd stayed on, he'd have been bound to get a house. I mean, he's considerably senior to my Arthur as it is, and they simply couldn't have gone on passing him over, could they?'

FRANK. There's a word for Betty Carstairs, my dear, that I would hesitate to employ before a lady.

MILLIE. She's got her eye on you, anyway.

FRANK. Betty Carstairs? What utter rot!

MILLIE. Oh yes, she has. I saw you at that concert. Don't think I didn't notice.

FRANK. Millie, darling! Really! I detest the woman.

MILLIE. Then what were you doing in her box at Lord's?

FRANK. Carstairs invited me. I went there because it was a good place to see the match from.

MILLIE. Yes, I'm sure it was. Much better than the grandstand, anyway.

FRANK (*remembering something suddenly*). Oh, my God!

MILLIE (*coming below the desk*). It's all right, my dear. Don't bother to apologize. We gave the seat away, as it happens.

FRANK. I'm most terribly sorry.

MILLIE. It's all right. (*She moves to* R. *of the desk.*) We couldn't afford a box, you see.

FRANK (*moving a few steps towards* R.C.). It wasn't that. You know it wasn't that. It's just that I—well, I clean forgot.

MILLIE. Funny you didn't forget the Carstairs invitation.

FRANK. Millie—don't be a fool.

MILLIE. It's you who are the fool. (*Appealingly.*) Frank— have you never been in love? I know you're not in love with me—but haven't you ever been in love with anyone? Don't you realize what torture you inflict on someone who loves you when you do a thing like that?

FRANK. I've told you I'm sorry—I don't know what more I can say.

MILLIE. Why not the truth?

FRANK. The truth is—I clean forgot.

MILLIE. The truth is—you had something better to do—and why not say it?

FRANK. All right. Believe that if you like. It happens to be a lie, but believe it all the same. Only for God's sake stop this. (*He turns and moves down* R.)

MILLIE. Then for God's sake show me some pity. Do you think it's any pleasanter for me to believe that you cut me because you forgot? Do you think that doesn't hurt either?

[FRANK *turns away.*

(*She moves above the up* R. *corner of the desk and faces the door up* L.) Oh damn! I was so determined to be brave and not mention Lord's. Why did I? Frank, just tell me one thing. Just tell me you're not running away from me—that's all I want to hear.

FRANK. I'm coming to Bradford.

MILLIE (*turning to* FRANK). I think, if you don't, I'll kill myself.

FRANK (*turning and taking a few steps in towards* MILLIE). I'm coming to Bradford.

[*The door up* R. *opens.* FRANK *stops at the sound.* MILLIE *recovers herself and crosses above the table* C. *to the sideboard.* ANDREW CROCKER-HARRIS *enters and appears from behind the screen. Despite the summer sun he wears a serge suit and a stiff collar. He carries a mackintosh and a rolled-up time-table and looks, as ever, neat, complacent and unruffled. He speaks in a very gentle voice which he rarely raises.*

ANDREW (*hanging his mackintosh on the hall-stand*). Is Taplow here?

[FRANK *eases towards the fireplace.*

MILLIE. I sent him to the chemist to get your prescription made up.

ANDREW. What prescription?

MILLIE. Your heart medicine. Don't you remember? You told me this morning it had run out.

ANDREW. Of course I remember, my dear, but there was no need to send Taplow for it. If you had telephoned the chemist he would have sent it round in plenty of time. He knows the prescription. (*He comes down to the* L. *end of the settee.*) Now Taplow will be late and I am so pressed for

time I hardly know how to fit him in. (*He sees* FRANK.)
Ah, Hunter! How are you? (*He moves* R. *to* FRANK.)

FRANK. Very well, thanks.

[*They shake hands.*

ANDREW. Most kind of you to drop in, but, as Millie should
have warned you, I am expecting a pupil for extra work
and . . .

MILLIE. He's staying to dinner, Andrew.

ANDREW. Good. Then I shall see something of you. However,
when Taplow returns I'm sure you won't mind . . .

FRANK (*making a move*). No, of course not. I'll make myself
scarce now, if you'd rather—I mean, if you're busy . . .

[*He turns away and moves* C.

ANDREW. Oh no. There is no need for that. Sit down, do.
Will you smoke? I don't, as you know, but Millie does.
(*He crosses below the desk and moves up* L. *of it.*) Millie, give
our guest a cigarette.

MILLIE (*moving down to the table* C.). I haven't any, I'm
afraid. I've had to cadge from him. (*She takes a copy of the
'Tatler' from the basket.*)

[ANDREW *opens the drawer that should contain the
scissors.* FRANK *takes out his cigarette case, crosses to* R.
*of the table* C., *and offers it to* MILLIE. *She exchanges a
glance with him as she takes a cigarette.*

ANDREW (*looking for the scissors*). We expected you at Lord's,
Hunter.

FRANK. What? Oh yes. I'm most terribly sorry. I . . .

MILLIE (*crossing behind the settee*). He clean forgot, Andrew.
Imagine.

ANDREW. Forgot?

MILLIE. Not everyone is blessed with your superhuman
memory, you see.

FRANK. I really can't apologize enough.

ANDREW. Please don't bother to mention it. On the second day we managed to sell the seat to a certain Dr. Lambert, who wore, I regret to say, the colours of the opposing faction, but who otherwise seemed a passably agreeable person. (*He moves above the table* c.) You liked him, didn't you, Millie?

MILLIE (*looking at* FRANK). Very much indeed. I thought him quite charming.

ANDREW. A charming old gentleman. (*To* FRANK.) You have had tea? (*He picks up the scissors.*)

FRANK. Yes—thank you.

ANDREW. Is there any other refreshment I can offer you?

FRANK. No, thank you.

ANDREW (*cutting the string round the time-table*). Would it interest you to see the new time-table I have drafted for next term?

FRANK. Yes, very much. (*He moves up* R. *of* ANDREW.)

[ANDREW *opens out a long roll of paper, made by pasting pieces of foolscap together, and which is entirely covered by his meticulous writing.*

FRANK. I never knew you drafted our time-tables.

ANDREW. Didn't you? I have done so for the last fifteen years.

[MILLIE *wanders down* R. *of the settee.*

Of course, they are always issued in mimeograph under the headmaster's signature. Now what form do you take? Upper fifth Science—there you are—that's the general picture; but on the back you will see each form specified under separate headings—there—that's a new idea of mine—Millie, this might interest you.

3

MILLIE (*sitting in the easy chair; suddenly harsh*). You know it bores me to death.

[FRANK *looks up, surprised and uncomfortable.* ANDREW *does not remove his eyes from the time-table.*

ANDREW. Millie has no head for this sort of work. There you see. Now here you can follow the upper fifth Science throughout every day of the week.

FRANK (*indicating the time-table*). I must say, I think this is a really wonderful job.

ANDREW. Thank you. It has the merit of clarity, I think. (*He starts to roll up the time-table.*)

FRANK. I don't know what they'll do without you.

ANDREW (*without expression*). They'll find somebody else, I expect.

[*There is a pause.*

FRANK. What sort of job is this you're going to?

ANDREW (*looking at* MILLIE *for the first time*). Hasn't Millie told you?

FRANK. She said it was a cr—— a private school.

ANDREW. A crammer's—for backward boys. It is run by an old Oxford contemporary of mine who lives in Dorset. (*He moves round* L. *of the table* C. *and finishes rolling up the time-table.*) The work will not be so arduous as here and my doctor seems to think I will be able to undertake it without—er danger.

FRANK (*with genuine sympathy*). It's the most rotten bad luck for you. I'm awfully sorry.

ANDREW (*raising his voice a little*). My dear Hunter, there is nothing whatever to be sorry for. I am looking forward to the change.

[*There is a knock at the door up* R.

Come in. (*He crosses below the table to* C.)

> [TAPLOW *enters up* R., *a trifle breathless and guilty-look-ing. He carries a medicine bottle wrapped and sealed*

Ah, Taplow. Good. You have been running, I see.

TAPLOW. Yes, sir. (*He crosses to the* L. *end of the settee.*)

ANDREW. There was a queue at the chemist's, I suppose?

TAPLOW. Yes, sir.

ANDREW. And doubtless an even longer one at Stewart's?

TAPLOW. Yes, sir—I mean—no, sir—I mean—(*he looks at* MILLIE) yes, sir. (*He crosses below the settee to* MILLIE *and hands her the medicine.*)

MILLIE. You were late yourself, Andrew.

ANDREW. Exactly. And for that I apologize, Taplow.

TAPLOW. That's all right, sir.

ANDREW (*crossing below the desk and moving* L. *of it*). Luckily we still have a good hour before lock-up, so nothing has been lost. (*He puts the time-table on the desk.*)

FRANK (*moving to the door up* L.; *to* MILLIE). May I use the short cut? I'm going back to my digs.

> [ANDREW *sits at his desk and opens a book.*

MILLIE (*rising and moving up* R. *of the settee*). Yes. Go ahead. Come back soon. If Andrew hasn't finished we can sit in the garden. (*She crosses above the table* C. *and picks up the shopping basket. She puts the medicine on the sideboard.*) I'd better go and see about dinner.

> [*She goes out up* C.

ANDREW (*to* FRANK). Taplow is desirous of obtaining a re-move from my form, Hunter, so that he can spend the rest of his career here playing happily with the crucibles, retorts and bunsen burners of your science fifth.

FRANK (*turning at the door*). Oh. Has he?

ANDREW. Has he what?

FRANK. Obtained his remove?

ANDREW (*after a pause*). He has obtained exactly what he deserves. No less; and certainly no more.

> [TAPLOW *mutters an explosion of mirth.* FRANK *nods, thoughtfully, and goes out.* ANDREW *has caught sight of* TAPLOW's *contorted face, but passes no remark on it. He beckons* TAPLOW *across and signs to him to sit in the chair* R. *of the desk.* TAPLOW *sits.* ANDREW *picks up a copy of 'The Agamemnon' and* TAPLOW *does the same.*

ANDREW. Line thirteen hundred and ninety-nine. Begin. (*He leans back.*)

TAPLOW (*reading slowly*). Chorus. We—are surprised at . . .

ANDREW (*automatically*). We marvel at.

TAPLOW. We marvel at—thy tongue—how bold thou art— that you . . .

ANDREW. Thou. (*His interruptions are automatic. His thoughts are evidently far distant.*)

TAPLOW. Thou—can . . .

ANDREW. Canst.

TAPLOW. Canst—boastfully speak . . .

ANDREW. Utter such a boastful speech.

TAPLOW. Utter such a boastful speech—over—(*in a sudden rush of inspiration*) the bloody corpse of the husband you have slain.

> [ANDREW *puts on his glasses and looks down at his text for the first time.* TAPLOW *looks apprehensive*

ANDREW (*after a pause*). Taplow—I presume you are using a different text from mine.

TAPLOW. No, sir.

ANDREW. That is strange, for the line as I have it reads: 'ἥτις τοιόνδ' ἐπ' ἀνδρὶ κομπάζεις λόγον'.[1] However diligently

[1] *Phonetically represented, this reads:* 'heetis toiond ep andri compadzise logon.'

I search I can discover no 'bloody'—no 'corpse'—no
'you have slain'. Simply 'husband'.

TAPLOW. Yes, sir. That's right.

ANDREW. Then why do you invent words that simply are
not there?

TAPLOW. I thought they sounded better, sir. More exciting.
After all, she did kill her husband, sir. (*With relish.*) She's
just been revealed with his dead body and Cassandra's
weltering in gore.

ANDREW. I am delighted at this evidence, Taplow, of your
interest in the rather more lurid aspects of dramaturgy,
but I feel I must remind you that you are supposed to be
construing Greek, not collaborating with Aeschylus. (*He
leans back.*)

TAPLOW (*greatly daring*). Yes, but still, sir, translator's
licence, sir—I didn't get anything wrong—and after all it
*is* a play and not just a bit of Greek construe.

ANDREW (*momentarily at a loss*). I seem to detect a note of
end of term in your remarks. I am not denying that *The
Agamemnon* is a play. It is perhaps the greatest play ever
written. (*He leans forward.*)

TAPLOW (*quickly*). I wonder how many people in the form
think that? (*He pauses; instantly frightened of what he has
said.*) Sorry, sir. Shall I go on?

[ANDREW *does not answer. He sits motionless, staring at
his book.*

Shall I go on, sir?

[*There is another pause.* ANDREW *raises his head slowly
from his book.*

ANDREW (*murmuring gently, not looking at* TAPLOW). When
I was a very young man, only two years older than
you are now, Taplow, I wrote, for my own pleasure, a

translation of *The Agamemnon*—a very free translation—I remember—in rhyming couplets.

TAPLOW. The whole *Agamemnon*—in verse? That must have been hard work, sir.

ANDREW. It was hard work; but I derived great joy from it. The play had so excited and moved me that I wished to communicate, however imperfectly, some of that emotion to others. When I had finished it, I remember, I thought it very beautiful—almost more beautiful than the original. (*He leans back.*)

TAPLOW. Was it ever published, sir?

ANDREW. No. Yesterday I looked for the manuscript while I was packing my papers. I was unable to find it. I fear it is lost—like so many other things. Lost for good.

TAPLOW. Hard luck, sir.

[ANDREW *is silent again.* TAPLOW *steals a timid glance at him.*

Shall I go on, sir?

[ANDREW, *with a slight effort, lowers his eyes again to his text.*

ANDREW (*leaning forward; raising his voice slightly*). No. Go back and get that last line right.

[TAPLOW, *out of* ANDREW's *vision, as he thinks, makes a disgusted grimace in his direction.*

TAPLOW. That—thou canst utter such a boastful speech over thy husband.

ANDREW. Yes. And now, if you would be so kind, you will do the line again, without the facial contortion which you just found necessary to accompany it.

[TAPLOW *is about to begin the line again.* MILLIE *enters up* C., *hurriedly. She is wearing an apron.* TAPLOW *rises.*

MILLIE. The headmaster's just coming up the drive. Don't tell him I'm in. The fish pie isn't in the oven yet.

[*She exits up* C.

TAPLOW (*turning hopefully to* ANDREW). I'd better go, hadn't I, sir? I mean—I don't want to be in the way.

ANDREW. We do not yet know that it is I the headmaster wishes to see. Other people live in this building.

[*There is a knock at the door up* R.

Come in.

[DR. FROBISHER *enters up* R. *He looks more like a distinguished diplomat than a doctor of literature and a classical scholar. He is in the middle fifties and goes to a very good tailor.* ANDREW *rises.*

FROBISHER. Ah, Crocker-Harris, I've caught you in. I'm so glad. (*He crosses behind the settee and comes down* L. *of it.*) I hope I'm not disturbing you?

ANDREW. I have been taking a pupil in extra work.

[TAPLOW *eases below the table* C.

FROBISHER. On the penultimate day of term? That argues either great conscientiousness on your part or considerable backwardness on his.

ANDREW. Perhaps a combination of both.

FROBISHER. Quite so, but as this is my only chance of speaking to you before tomorrow, I think that perhaps your pupil will be good enough to excuse us. (*He turns politely to* TAPLOW.)

TAPLOW. Oh yes, sir. That's really quite all right. (*He grabs his books off* ANDREW's *desk.*)

ANDREW (*crossing to* TAPLOW). I'm extremely sorry, Taplow. You will please explain to your father exactly what occurred over this lost hour and tell him that I shall in due course be writing to him to return the money involved.

[FROBISHER *moves below the settee to the fireplace.*

TAPLOW (*hurriedly*). Yes, sir. But please don't bother, sir. (*He dashes to the door up* R.) I know it's all right, sir. Thank you, sir.

[*He darts out.*

FROBISHER (*idly picking up an ornament on the mantelpiece*). Have the Gilberts called on you yet? (*He turns to* ANDREW).

ANDREW (*moving* C.). The Gilberts, sir? Who are they?

FROBISHER. Gilbert is your successor with the lower fifth. He is down here today with his wife, and as they will be taking over this flat I thought perhaps you wouldn't mind if they came in to look it over.

ANDREW. Of course not.

FROBISHER. I've told you about him, I think. He is a very brilliant young man and won exceptionally high honours at Oxford.

ANDREW. So I understand, sir.

FROBISHER. Not, of course, as high as the honours you yourself won there. He didn't, for instance, win the Chancellor's prize for Latin verse or the Gaisford.

ANDREW. He won the Hertford Latin, then?

FROBISHER (*replacing the ornament*). No. (*Mildly surprised.*) Did you win that, too?

[ANDREW *nods.*

It's sometimes rather hard to remember that you are perhaps the most brilliant classical scholar we have ever had at the school.

ANDREW. You are very kind.

FROBISHER (*urbanely correcting his gaffe*). Hard to remember, I mean—because of your other activities—your brilliant work on the school time-table, for instance, and also for your heroic battle for so long and against such odds with the soul-destroying lower fifth.

ANDREW. I have not found that my soul has been destroyed by the lower fifth, Headmaster.

FROBISHER. I was joking, of course.

ANDREW. Oh. I see.

FROBISHER. Is your wife in?

ANDREW. Er—no. Not at the moment.

FROBISHER. I shall have a chance of saying good-bye to her tomorrow. (*He moves in a few steps below the settee.*) I am rather glad I have got you to myself. I have a delicate matter—two rather delicate matters—to broach.

ANDREW (*moving in slightly; indicating the settee*). Please sit down. (*He stands at the L. end of the settee.*)

FROBISHER. Thank you. (*He sits.*) Now you have been with us, in all, eighteen years, haven't you?

[ANDREW *nods.*

It is extremely unlucky that you should have had to retire at so comparatively an early age and so short a time before you would have been eligible for a pension. (*He is regarding his nails, as he speaks, studiously avoiding meeting* ANDREW's *gaze.*)

[ANDREW *crosses below the settee to the fireplace and stands facing it.*

ANDREW (*after a pause*). You have decided, then, not to award me a pension?

FROBISHER. Not I, my dear fellow. It has nothing at all to do with me. It's the governors who, I'm afraid, have been forced to turn down your application. I put your case to them as well as I could——

[ANDREW *turns and faces* FROBISHER.

—but they decided with great regret, that they couldn't make an exception to the rule.

ANDREW. But I thought—my wife thought, that an exception was made some five years ago . . .

FROBISHER. Ah! In the case of Buller, you mean? True. But the circumstances with Buller were quite remarkable. It was, after all, in playing rugger against the school that he received that injury.

ANDREW. Yes. I remember.

FROBISHER. And then the governors received a petition from boys, old boys and parents, with over five hundred signatures.

ANDREW. I would have signed that petition myself, but through some oversight I was not asked.

FROBISHER. He was a splendid fellow, Buller. Splendid. Doing very well, too, now, I gather.

ANDREW. I'm delighted to hear it.

FROBISHER. Your own case, of course, is equally deserving. If not more so—for Buller was a younger man. Unfortunately—rules are rules—and are not made to be broken every few years; at any rate that is the governors' view.

ANDREW. I quite understand.

FROBISHER. I knew you would. Now might I ask you a rather impertinent question?

ANDREW. Certainly.

FROBISHER. You have, I take it, private means?

ANDREW. My wife has some.

FROBISHER. Ah, yes. Your wife has often told me of her family connexions. I understand her father has a business in—Bradford—isn't it?

ANDREW. Yes. He runs a men's clothing shop in the Arcade.

FROBISHER. Indeed? Your wife's remarks had led me to imagine something a little more—extensive.

ANDREW. My father-in-law made a settlement on my wife at the time of our marriage. She has about three hundred a year of her own. I have nothing. Is that the answer to your question, Headmaster?

FROBISHER. Yes. Thank you for your frankness. Now, this private school you are going to . . .

ANDREW. My salary at the crammer's is to be two hundred pounds a year.

FROBISHER. Quite so. With board and lodging, of course?

ANDREW. For eight months of the year.

FROBISHER. Yes, I see. (*He ponders a second.*) Of course, you know, there is the School Benevolent Fund that deals with cases of actual hardship.

ANDREW. There will be no actual hardship, Headmaster.

FROBISHER. No. I am glad you take that view. I must admit, though, I had hoped that your own means had proved a little more ample. Your wife had certainly led me to suppose . . .

ANDREW. I am not denying that a pension would have been very welcome, Headmaster, but I see no reason to quarrel with the governors' decision. What is the other delicate matter you have to discuss?

FROBISHER. Well, it concerns the arrangements at prize-giving tomorrow. You are, of course, prepared to say a few words?

ANDREW. I had assumed you would call on me to do so.

FROBISHER. Of course. It is always done, and I know the boys appreciate the custom.

ANDREW (*crossing to the upstage end of the desk*). I have already made a few notes of what I am going to say. Perhaps you would care . . .

FROBISHER. No, no. That isn't necessary at all. I know I can trust your discretion—not to say your wit. It will be, I know, a very moving moment for you—indeed for us all—but, as I'm sure you realize, it is far better to keep these occasions from becoming too heavy and distressing. You know how little the boys appreciate sentiment.

ANDREW. I do.

FROBISHER. That is why I've planned my own reference to you at the end of my speech to be rather more light and jocular than I would otherwise have made it.

ANDREW. I quite understand. (*He moves to* L. *of the desk, puts on his glasses and picks up his speech.*) I too have prepared a few little jokes and puns for my speech. One—a play of words on *vale*, farewell and Wally, the Christian name of a backward boy in my class, is, I think, rather happy.

FROBISHER. Yes. (*He laughs belatedly.*) Very neat. That should go down extremely well.

ANDREW. I'm glad you like it.

FROBISHER (*rising and crossing to* R. *of the desk*). Well, now—there is a particular favour I have to ask of you in connexion with the ceremony, and I know I shall not have to ask in vain. Fletcher, as you know, is leaving too.

ANDREW. Yes. He is going into the city, they tell me.

FROBISHER. Yes. Now he is, of course, considerably junior to you. He has only been here—let me see—five years. But, as you know, he has done great things for our cricket —positive wonders, when you remember what doldrums we were in before he came.

ANDREW. Our win at Lord's this year was certainly most inspiring.

FROBISHER. Exactly. (*He moves above the desk.*) Now I'm sure that tomorrow the boys will make the occasion of his farewell speech a tremendous demonstration of gratitude. The applause might go on for minutes—you know what the boys feel about Lord's—and I seriously doubt my ability to cut it short or even, I admit, the propriety of trying to do so. Now, you see the quandary in which I am placed?

ANDREW. Perfectly. You wish to refer to me and for me to make my speech before you come to Fletcher?

FROBISHER. It's extremely awkward, and I feel wretched about asking it of you—but it's more for your own sake than for mine or Fletcher's that I do. After all, a climax is what one must try to work up to on these occasions.

ANDREW. Naturally, Headmaster, I wouldn't wish to provide an anti-climax.

FROBISHER. You really mustn't take it amiss, my dear fellow. The boys, in applauding Fletcher for several minutes and yourself say—for—well, for not quite so long—won't be making any personal demonstration between you. It will be quite impersonal—I assure you— quite impersonal.

ANDREW. I understand.

FROBISHER (*patting* ANDREW's *shoulder; warmly*). I knew you would (*he looks at his watch*) and I can hardly tell you how wisely I think you have chosen. Well now—as this is all my business, I think perhaps I had better be getting along. (*He crosses to* R. *of the table* C.) This has been a terribly busy day for me—for you too, I imagine.

ANDREW. Yes.

[MILLIE *enters up* C. *She has taken off her apron, and tidied herself up. She comes to* L. *of* FROBISHER.

MILLIE (*in her social manner*). Ah, Headmaster. How good of you to drop in.

FROBISHER (*more at home with her than with* ANDREW). Mrs. Crocker-Harris. How are you?

[*They shake hands.*

You're looking extremely well, I must say. (*To* ANDREW.) Has anyone ever told you, Crocker-Harris, that you have a very attractive wife?

ANDREW. Many people, sir. But then I hardly need to be told.

MILLIE. Can I persuade you to stay a few moments and have a drink, Headmaster? It's so rarely we have the pleasure of seeing you.

FROBISHER. Unfortunately, dear lady, I was just on the point of leaving. I have two frantic parents waiting for me at home. You are dining with us tomorrow—both of you, aren't you?

MILLIE. Yes, indeed—and so looking forward to it.

[FROBISHER *and* MILLIE *move to the door up* R.

FROBISHER. I'm so glad. We can say our sad farewells then. (*To* ANDREW.) Au revoir, Crocker-Harris, and thank you very much. (*He opens the door.*)

[ANDREW *gives a slight bow.* MILLIE *holds the door open.* FROBISHER *goes out.*

MILLIE (*to* ANDREW). Don't forget to take your medicine, dear, will you?

[*She goes out.*

ANDREW. No.

FROBISHER (*off*). Lucky invalid! To have such a very charming nurse.

MILLIE (*off*). I really don't know what to say to all these compliments, Headmaster. I don't believe you mean a word of them.

[ANDREW *turns and looks out of the window.*

FROBISHER (*off*). Every word. Till tomorrow, then? Goodbye.

[*The outer door is heard to slam.* ANDREW *is staring out of the window.* MILLIE *enters up* R.

MILLIE. Well? Do we get it? (*She stands on the step.*)

ANDREW (*turning and moving below the chair* L. *of his desk; absently*). Get what?

MILLIE. The pension, of course. Do we get it?

ANDREW. No.

MILLIE (*crossing above the settee to* C.). My God! Why not?

ANDREW (*sitting at his desk*). It's against the rules.

MILLIE. Buller got it, didn't he? Buller got it? What's the idea of giving it to him and not to us?

ANDREW. The governors are afraid of establishing a precedent.

MILLIE. The mean old brutes! My God, what I wouldn't like to say to them! (*She moves above the desk and rounds on* ANDREW.) And what did you say? Just sat there and made a joke in Latin, I suppose?

ANDREW. There wasn't very much I could say, in Latin or any other language.

MILLIE. Oh, wasn't there? I'd have said it all right. I wouldn't just have sat there twiddling my thumbs and taking it from that old phoney of a headmaster. But, then, of course, I'm not a man.

[ANDREW *is turning the pages of 'The Agamemnon', not looking at her.*

What do they expect you to do? Live on my money, I suppose.

ANDREW. There has never been any question of that. I shall be perfectly able to support myself.

MILLIE. Yourself? Doesn't the marriage service say something about the husband supporting his wife? (*She leans on the desk.*) Doesn't it? You ought to know.

ANDREW. Yes, it does.

MILLIE. And how do you think you're going to do that on two hundred a year?

ANDREW. I shall do my utmost to save some of it. You're welcome to it, if I can.

MILLIE. Thank you for precisely nothing.

[ANDREW *underlines a word in the text he is reading.*

What else did the old fool have to say? (*She moves to* R. *of the chair,* R. *of the desk.*)

ANDREW. The headmaster? He wants me to make my speech tomorrow before instead of after Fletcher.

MILLIE (*sitting* R. *of the desk*). Yes. I knew he was going to ask that.

ANDREW (*without surprise*). You knew?

MILLIE. Yes. He asked my advice about it a week ago. I told him to go ahead. I knew you wouldn't mind, and as there isn't a Mrs. Fletcher to make *me* look a fool, I didn't give two hoots.

[*There is a knock on the door up* R.

Come in.

[MR. *and* MRS. GILBERT *enter up* R. *He is about twenty-two, and his wife a year or so younger.* MILLIE *rises and stands at the downstage corner of the desk.*

GILBERT. Mr. Crocker-Harris?

ANDREW. Yes. (*He rises.*) Is it Mr. and Mrs. Gilbert? The headmaster told me you might look in.

MRS. GILBERT (*crossing above the settee to* C.). I do hope we're not disturbing you.

[GILBERT *follows* MRS. GILBERT *and stands down stage of, and slightly behind, her.*

ANDREW. Not at all. This is my wife.

MRS. GILBERT. How do you do?

ANDREW. Mr. and Mrs. Gilbert are our successors to this flat, my dear.

MILLIE. Oh yes. (*She moves to* L. *of* MRS. GILBERT.) How nice to meet you both.

GILBERT. How do you do? We really won't keep you more than a second—my wife thought as we were here you wouldn't mind us taking a squint at our future home.

MRS. GILBERT (*unnecessarily*). This is the drawing-room, I suppose?

> [GILBERT *crosses to the fireplace. He looks for a moment at the picture above the mantelpiece, then turns and watches the others.*

MILLIE. Well, it's really a living-room. Andrew uses it as a study.

MRS. GILBERT. How charmingly you've done it!

MILLIE. Oh, do you think so? I'm afraid it isn't nearly as nice as I'd like to make it—but a schoolmaster's wife has to think of so many other things besides curtains and covers. Boys with dirty books and a husband with leaky fountain pens, for instance.

MRS. GILBERT. Yes, I suppose so. Of course, I haven't been a schoolmaster's wife for very long, you know.

GILBERT. Don't swank, darling. You haven't been a school-master's wife at all yet.

MRS. GILBERT. Oh yes, I have—for two months. You were a schoolmaster when I married you.

GILBERT. Prep school doesn't count.

MILLIE. Have you only been married two months?

MRS. GILBERT. Two months and sixteen days.

GILBERT. Seventeen.

MILLIE (*sentimentally*). Andrew, did you hear? They've only been married two months.

4

ANDREW. Indeed? Is that all?

MRS. GILBERT (*crossing above* MILLIE *to the window*). Oh, look, darling. They've got a garden. It is yours, isn't it?

MILLIE. Oh, yes. It's only a pocket handkerchief, I'm afraid, but it's very useful to Andrew. He often works out there, don't you, dear?

ANDREW. Yes, indeed. I find it very agreeable.

MILLIE (*moving to the door up* c.). Shall I show you the rest of the flat? It's a bit untidy, I'm afraid, but you must forgive that. (*She opens the door.*)

MRS. GILBERT (*moving up to* L. *of* MILLIE). Oh, of course.

MILLIE. And the kitchen is in a terrible mess. I'm in the middle of cooking dinner.

MRS. GILBERT (*breathlessly*). Oh, do you cook?

MILLIE. Oh, yes. I have to. We haven't had a maid for five years.

MRS. GILBERT. Oh! I do think that's wonderful of you. I'm scared stiff of having to do it for Peter—I know the first dinner I have to cook for him will wreck our married life.

GILBERT. Highly probable.

[MRS. GILBERT *exits up* c.

MILLIE (*following* MRS. GILBERT). Well, these days we've all got to try and do things we weren't really brought up to do.

[*She goes out, closing the door.*

ANDREW (*to* GILBERT). Don't you want to see the rest of the flat?

GILBERT (*crossing to* c.). No. I leave all that sort of thing to my wife. She's the boss. I thought perhaps you could tell me something about the lower fifth.

ANDREW. What would you like to know?

GILBERT. Well, sir, quite frankly, I'm petrified.

ANDREW. I don't think you need to be. May I give you some sherry? (*He comes down* L. *to the cupboard.*)

GILBERT. Thank you.

ANDREW. They are mostly boys of about fifteen or sixteen. They are not very difficult to handle. (*He takes out a bottle and a glass.*)

GILBERT. The headmaster said you ruled them with a rod of iron. He called you 'the Himmler of the lower fifth'.

ANDREW (*turning, bottle and glass in hand*). Did he? 'The Himmler of the lower fifth.' I think he exaggerated. I hope he exaggerated. 'The Himmler of the lower fifth.' (*He puts the bottle on the desk, then fills the glass.*)

GILBERT (*puzzled*). He only meant that you kept the most wonderful discipline. I must say I do admire you for that. I couldn't even manage that with eleven-year-olds, so what I'll be like with fifteens and sixteens I shudder to think. (*He moves below the chair* R. *of the desk.*)

ANDREW. It is not so difficult. (*He hands* GILBERT *the glass.*) They aren't bad boys. Sometimes a little wild and unfeeling, perhaps—but not bad. 'The Himmler of the lower fifth.' Dear me! (*He turns to the cabinet with the bottle.*)

GILBERT. Perhaps I shouldn't have said that. I've been tactless, I'm afraid.

ANDREW. Oh no. (*He puts the bottle in the cupboard.*) Please sit down. (*He stands by the downstage end of the desk.*)

GILBERT. Thank you, sir. (*He sits* R. *of the desk.*)

ANDREW. From the very beginning I realized that I didn't possess the knack of making myself liked—a knack that you will find you do possess.

GILBERT. Do you think so?

ANDREW. Oh yes. I am quite sure of it. (*He moves up* L. *of the desk.*) It is not a quality of great importance to a schoolmaster though, for too much of it, as you may also find, is as great a danger as the total lack of it. Forgive me lecturing, won't you?

GILBERT. I want to learn.

ANDREW. I can only teach you from my own experience. For two or three years I tried very hard to communicate to the boys some of my own joy in the great literature of the past. Of course I failed, as you will fail, nine hundred and ninety-nine times out of a thousand. But a single success can atone, and more than atone, for all the failures in the world. And sometimes—very rarely, it is true—but sometimes I had that success. That was in the early years.

GILBERT (*eagerly listening*). Please go on, sir.

ANDREW. In early years too, I discovered an easy substitute for popularity. (*He picks up his speech.*) I had of course acquired—we all do—many little mannerisms and tricks of speech, and I found that the boys were beginning to laugh at me. I was very happy at that, and encouraged the boys' laughter by playing up to it. It made our relationship so very much easier. They didn't like me as a man, but they found me funny as a character, and you can teach more things by laughter than by earnestness—for I never did have much sense of humour. So, for a time, you see, I was quite a success as a schoolmaster . . . (*He stops.*) I fear this is all very personal and embarrassing to you. Forgive me. You need have no fears about the lower fifth. (*He puts the speech into his pocket and turns to the window.*)

[GILBERT *rises and moves above the desk.*

GILBERT (*after a pause*). I'm afraid I said something that hurt you very much. It's myself you must forgive, sir. Believe me, I'm desperately sorry.

ANDREW (*turning down stage and leaning slightly on the back of the swivel chair*). There's no need. You were merely telling me what I should have known for myself. Perhaps I did in my heart, and hadn't the courage to acknowledge it. I knew, of course, that I was not only not liked, but now positively disliked. I had realized too that the boys— for many long years now—had ceased to laugh at me. I don't know why they no longer found me a joke. Perhaps it was my illness. No, I don't think it was that. Something deeper than that. Not a sickness of the body, but a sickness of the soul. At all events it didn't take much discernment on my part to realize I had become an utter failure as a schoolmaster. Still, stupidly enough, I hadn't realized that I was also feared. 'The Himmler of the lower fifth.' I suppose that will become my epitaph.

[GILBERT *is now deeply embarrassed and rather upset, but he remains silent.*

(*He sits on the upstage end of the window seat. With a mild laugh.*) I cannot for the life of me imagine why I should choose to unburden myself to you—a total stranger— when I have been silent to others for so long. Perhaps it is because my very unworthy mantle is about to fall on your shoulders. If that is so I shall take a prophet's privilege and foretell that you will have a very great success with the lower fifth.

GILBERT. Thank you, sir. I shall do my best.

ANDREW. I can't offer you a cigarette, I'm afraid. I don't smoke.

GILBERT. That's all right, sir. Nor do I.

MRS. GILBERT (*off*). Thank you so much for showing me round.

[MILLIE *and* MRS. GILBERT *enter up* C. ANDREW *rises.* MILLIE *comes down* R. *of the table* C., *picks up the papers on the settee and puts them on the fender down* R. MRS. GILBERT *comes down* L. *of the table* C. *to* R. *of* GILBERT.

ANDREW. I trust your wife has found no major snags in your new flat.

MRS. GILBERT. No. None at all.

MRS. GILBERT. Just imagine, Peter. Mr. and Mrs. Crocker-Harris first met each other on a holiday in the Lake District. Isn't that a coincidence?

GILBERT (*a little distrait*). Yes. Yes, it certainly is. On a walking tour, too?

[ANDREW *turns and looks out of the window.*

MILLIE. Andrew was on a walking tour. No walking for me. I can't abide it. I was staying with my uncle—that's Sir William Bartop, you know—you may have heard of him.

[GILBERT *and* MRS. GILBERT *try to look as though they had heard of him constantly.*

(*She moves below the settee.*) He'd taken a house near Windermere—quite a mansion it was really—rather silly for an old gentleman living alone—and Andrew knocked on our front door one day and asked the footman for a glass of water. So my uncle invited him in to tea.

MRS. GILBERT (*moving* C.). Our meeting wasn't quite as romantic as that.

GILBERT. I knocked her flat on her face. (*He moves behind* MRS. GILBERT *and puts his hands on her shoulders.*)

MRS. GILBERT. Not with love at first sight. With the swing doors of our hotel bar. So of course then he apologized and . . .

[ANDREW *turns and faces into the room.*

GILBERT (*brusquely*). Darling. The Crocker-Harris's, I'm sure, have far more important things to do than to listen to your detailed but inaccurate account of our very sordid little encounter. Why not just say I married you for your money and leave it at that? Come on, we must go.

MRS. GILBERT (*moving above the settee; to* MILLIE). Isn't he awful to me?

MILLIE (*moving round the* R. *end of the settee to the door up* R.). Men have no souls, my dear. My husband is just as bad.

MRS. GILBERT. Good-bye, Mr. Crocker-Harris.

ANDREW (*with a slight bow*). Good-bye.

MRS. GILBERT (*moving to the door up* R.; *to* MILLIE). I think your idea about the dining-room is awfully good—if only I can get the permit . . .

[MILLIE *and* MRS. GILBERT *go out.* GILBERT *has dallied to say good-bye alone to* ANDREW.

GILBERT. Good-bye, sir.

ANDREW (*crossing* C. *to* L. *of* GILBERT). Er—you will, I know, respect the confidences I have just made to you.

GILBERT. I should hate you to think I wouldn't.

ANDREW. I am sorry to have embarrassed you. I don't know what came over me. I have not been very well, you know. Good-bye, my dear fellow, and my best wishes.

GILBERT. Thank you. The very best of good luck to you too, sir, in your future career.

ANDREW. My future career? Yes. Thank you.

GILBERT. Well, good-bye, sir.

[*He crosses up* R. *and goes out.* ANDREW *moves to the chair* R. *of the desk and sits. He picks up a book and looks idly at it.* MILLIE *enters up* R. *She crosses above the table* C., *picks up the box of chocolates and eats one as she speaks.*

MILLIE. Good-looking couple.

ANDREW. Very.

MILLIE. He looks as if he'd got what it takes. I should think he'll be a success all right.

ANDREW. That's what I thought.

MILLIE. I don't think it's much of a career, though—a schoolmaster—for a likely young chap like that.

ANDREW. I know you don't.

MILLIE (*crossing down to the desk and picking up the luggage labels*). Still, I bet when he leaves this place it won't be without a pension. It'll be roses, roses all the way, and tears and cheers and good-bye, Mr. Chips.

ANDREW. I expect so.

MILLIE. What's the matter with you?

ANDREW. Nothing.

MILLIE. You're not going to have another of your attacks, are you? You look dreadful.

ANDREW. I'm perfectly all right.

MILLIE (*indifferently*). You know best. Your medicine's there, anyway, if you want it.

[*She goes out up* C. ANDREW, *left alone, continues for a time staring at the text he has been pretending to read. Then he puts one hand over his eyes. There is a knock on the door up* R.

ANDREW. Come in.

[TAPLOW *enters up* R. *and appears timidly from behind the screen. He is carrying a small book behind his back.*

(*Sharply.*) Yes, Taplow? What is it?

TAPLOW. Nothing, sir.

ANDREW. What do you mean, nothing?

TAPLOW (*timidly*). I just came back to say good-bye, sir.

ANDREW. Oh. (*He puts down the book and rises.*)

TAPLOW (*moving* C.). I didn't have a chance with the head here. I rather dashed out, I'm afraid. I thought I'd just come back and—wish you luck, sir.

ANDREW. Thank you, Taplow. That's good of you.

TAPLOW. I—er—thought this might interest you, sir. (*He quickly thrusts the small book towards* ANDREW.)

ANDREW (*taking out his glasses and putting them on*). What is it?

TAPLOW. Verse translation of *The Agamemnon*, sir. The Browning version. It's not much good. I've been reading it in the Chapel gardens.

ANDREW (*taking the book*). Very interesting, Taplow. (*He seems to have a little difficulty in speaking. He clears his throat and then goes on in his level, gentle voice.*) I know the translation, of course. It has its faults, I agree, but I think you will enjoy it more when you get used to the metre he employs. (*He hands the book to* TAPLOW.)

TAPLOW (*brusquely thrusting the book back to* ANDREW). It's for you, sir.

ANDREW. For me?

TAPLOW. Yes, sir. I've written in it.

[ANDREW *opens the fly-leaf and reads whatever is written there.*

ANDREW. Did you buy this?

TAPLOW. Yes, sir. It was only second-hand.

ANDREW. You shouldn't have spent your pocket-money this way.

TAPLOW. That's all right, sir. It wasn't very much. (*Suddenly appalled.*) The price isn't still inside, is it?

[ANDREW *carefully wipes his glasses and puts them on again.*

ANDREW (*at length*). No. Just what you've written. Nothing else.

TAPLOW. Good. I'm sorry you've got it already. I thought you probably would have.

ANDREW. I haven't got it already. I may have had it once. I can't remember. But I haven't got it now.

TAPLOW. That's all right, then.

[ANDREW *continues to stare at* TAPLOW'S *inscription on the fly-leaf.*

(*Suspiciously.*) What's the matter, sir? Have I got the accent wrong on εὐμενῶς ?[1]

ANDREW. No. The perispomenon is perfectly correct. (*His hands are shaking. He lowers the book and turns away above the chair* R. *of the desk.*) Taplow, would you be good enough to take that bottle of medicine, which you so kindly brought in, and pour me out one dose in a glass which you will find in the bathroom?

TAPLOW (*seeing something is wrong*). Yes, sir. (*He moves up to the sideboard and picks up the bottle.*)

ANDREW. The doses are clearly marked on the bottle. I usually put a little water with it.

TAPLOW. Yes, sir.

[*He darts out up* C. ANDREW, *the moment he is gone, breaks down and begins to sob uncontrollably. He sits in the chair* L. *of the desk and makes a desperate attempt, after a moment, to control himself, but when* TAPLOW *comes back his emotion is still very apparent.* TAPLOW *re-enters with the bottle and a glass, comes to the upstage end of the desk and holds out the glass.*

ANDREW (*taking the glass*). Thank you. (*He drinks, turning his back on* TAPLOW *as he does so.*) You must forgive this exhibition of weakness, Taplow. The truth is I have been going through rather a strain lately.

TAPLOW (*putting the bottle on the desk*). Of course, sir. I quite understand. (*He eases towards* C.)

[*There is a knock on the door up* L.

[1] *Phonetically represented, this reads:* 'eumenose'.

ANDREW. Come in.

[FRANK *enters up* L.

FRANK. Oh, sorry. I thought you'd be finished by now. (*He moves to* L. *of* TAPLOW.)

ANDREW. Come in, Hunter, do. It's perfectly all right. Our lesson was over some time ago, but Taplow most kindly came back to say good-bye.

[FRANK, *taking in* TAPLOW's *rather startled face and* ANDREW's *obvious emotion, looks a little puzzled.*

FRANK. Are you sure I'm not intruding?

ANDREW. No, no. I want you to see this book that Taplow has given me, Hunter. Look. A translation of *The Agamemnon,* by Robert Browning. (*He rises.*) Do you see the inscription he has put into it? (*He hands the book open to* FRANK *across the desk.*)

FRANK (*glancing at the book*). Yes, but it's no use to me, I'm afraid. I never learnt Greek.

ANDREW. Then we'll have to translate it for him, won't we, Taplow? (*He recites by heart.*) τὸν κρατοῦντα μαλθακῶς θεὸς πρόσωθεν εὐμενῶς προσδέρκεται.[1] That means—in a rough translation: 'God from afar looks graciously upon a gentle master.' It comes from a speech of Agamemnon's to Clytaemnestra.

FRANK. I see. Very pleasant and very apt. (*He hands the book back to* ANDREW.)

ANDREW. Very pleasant. But perhaps not, after all, so very apt. (*He turns quickly away from both of them as emotion once more seems about to overcome him.*)

[FRANK *brusquely jerks his head to the bewildered* TAPLOW *to get out.* TAPLOW *nods.*

[1] *Phonetically rendered, this reads:* 'ton kratownta malthecose theos prosothen eumenose prosdirkati'.

TAPLOW. Good-bye, sir, and the best of luck.

ANDREW. Good-bye, Taplow, and thank you very much.

[TAPLOW *flees quickly up* R. *and goes out.* FRANK *watches* ANDREW'S *back with a mixture of embarrassment and sympathy.*

ANDREW (*turning at length, slightly recovered*). Dear me, what a fool I made of myself in front of that boy. And in front of you, Hunter. (*He moves in to the desk.*) I can't imagine what you must think of me.

FRANK. Nonsense.

ANDREW. I am not a very emotional person, as you know, but there was something so very touching and kindly about his action, and coming as it did just after . . . (*He stops, then glances at the book in his hand.*) This is a very delightful thing to have, don't you think?

FRANK. Delightful.

ANDREW. The quotation, of course, he didn't find entirely by himself. I happened to make some little joke about the line in form the other day. But he must have remembered it all the same to have found it so readily—and perhaps he means it.

FRANK. I'm sure he does, or he wouldn't have written it.

[MILLIE *enters up* C. *with a tray of supper things. She puts the tray on the sideboard. She puts table napkins, mats and bread on the table.* ANDREW *turns and looks out of the window.*

MILLIE. Hullo, Frank. I'm glad you're in time. Lend me a cigarette. I've been gasping for one for an hour.

[FRANK *moves up* L *of the table* C. *and once more extends his case.* MILLIE *takes a cigarette.*

FRANK. Your husband has just had a very nice present.

MILLIE. Oh? Who from?

FRANK. Taplow. (*He comes down* L. *of the table.*)

MILLIE (*coming down* R. *of the table; smiling*). Oh, Taplow.

[FRANK *lights* MILLIE'S *cigarette.*

ANDREW (*moving above the desk to the chair* R. *of it*). He bought it with his own pocket-money, Millie, and wrote a very charming inscription inside.

FRANK. 'God looks kindly upon a gracious master.'

ANDREW. No—not gracious—gentle, I think. τὸν κρατοῦντα μαλθακῶς—yes, I think gentle is the better translation. I would rather have had this present, I think, than almost anything I can think of.

[*There is a pause.* MILLIE *laughs suddenly.*

MILLIE (*holding out her hand*). Let's see it. The artful little beast.

[ANDREW *hands the book across to* MILLIE. MILLIE *opens it.*

FRANK (*urgently*). Millie.

[MILLIE *looks at* ANDREW.

ANDREW. Artful?

[MILLIE *looks at* FRANK.

Why artful?

[FRANK *stares meaningly at* MILLIE. MILLIE *looks at* ANDREW.

Why artful, Millie?

[MILLIE *laughs again, quite lightly.*

MILLIE. My dear, because I came into this room this afternoon to find him giving an imitation of you to Frank here. Obviously he was scared stiff I was going to tell you, and you'd ditch his remove or something. I don't blame him for trying a few bobs' worth of appeasement. (*She gives the book to* ANDREW, *then moves up* R. *of the table to the sideboard, where she stubs out her cigarette, picks up some cutlery and starts to lay the table.*)

[ANDREW *stands quite still, looking down at the book.*

ANDREW (*after a pause; nodding*). I see. (*He puts the book gently on the desk, picks up the bottle of medicine and moves up* L. *of the table to the door up* C.)

MILLIE. Where are you going, dear? Dinner's nearly ready.

ANDREW (*opening the door*). Only to my room for a moment. I won't be long.

MILLIE. You've just had a dose of that, dear. I shouldn't have another, if I were you.

ANDREW. I am allowed two at a time.

MILLIE. Well, see it is two and no more, won't you?

[ANDREW *meets her eye for a moment, then goes out quietly.* MILLIE *moves to* L. *of the table and lays the last knife and fork. She looks at* FRANK *with an expression half defiant and half ashamed.*

FRANK (*with a note of real repulsion in his voice*). Millie! My God! How could you?

MILLIE. Well, why not? (*She crosses above the table and comes down* L. *of the settee.*) Why should he be allowed his comforting little illusions? I'm not.

FRANK (*advancing on her*). Listen. You're to go to his room now and tell him that was a lie.

MILLIE. Certainly not. It wasn't a lie.

FRANK. If you don't, I will.

MILLIE. I shouldn't, if I were you. It'll only make things worse. He won't believe you.

FRANK (*moving up* R. *of the table* C.). We'll see about that.

MILLIE. Go ahead. See what happens. He knows I don't lie to him. He knows what I told him was the truth, and he won't like your sympathy. He'll think you're making fun of him, like Taplow.

[FRANK *hesitates, then comes slowly down* C. *again.* MILLIE *watches him, a little frightened.*

FRANK (*after a pause*). We're finished, Millie—you and I.

MILLIE (*laughing*). Frank, really! Don't be hysterical.

FRANK. I'm not. I mean it.

MILLIE (*lightly*). Oh yes, you mean it. Of course you mean it. Now just sit down, dear, and relax and forget all about artful little boys and their five bob presents, and talk to me. (*She pulls at his coat.*)

FRANK (*pulling away*). Forget? If I live to be a hundred I shall never forget that little glimpse you've just given me of yourself.

MILLIE. Frank—you're making a frightening mountain out of an absurd little molehill.

FRANK. Of course, but the mountain I'm making in my imagination is so frightening that I'd rather try to forget both it and the repulsive little molehill that gave it birth. But as I know I never can, I tell you, Millie—from this moment you and I are finished.

MILLIE (*quietly*). You can't scare me, Frank. (*She turns away towards the fireplace.*) I know that's what you're trying to do, but you can't do it.

FRANK (*quietly*). I'm not trying to scare you, Millie. I'm telling you the simple truth. I'm not coming to Bradford.

[*There is a pause.*

MILLIE (*turning to face* FRANK; *with an attempt at bravado*). All right, my dear, if that's the way you feel about it. Don't come to Bradford.

FRANK. Right. Now I think you ought to go to your room

and look after Andrew. (*He crosses towards the door up* L.) I'm leaving.

MILLIE (*following* FRANK). What is this? Frank, I don't understand, really I don't. What have I done?

FRANK. I think you know what you've done, Millie. Go and look after Andrew.

MILLIE (*moving to the* L. *end of the settee*). Andrew? Why this sudden concern for Andrew?

FRANK. Because I think he's just been about as badly hurt as a human being can be; and as he's a sick man and in a rather hysterical state it might be a good plan to go and see how he is.

MILLIE (*scornfully*). Hurt? Andrew hurt? You can't hurt Andrew. He's dead.

FRANK (*moving to* R. *of* MILLIE). Why do you hate him so much, Millie?

MILLIE. Because he keeps me from you.

FRANK. That isn't true.

MILLIE. Because he's not a man at all.

FRANK. He's a human being.

MILLIE. You've got a fine right to be so noble about him, after deceiving him for six months.

FRANK. Twice in six months—at your urgent invitation.

[MILLIE *slaps his face, in a violent paroxysm of rage.*

Thank you for that. I deserved it. (*He crosses to the chair* R. *of the desk.*) I deserve a lot worse than that, too.

MILLIE (*running to him*). Frank, forgive me—I didn't mean it.

FRANK (*quietly*). You'd better have the truth, Millie, it had to come some time. (*He turns to face* MILLIE.) I've never loved you. I've never told you I loved you.

MILLIE. I know, Frank, I know. (*She backs away slightly.*) I've always accepted that.

FRANK. You asked me just now if I was running away from you. Well, I was.

MILLIE. I knew that, too.

FRANK. But I was coming to Bradford. It was going to be the very last time I was ever going to see you and at Bradford I would have told you that.

MILLIE. You wouldn't. You wouldn't. You've tried to tell me that so often before—(*she crosses to the fireplace*) and I've always stopped you somehow—somehow. I would have stopped you again.

FRANK (*quietly*). I don't think so, Millie. Not this time.

MILLIE (*crossing to R. of the table C.*). Frank, I don't care what humiliations you heap on me. I know you don't give two hoots for me as a person. I've always known that. I've never minded so long as you care for me as a woman. And you do, Frank. You do. You do, don't you?

[FRANK *is silent. He crosses slowly to the fireplace.*

It'll be all right at Bradford, you see. It'll be all right, there.

FRANK. I'm not coming to Bradford, Millie.

[*The door up* C. *opens slowly and* ANDREW *enters. He is carrying the bottle of medicine. He hands it to* MILLIE *and passes on crossing down* L. *below the desk.* MILLIE *holds the bottle up to the light.*

ANDREW (*gently*). You should know me well enough by now, my dear, to realize how unlikely it is that I should ever take an overdose.

[MILLIE, *without a word, puts the bottle on the sideboard and goes out up* C. ANDREW *goes to the cupboard down* L. *and takes out the sherry and one glass.*

FRANK. I'm not staying to dinner, I'm afraid.

5

ANDREW. Indeed? I'm sorry to hear that. You'll have a glass of sherry?

FRANK. No, thank you.

ANDREW. You will forgive me if I do.

FRANK. Of course. Perhaps I'll change my mind. (*He crosses to* c.)

(ANDREW *takes out a second glass and fills both of them.*) About Taplow . . .

ANDREW. Oh yes?

FRANK. It *is* perfectly true that he was imitating you. I, of course, was mostly to blame in that, and I'm very sorry.

ANDREW. That is perfectly all right. Was it a good imitation?

FRANK. No.

ANDREW. I expect it was. Boys are often very clever mimics.

FRANK. We talked about you, of course, before that. (*He moves in to* R. *of the desk.*) He said—you probably won't believe this, but I thought I ought to tell you—he said he liked you very much.

[ANDREW *smiles slightly.*

ANDREW. Indeed? (*He drinks.*)

FRANK. I can remember very clearly his exact words. He said: 'He doesn't seem to like people to like him—but in spite of that, I do—very much.' (*Lightly.*) So you see it looks after all as if the book might not have been a mere question of—appeasement.

ANDREW. The book? (*He picks it up.*) Dear me! What a lot of fuss about a little book—and a not very good little book at that. (*He drops it on the desk.*)

FRANK. I would like you to believe me.

ANDREW. Possibly you would, my dear Hunter; but I can assure you I am not particularly concerned about

Taplow's views of my character: or about yours either, if it comes to that.

FRANK (*hopelessly*). I think you should keep that book all the same. You may find it'll mean something to you after all.

ANDREW (*turning to the cupboard and pouring himself another sherry*). Exactly. It will mean a perpetual reminder to myself of the story with which Taplow is at this very moment regaling his friends in the House. 'I gave the Crock a book, to buy him off, and he blubbed. The Crock blubbed. I tell you I was there. I saw it. The Crock blubbed.' My mimicry is not as good as his, I fear. Forgive me. (*He moves up* L. *of the desk.*) And now let us leave this idiotic subject and talk of more pleasant things. Do you like this sherry? I got it on my last visit to London.

FRANK. If Taplow ever breathes a word of that story to anyone at all, I'll murder him. But he won't. And if you think I will you greatly underestimate my character as well as his. (*He drains his glass and puts it on the desk. He moves to the door up* L.)

[ANDREW *comes down* L., *puts his glass on the cupboard, and stands facing down stage.*

Good-bye.

ANDREW. Are you leaving so soon? Good-bye, my dear fellow.

[FRANK *stops. He takes out his cigarette case and places it on the* L. *end of the table* C.

FRANK. As this is the last time I shall probably ever see you, I'm going to offer you a word of advice.

ANDREW (*politely*). I shall be glad to listen to it.

FRANK. Leave your wife.

[*There is a pause.* ANDREW *looks out of the window.*

ANDREW. So that you may the more easily carry on your intrigue with her?

FRANK (*moving in to the upstage end of the desk*). How long have you known that?

ANDREW. Since it first began.

FRANK. How did you find out?

ANDREW. By information.

FRANK. By whose information?

ANDREW. By someone's whose word I could hardly discredit.

[*There is a pause.*

FRANK (*slowly, with repulsion*). No! That's too horrible to think of.

ANDREW (*turning to* FRANK). Nothing is ever too horrible to think of, Hunter. It is simply a question of facing facts.

FRANK. She might have told you a lie. Have you faced that fact?

ANDREW. She never tells me a lie. In twenty years she has never told me a lie. Only the truth.

FRANK. This was a lie.

ANDREW (*moving up* L. *of* FRANK). No, my dear Hunter. Do you wish me to quote you dates?

FRANK (*still unable to believe it*). And she told you six months ago?

ANDREW (*moving down* L.). Isn't it seven?

FRANK (*savagely*). Then why have you allowed me inside your home? Why haven't you done something—reported me to the governors—anything—made a scene, knocked me down?

ANDREW. Knocked you down?

FRANK. You didn't have to invite me to dinner.

ANDREW. My dear Hunter, if, over the last twenty years, I had allowed such petty considerations to influence my choice of dinner guests I would have found it increasingly hard to remember which master to invite and which to refuse. You see, Hunter, you mustn't flatter yourself you are the first. My information is a good deal better than yours, you understand. It's authentic.

[*There is a pause.*

FRANK. She's evil.

ANDREW. That's hardly a kindly epithet to apply to a lady whom, I gather, you have asked to marry.

FRANK. Did she tell you that?

ANDREW. She's a dutiful wife. She tells me everything.

FRANK. That, at least, was a lie.

ANDREW. She never lies.

FRANK (*leaning on the desk*). That was a lie. Do you want the truth? Can you bear the truth?

ANDREW. I can bear anything. (*He crosses to the fireplace.*)

FRANK (*turning to face* ANDREW). What I did I did cold-bloodedly out of weakness and ignorance and crass stupidity. I'm bitterly, bitterly ashamed of myself, but, in a sense, I'm glad you know (*he moves* c.) though I'd rather a thousand times that you'd heard it from me than from your wife. I won't ask you to forgive me. I can only tell you, with complete truth, that the only emotion she has ever succeeded in arousing in me she aroused in me for the first time ten minutes ago—an intense and passionate disgust.

ANDREW. What a delightfully chivalrous statement.

FRANK (*moving below the settee*). Forget chivalry, Crock, for God's sake. Forget all your fine mosaic scruples. You must leave her—it's your only chance.

ANDREW. She's my wife, Hunter. You seem to forget that. As long as she wishes to remain my wife, she may.

FRANK. She's out to kill you.

ANDREW. My dear Hunter, if that was indeed her purpose, you should know by now that she fulfilled it long ago.

FRANK. Why won't you leave her?

ANDREW. Because I wouldn't wish to add another grave wrong to one I have already done her.

FRANK. What wrong have you done her?

ANDREW. To marry her.

[*There is a pause.* FRANK *stares at him in silence.*

You see, my dear Hunter, she is really quite as much to be pitied as I. We are both of us interesting subjects for your microscope. (*He sits on the fender.*) Both of us needing from the other something that would make life supportable for us, and neither of us able to give it. Two kinds of love. Hers and mine. Worlds apart, as I know now, though when I married her I didn't think they were incompatible. In those days I hadn't thought that her kind of love—the love she requires and which I was unable to give her—was so important that its absence would drive out the other kind of love—the kind of love that I require and which I thought, in my folly, was by far the greater part of love. (*He rises.*) I may have been, you see, Hunter, a brilliant classical scholar, but I was woefully ignorant of the facts of life. I know better now, of course. I know that in both of us, the love that we should have borne each other has turned to bitter hatred. That's all the problem is. Not a very unusual one, I venture to think—nor nearly as tragic as you seem to imagine. Merely the problem of an unsatisfied wife and a henpecked husband. You'll find it all over the world. It is usually, I believe, a subject for farce. (*He turns to the mantelpiece and adjusts the hands of the clock.*) And now, if you have to leave us, my dear fellow, please don't let me detain you any longer.

[FRANK *makes no move to go.*

FRANK. Don't go to Bradford. Stay here, until you take up your new job.

ANDREW. I think I've already told you I'm not interested in your advice.

FRANK. Leave her. It's the only way.

ANDREW (*violently*). Will you please go!

FRANK. All right. I'd just like you to say good-bye to me, properly, though. Will you? I shan't see you again. I know you don't want my pity, but, I would like to be of some help.

[ANDREW *turns and faces* FRANK.

ANDREW. If you think, by this expression of kindness, Hunter, that you can get me to repeat the shameful exhibition of emotion I made to Taplow a moment ago, I must tell you that you have no chance. My hysteria over that book just now was no more than a sort of reflex action of the spirit. The muscular twitchings of a corpse. It can never happen again.

FRANK. A corpse can be revived.

ANDREW. I don't believe in miracles.

FRANK. Don't you? Funnily enough, as a scientist, I do.

ANDREW (*turning to the fireplace*). Your faith would be touching, if I were capable of being touched by it.

FRANK. You are, I think. (*He moves behind* ANDREW. *After a pause.*) I'd like to come and visit you at this crammer's.

ANDREW. That is an absurd suggestion.

FRANK. I suppose it is rather, but all the same I'd like to do it. May I?

ANDREW. Of course not.

FRANK (*sitting on the settee*). Your term begins on the first of September, doesn't it? (*He takes out a pocket diary.*)

ANDREW. I tell you the idea is quite childish.

FRANK. I could come about the second week.

ANDREW. You would be bored to death. So, probably, would I.

FRANK (*glancing at his diary*). Let's say Monday the twelfth, then.

ANDREW (*turning to face* FRANK, *his hands beginning to tremble*). Say anything you like, only please go. Please go, Hunter.

FRANK (*writing in his book and not looking at* ANDREW). That's fixed then. Monday, September the twelfth. Will you remember that?

ANDREW (*after a pause; with difficulty*). I suppose I'm at least as likely to remember it as you are.

FRANK. That's fixed, then. (*He rises, slips the book into his pocket, and puts out his hand.*) Good-bye, until then. (*He moves in to* ANDREW.)

[ANDREW *hesitates, then shakes his hand.*

ANDREW. Good-bye.

FRANK. May I go out through your garden? (*He crosses to c.*)

ANDREW (*nodding*). Of course.

FRANK. I'm off to have a quick word with Taplow. By the way, may I take him a message from you?

ANDREW. What message?

FRANK. Has he or has he not got his remove?

ANDREW. He has.

FRANK. May I tell him?

ANDREW. It is highly irregular. Yes, you may.

FRANK. Good. (*He turns to go, then turns back.*) Oh, by the way, I'd better have the address of that crammer's. (*He moves below the settee, takes out his diary, and points his pencil, ready to write.*)

[MILLIE *enters up* C. *She carries a casserole on three plates.*

MILLIE (*coming above the table* C.). Dinner's ready. You're staying, Frank, aren't you? (*She puts the casserole and plates on the table.*)

FRANK (*politely*). No. I'm afraid not. (*To* ANDREW.) What's that address?

ANDREW (*after great hesitation*). The Old Deanery, Malcombe, Dorset.

FRANK. I'll write to you and you can let me know about trains. Good-bye. (*To* MILLIE.) Good-bye.

[*He crosses to the door up* L. *and goes out.* MILLIE *is silent for a moment. Then she laughs.*

MILLIE. That's a laugh, I must say.

ANDREW. What's a laugh, my dear?

MILLIE. You inviting him to stay with you.

ANDREW. I didn't. He suggested it.

MILLIE (*moving to the* L. *end of the settee*). He's coming to Bradford.

ANDREW. Yes. I remember your telling me so.

MILLIE. He's coming to Bradford. He's not going to you.

ANDREW. The likeliest contingency is, that he's not going to either of us.

MILLIE. He's coming to Bradford.

ANDREW. I expect so. Oh, by the way, I'm not. I shall be staying here until I go to Dorset.

MILLIE (*indifferently*). Suit yourself. What makes you think I'll join you there?

ANDREW. I don't.

MILLIE. You needn't expect me.

ANDREW. I don't think either of us has the right to expect anything further from the other.

[*The telephone rings.*

Excuse me. (*He moves to the table down* R. *and lifts the receiver.*) Hullo . . .

[*While he is speaking* MILLIE *crosses to* L. *of the table* C. *About to sit, she sees the cigarette case. She picks it up, fingers it for a moment, and finally drops it into her pocket.*

Yes, Headmaster . . . The time-table? . . . It's perfectly simple. The middle fourth B division will take a ten-minute break on Tuesdays and a fifteen-minute break on alternate Wednesdays; while exactly the reverse procedure will apply to the lower Shell, C division. I thought I had sufficiently explained that on my chart . . . Oh, I see . . . Thank you, that is very good of you . . . Yes. I think you will find it will work out quite satisfactorily . . . Oh, by the way, Headmaster. I have changed my mind about the prize-giving ceremony. I intend to speak after, instead of before, Fletcher, as is my privilege . . . Yes, I quite understand, but I am now seeing the matter in a different light . . . I know, but I am of opinion that occasionally an anti-climax can be surprisingly effective. Good-bye. (*He replaces the receiver, crosses to* R. *of the table* C., *and sits.*) Come along, my dear. We mustn't let our dinner get cold. (*He unrolls his table napkin.*)

MILLIE *sits* L. *of the table and unrolls her table napkin.* ANDREW *offers her the bread. She ignores it. He takes a piece. She removes the lid of the casserole as—*

the CURTAIN *falls.*

# A PHOENIX TOO FREQUENT
by Christopher Fry

'To whom conferr'd a peacock's undecent,
A squirrel's harsh, a phoenix too frequent.'
*Robert Burton quoting Martial*

# CHARACTERS

DYNAMENE

DOTO

TEGEUS-CHROMIS

*Scene*

The tomb of Virilius, near Ephesus; night

*Note*

The story was got from Jeremy Taylor who
had it from Petronius

# A PHOENIX TOO FREQUENT

*An underground tomb, in darkness except for the very low light
of an oil-lamp. Above ground the starlight shows a line of trees
on which hang the bodies of several men. It also penetrates a
gate and falls on to the first of the steps which descend into the
darkness of the tomb.* DOTO *talks to herself in the dark.*

DOTO. Nothing but the harmless day gone into black
   Is all the dark is. And so what's my trouble?
   Demons is so much wind. Are so much wind.
   I've plenty to fill my thoughts. All that I ask
   Is don't keep turning men over in my mind,
   Venerable Aphrodite. I've had my last one
   And thank you. I thank thee. He smelt of sour grass
   And was likeable. He collected ebony quoits.

   [*An owl hoots near at hand.*

O Zeus! O some god or other, where is the oil?
Fire's from Prometheus. I thank thee. If I
Mean to die I'd better see what I'm doing.

   [*She fills the lamp with oil. The flame burns up brightly
   and shows* DYNAMENE, *beautiful and young, leaning
   asleep beside a bier.*

Honestly, I would rather have to sleep
With a bald bee-keeper who was wearing his boots
Than spend more days fasting and thirsting and crying
In a tomb. I shouldn't have said that. Pretend
I didn't hear myself. But life and death
Is cat and dog in this double-bed of a world.
My master, my poor master, was a man

Whose nose was as straight as a little buttress,
And now he has taken it into Elysium
Where it won't be noticed among all the other straight-
ness.

[*The owl cries again and wakens* DYNAMENE.

Oh, them owls. Those owls. It's woken her.

DYNAMENE. Ah! I'm breathless. I caught up with the ship
But it spread its wings, creaking a cry of *Dew*,
*Dew*! and flew figurehead foremost into the sun.

DOTO. How crazy, madam.

DYNAMENE. Doto, draw back the curtains.
I'll take my barley-water.

DOTO. We're not at home
Now, madam. It's the master's tomb.

DYNAMENE. Of course!
Oh, I'm wretched. Already I have disfigured
My vigil. My cynical eyelids have soon dropped me
In a dream.

DOTO. But then it's possible, madam, you might
Find yourself in bed with him again
In a dream, madam. Was he on the ship?

DYNAMENE. He was the ship.

DOTO. Oh. That makes it different.

DYNAMENE. He was the ship. He had such a deck, Doto,
Such a white, scrubbed deck. Such a stern prow,
Such a proud stern, so slim from port to starboard.
If ever you meet a man with such fine masts
Give your life to him, Doto. The figurehead
Bore his own features, so serene in the brow
And hung with a little seaweed. O Virilius,
My husband, you have left a wake in my soul.
You cut the glassy water with a diamond keel.
I must cry again.

DOTO.                    What, when you mean to join him?
Don't you believe he will be glad to see you, madam?
*Thankful* to see you, I should imagine, among
Them shapes and shades; all shapes of shapes and all
Shades of shades, from what I've heard. I know
I shall feel odd at first with Cerberus,
Sop or no sop. Still, I know how you feel, madam.
You think he may find a temptation in Hades.
I shouldn't worry. It would help him to settle down.

  [DYNAMENE *weeps.*

It would only be *fun*, madam. He couldn't go far
With a shade.
DYNAMENE.       He was one of the coming men.
He was certain to have become the most well-organized
    provost
The town has known, once they had made him provost.
He was so punctual, you could regulate
The sun by him. He made the world succumb
To his daily revolution of habit. But who,
In the world he has gone to, will appreciate that?
O poor Virilius! To be a coming man
Already gone—it must be distraction.
Why did you leave me walking about our ambitions
Like a cat in the ruins of a house? Promising husband,
Why did you insult me by dying? Virilius,
Now I keep no flower, except in the vase
Of the tomb.
DOTO.            O poor madam! O poor master!
I presume so far as to cry somewhat for myself
As well. I know you won't mind, madam. It's two
Days not eating makes me think of my uncle's
Shop in the country, where he has a hardware business,
Basins, pots, ewers, and alabaster birds.

He makes you die of laughing. O madam,
Isn't it sad?

[*They both weep.*

DYNAMENE.    How could I have allowed you
To come and die of my grief? Doto, it puts
A terrible responsibility on me. Have you
No grief of your own you could die of?

DOTO.                                          Not really, madam.

DYNAMENE.    Nothing?

DOTO.                    Not really. They was all one to me.
Well, all but two was all one to me. And they,
I could never be sure if they had gone for good
Or not; and so that kept things cheerful, madam.
One always gave a wink before he deserted me,
The other slapped me as it were behind, madam;
Then they would be away for some months.

DYNAMENE.                              Oh Doto,
What an unhappy life you were having to lead.

DOTO. Yes, I'm sure. But never mind, madam,
It seemed quite lively then. And now I know
It's what you say; life is more big than a bed
And full of miracles and mysteries like
One man made for one woman, etcetera, etcetera.
Lovely. I feel sung, madam, by a baritone
In mixed company with everyone pleased.
And so I had to come with you here, madam,
For the last sad chorus of me. It's all
Fresh to me. Death's a new interest in life,
If it doesn't disturb you, madam, to have me crying.
It's because of us not having breakfast again.
And the master, of course. And the beautiful world.
And you crying too, madam. Oh—Oh!

DYNAMENE. I can't forbid your crying; but you must cry

On the other side of the tomb. I'm becoming confused.
This is my personal grief and my sacrifice
Of self, solus. Right over there, darling girl.
DOTO. What here?
DYNAMENE.        Now, if you wish, you may cry, Doto.
But our tears are very different. For me
The world is all with Charon, all, all,
Even the metal and plume of the rose garden,
And the forest where the sea fumes overhead
In vegetable tides, and particularly
The entrance to the warm baths in Arcite Street
Where we first met;—all!—the sun itself
Trails an evening hand in the sultry river
Far away down by Acheron. I am lonely,
Virilius. Where is the punctual eye
And where is the cautious voice which made
Balance-sheets sound like Homer and Homer sound
Like balance-sheets? The precision of limbs, the amiable
Laugh, the exact festivity? Gone from the world.
You were the peroration of nature, Virilius.
You explained everything to me, even the extremely
Complicated gods. You wrote them down
In seventy columns. Dear curling calligraphy!
Gone from the world, once and for all. And I taught you
In your perceptive moments to appreciate me.
You said I was harmonious, Virilius,
Moulded and harmonious, little matronal
Ox-eye, your package. And then I would walk
Up and down largely, as it were making my own
Sunlight. What a mad blacksmith creation is
Who blows his furnaces until the stars fly upward
And iron Time is hot and politicians glow
And bulbs and roots sizzle into hyacinth
And orchis, and the sand puts out the lion,

6

Roaring yellow, and oceans bud with porpoises,
Blenny, tunny and the almost unexisting
Blindfish; throats are cut, the masterpiece
Looms out of labour; nations and rebellions
Are spat out to hang on the wind—and all is gone
In one Virilius, wearing his office tunic,
Checking the pence column as he went.
Where's animation now? What is there that stays
To dance? The eye of the one-eyed world is out.

[*She weeps.*

DOTO. I shall try to grieve a little, too.
It would take lessons, I imagine, to do it out loud
For long. If I could only remember
Any one of those fellows without wanting to laugh.
Hopeless, I am. Now those good pair of shoes
I gave away without thinking, that's a different—
Well, I've cried enough about *them*, I suppose.
Poor madam, poor master.

[TEGEUS *comes through the gate to the top of the steps.*

TEGEUS.                     What's your trouble?
DOTO.                                         Oh!
Oh! Oh, a man. I thought for a moment it was something
With harm in it. Trust a man to be where it's dark.
What is it? Can't you sleep?
TEGEUS.                     Now, listen—
DOTO.                                    Hush!
Remember you're in the grave. You must go away.
Madam is occupied.
TEGEUS.           What, here?
DOTO.                          Becoming
Dead. We both are.
TEGEUS.           What's going on here?

DOTO.                                         Grief.
Are you satisfied now?

TEGEUS.                    Less and less. Do you know
What the time is?

DOTO.                   I'm not interested.
We've done with all that. Go away. Be a gentleman.
If we can't be free of men in a grave
Death's a dead loss.

TEGEUS.                    It's two in the morning. All
I ask is what are women doing down here
At two in the morning?

DOTO.                    Can't you see she's crying?
Or is she sleeping again? Either way
She's making arrangements to join her husband.

TEGEUS.                                         Where?

DOTO. Good god, in the Underworld, dear man. Haven't you
   learnt
About life and death?

TEGEUS.                   In a manner, yes; in a manner;
The rudiments. So the lady means to die?

DOTO. For love; beautiful, curious madam.

TEGEUS.                                  Not curious;
I've had thoughts like it. Death is a kind of love.
Not anything I can explain.

DOTO.                       You'd better come in
And sit down.

TEGEUS.          I'd be grateful.

DOTO.                             Do. It will be my last
Chance to have company, in the flesh.

TEGEUS.                               Do you mean
You're going too?

DOTO.              Oh, certainly I am.
Not anything I can explain.
It all started with madam saying a man

Was two men really, and I'd only noticed one,
One each, I mean. It seems he has a soul
As well as his other troubles. And I like to know
What I'm getting with a man. I'm inquisitive,
I suppose you'd call me.
TEGEUS.                    It takes some courage.
DOTO.                                        Well, yes
And no. I'm fond of change.
TEGEUS.                    Would you object
To have me eating my supper here?
DOTO.                    Be careful
Of the crumbs. We don't want a lot of squeaking mice
Just when we're dying.
TEGEUS.          What a sigh she gave then.
Down the air like a slow comet.
And now she's all dark again. Mother of me.
How long has this been going on?
DOTO.                    Two days.
It should have been three by now, but at first
Madam had difficulty with the Town Council. They said
They couldn't have a tomb used as a private residence.
But madam told them she wouldn't be eating here,
Only suffering, and they thought that would be all right.
TEGEUS. Two of you. Marvellous. Who would have said
I should ever have stumbled on anything like this?
Do you have to cry? Yes, I suppose so. It's all
Quite reasonable.
DOTO.          Your supper and your knees.
That's what's making me cry. I can't bear sympathy
And they're sympathetic.
TEGEUS.                    Please eat a bit of something.
I've no appetite left.
DOTO.          And see her go ahead of me?
Wrap it up; put it away. You sex of wicked beards!

It's no wonder you have to shave off your black souls
Every day as they push through your chins.
I'll turn my back on you. It means utter
Contempt. Eat? Utter contempt. Oh, little new rolls!
TEGEUS. Forget it, forget it; please forget it. Remember
I've had no experience of this kind of thing before.
Indeed I'm as sorry as I know how to be. Ssh,
We'll disturb her. She sighed again. O Zeus,
It's terrible! Asleep, and still sighing.
Mourning has made a warren in her spirit,
All that way below. Ponos! the heart
Is the devil of a medicine.
DOTO.                    And I don't intend
To turn round.
TEGEUS.          I understand how you must feel.
Would it be—have you any objection
To my having a drink? I have a little wine here.
And, you probably see how it is: grief's in order,
And death's in order, and women—I can usually
Manage that too; but not all three together
At this hour of the morning. So you'll excuse me.
How about you? It would make me more comfortable
If you'd take a smell of it.
DOTO.                    One for the road?
TEGEUS. One for the road.
DOTO.                    It's the dust in my throat. The tomb
Is so dusty. Thanks, I will. There's no point in dying
Of everything, simultaneous.
TEGEUS.                    It's lucky
I brought two bowls. I was expecting to keep
A drain for my relief when he comes in the morning.
DOTO. Are you on duty?
TEGEUS.          Yes.
DOTO.                    It looks like it.

TEGEUS.                                        Well,
Here's your good health.

DOTO.                          What good is that going to do me?
Here's to an easy crossing and not too much waiting
About on the bank. Do you have to tremble like that?

TEGEUS. The idea—I can't get used to it.

DOTO.                                        For a member
Of the forces, you're peculiarly queasy. I wish
Those owls were in Hades—oh no; let them stay where
   they are.
Have you never had nothing to do with corpses before?

TEGEUS. I've got six of them outside.

DOTO.                          Morpheus, that's plenty.
What are they doing there?

TEGEUS.                     Hanging.

DOTO.                               Hanging?

TEGEUS.                                        On trees.
Five plane trees and a holly. The holly-berries
Are just reddening. Another drink?

DOTO.                               Why not?

TEGEUS. It's from Samos. Here's—

DOTO.                          All right. Let's just drink it.
—How did they get in that predicament?

TEGEUS. The sandy-haired fellow said we should collaborate
With everybody; the little man said he wouldn't
Collaborate with anybody; the old one
Said that the Pleiades weren't sisters but cousins
And anyway were manufactured in Lacedaemon.
The fourth said that we hanged men for nothing.
The other two said nothing. Now they hang
About at the corner of the night, they're present
And absent, horribly obsequious to every
Move in the air, and yet they keep me standing
For five hours at a stretch.

DOTO.                    The wine has gone
  Down to my knees.
TEGEUS.            And up to your cheeks. You're looking
  Fresher. If only—
DOTO.              Madam? She never would.
  Shall I ask her?
TEGEUS.          No; no, don't dare, don't breathe it.
  This is privilege, to come so near
  To what is undeceiving and uncorrupt
  And undivided; this is the clear fashion
  For all souls, a ribbon to bind the unruly
  Curls of living, a faith, a hope, Zeus
  Yes, a fine thing. I am human, and this
  Is human fidelity, and we can be proud
  And unphilosophical.
DOTO.                I need to dance
  But I haven't the use of my legs.
TEGEUS.                      No, no, don't dance,
  Or, at least, only inwards; don't dance; cry
  Again. We'll put a moat of tears
  Round her bastion of love, and save
  The world. It's something, it's more than something,
  It's regeneration, to see how a human cheek
  Can become as pale as a pool.
DOTO.                      Do  you  love  me,  hand-
    some?
TEGEUS. To have found life, after all, unambiguous!
DOTO. Did you say Yes?
TEGEUS.              Certainly; just now I love all men.
DOTO. So do I.
TEGEUS.        And the world is a good creature again.
  I'd begun to see it as mildew, verdigris,
  Rust, woodrot, or as though the sky had uttered
  An oval twirling blasphemy with occasional vistas

In country districts. I was within an ace
Of volunteering for overseas service. Despair
Abroad can always nurse pleasant thoughts of home.
Integrity, by god!

DOTO.                   I love all the world
And the movement of the apple in your throat.
So shall you kiss me? It would be better, I should think,
To go moistly to Hades.

TEGEUS.                   Hers is the way,
Luminous with sorrow.

DOTO.                   Then I'll take
Another little swiggy. I love all men,
Everybody, even you, and I'll pick you
Some outrageous honeysuckle for your helmet,
If only it lived here. Pardon.

DYNAMENE.                   Doto. Who is it?

DOTO. Honeysuckle, madam. Because of the bees.
Go back to sleep, madam.

DYNAMENE.                   What person is it?

DOTO. Yes, I see what you mean, madam, It's a kind of
Corporal talking to his soul, on a five-hour shift,
Madam, with six bodies. He's been having his supper.

TEGEUS. I'm going. It's terrible that we should have disturbed her.

DOTO. He was delighted to see you so sad, madam.
It has stopped him going abroad.

DYNAMENE.                   One with six bodies?
A messenger, a guide to where we go.
It is possible he has come to show us the way
Out of these squalid suburbs of life, a shade,
A gorgon, who has come swimming up, against
The falls of my tears (for which in truth he would need
Many limbs) to guide me to Virilius.
I shall go quietly.

TEGEUS.                    I do assure you—
  Such clumsiness, such a vile and unforgivable
  Intrusion. I shall obliterate myself
  Immediately.
DOTO.                    Oblit—oh, what a pity
  To oblit. Pardon. Don't let him, the nice fellow.
DYNAMENE. Sir: your other five bodies: where are they?
TEGEUS.                                        Madam—
  Outside; I have them outside. On trees.
DYNAMENE.                              Quack!
TEGEUS. What do I reply?
DYNAMENE.                 Quack, charlatan!
  You've never known the gods. You came to mock me.
  Doto, this never was a gorgon, never.
  Nor a gentleman either. He's completely spurious.
  Admit it, you creature. Have you even a feather
  Of the supernatural in your system? Have you?
TEGEUS. Some of my relations—
DYNAMENE.                      Well?
TEGEUS.                            Are dead, I think;
  That is to say I have connexions—
DYNAMENE.                           Connexions
  With pickpockets. It's a shameless imposition.
  Does the army provide you with no amusements?
  If I were still of the world, and not cloistered
  In a colourless landscape of winter thought
  Where the approaching Spring is desired oblivion,
  I should write sharply to your commanding officer.
  It should be done, it should be done. If my fingers
  Weren't so cold I would do it now. But they are,
  Horribly cold. And why should insolence matter
  When my colour of life is unreal, a blush on death,
  A partial mere diaphane? I don't know
  Why it should matter. Oafish, non-commissioned

Young man! The boots of your conscience will pinch for
ever
If life's dignity has any self-protection.
Oh, I have to sit down. The tomb's going round.

DOTO. Oh, madam, don't give over. I can't remember
When things were so lively. He looks marvellously
Marvellously uncomfortable. Go on, madam.
Can't you, madam? Oh, madam, don't you feel up to
it?
There, do you see her, you acorn-chewing infantryman?
You've made her cry, you square-bashing barbarian.

TEGEUS. O history, my private history, why
Was I led here? What stigmatism has got
Into my stars? Why wasn't it my brother?
He has a tacit misunderstanding with everybody
And washes in it. Why wasn't it my mother?
She makes a collection of other people's tears
And dries them all. Let them forget I came;
And lie in the terrible black crystal of grief
Which held them, before I broke it. Outside, Tegeus.

DOTO. Hey, I don't think so, I shouldn't say so. Come
Down again, uniform. Do you think you're going
To half kill an unprotected lady and then
Back out upwards? Do you think you can leave her like
this?

TEGEUS. Yes, yes, I'll leave her. O directorate of gods,
How can I? Beauty's bit is between my teeth.
She has added another torture to me. Bottom
Of Hades' bottom.

DOTO.                    Madam. Madam, the corporal
Has some wine here. It will revive you, madam.
And then you can go at him again, madam.

TEGEUS. It's the opposite of everything you've said,
I swear. I swear by Horkos and the Styx,

I swear by the nine acres of Tityos,
I swear the Hypnotic oath, by all the Titans—
By Koeos, Krios, Iapetos, Kronos, and so on—
By the three Hekatoncheires, by the insomnia
Of Tisiphone, by Jove, by jove, and the dew
On the feet of my boyhood, I am innocent
Of mocking you. Am I a Salmoneus
That, seeing such a flame of sorrow—

DYNAMENE.                              You needn't
Labour to prove your secondary education.
Perhaps I jumped to a wrong conclusion, perhaps
I was hasty.

DOTO.       How easy to swear if you're properly educated.
Wasn't it pretty, madam? Pardon.

DYNAMENE.                          If I misjudged you
I apologize, I apologize. Will you please leave us?
You were wrong to come here. In a place of mourning
Light itself is a trespasser; nothing can have
The right of entrance except those natural symbols
Of mortality, the jabbing, funeral, sleek-
With-omen raven, the death-watch beetle which mocks
Time: particularly, I'm afraid, the spider
Weaving his home with swift self-generated
Threads of slaughter; and, of course, the worm.
I wish it could be otherwise. Oh dear,
They aren't easy to live with.

DOTO.                       Not even a *little* wine, madam?

DYNAMENE. Here, Doto?

DOTO.                 Well, on the steps perhaps,
Except it's so draughty.

DYNAMENE.              Doto! Here?

DOTO.                            No, madam;
I quite see.

DYNAMENE. I might be wise to strengthen myself

In order to fast again; it would make me abler
For grief, I will breathe a little of it, Doto.

DOTO. Thank god. Where's the bottle?

DYNAMENE.                              What an exquisite bowl.

TEGEUS. Now that it's peacetime we have pottery classes.

DYNAMENE. You made it yourself?

TEGEUS.                              Yes. Do you see the design?
The corded god, tied also by the rays
Of the sun, and the astonished ship erupting
Into vines and vine-leaves, inverted pyramids
Of grapes, the uplifted hands of the men (the raiders),
And here the headlong sea, itself almost
Venturing into leaves and tendrils, and Proteus
With his beard braiding the wind, and this
Held by other hands is a drowned sailor—

DYNAMENE. Always, always.

DOTO.                              Hold the bowl steady, madam.
Pardon.

DYNAMENE. Doto, have you been drinking?

DOTO.                              Here, madam?
I coaxed some a little way towards my mouth, madam,
But I scarcely swallowed except because I had to. The
   hiccup
Is from no breakfast, madam, and not meant to be
   funny.

DYNAMENE. You may drink this too. Oh, how the inveterate
   body,
Even when cut from the heart, insists on leaf,
Puts out, with a separate meaningless will,
Fronds to intercept the thankless sun.
How it does, oh, how it does. And how it confuses
The nature of the mind.

TEGEUS.                      Yes, yes, the confusion;
That's something I understand better than anything.

DYNAMENE. When the thoughts would die, the instincts will
    set sail
  For life. And when the thoughts are alert for life
  The instincts will rage to be destroyed on the rocks.
  To Virilius it was not so; his brain was an ironing-board
  For all crumpled indecision: and I follow him,
  The hawser of my world. You don't belong here,
  You see; you don't belong here at all.

TEGEUS.                         If only
  I did. If only you knew the effort it costs me
  To mount those steps again into an untrustworthy,
  Unpredictable, unenlightened night,
  And turn my back on—on a state of affairs,
  I can only call it a vision, a hope, a promise,
  A— By that I mean loyalty, enduring passion,
  Unrecking bravery and beauty all in one.

DOTO. He means you, or you and me; or me, madam.

TEGEUS. It only remains for me to thank you, and to say
  That whatever awaits me and for however long
  I may be played by this poor musician, existence,
  Your person and sacrifice will leave their trace
  As clear upon me as the shape of the hills
  Around my birthplace. Now I must leave you to your
    husband.

DOTO. Oh! You, madam.

DYNAMENE.             I'll tell you what I will do.
  I will drink with you to the memory of my husband,
  Because I have been curt, because you are kind,
  And because I'm extremely thirsty. And then we will say
  Good-bye and part to go to our opposite corruptions,
  The world and the grave.

TEGEUS.               The climax to the vision.

DYNAMENE (*drinking*). My husband, and all he stood for.

TEGEUS.                  Stands for.

DYNAMENE.                                        Stands for.

TEGEUS. Your husband.

DOTO.                        The master.

DYNAMENE.                              How good it is,
  How it sings to the throat, purling with summer.

TEGEUS. It has a twin nature, winter and warmth in one,
  Moon and meadow. Do you agree?

DYNAMENE.                              Perfectly;
  A cold bell sounding in a golden month.

TEGEUS. Crystal in harvest.

DYNAMENE.              Perhaps a nightingale
  Sobbing among the pears.

TEGEUS.                  In an old autumnal midnight.

DOTO. Grapes—Pardon. There's some more here.

TEGEUS.                                      Plenty.
  I drink to the memory of your husband.

DYNAMENE.                              My husband.

DOTO.                                  The master.

DYNAMENE. He was careless in his choice of wines.

TEGEUS.                                  And yet
  Rendering to living its rightful poise is not
  Unimportant.

DYNAMENE.    A mystery's in the world
  Where a little liquid, with flavour, quality, and fume
  Can be as no other, can hint and flute our senses
  As though a music played in harvest hollows
  And a movement was in the swathes of our memory.
  Why should scent, why should flavour come
  With such wings upon us? Parsley, for instance.

TEGEUS. Seaweed.

DYNAMENE.      Lime trees.

DOTO.                  Horses.

TEGEUS.                  Fruit in the fire.

DYNAMENE. Do I know your name?

TEGEUS.                              Tegeus.

DYNAMENE.                        That's very thin for you,
It hardly covers your bones. Something quite different,
Altogether other. I shall think of it presently.

TEGEUS. Darker vowels, perhaps.

DYNAMENE.                        Yes, certainly darker vowels
And your consonants should have a slight angle,
And a certain temperature. Do you know what I mean?
It will come to me.

TEGEUS.                  Now *your* name—

DYNAMENE.                              It is nothing
To any purpose. I'll be to you the She
In the tomb. You have the air of a natural-historian
As though you were accustomed to handling birds' eggs,
Or tadpoles, or putting labels on moths. You see?
The genius of dumb things, that they are nameless.
Have I found the seat of the weevil in human brains?
Our names. They make us broody; we sit and sit
To hatch them into reputation and dignity.
And then they set upon us and become despair,
Guilt and remorse. We go where they lead. We dance
Attendance on something wished upon us by the wife
Of our mother's physician. But insects meet and part
And put the woods about them, fill the dusk
And freckle the light and go and come without
A name among them, without the wish of a name
And very pleasant too. Did I interrupt you?

TEGEUS. I forget. We'll have no names then.

DYNAMENE.                              I should like
You to have a name, I don't know why; a small one
To fill out the conversation.

TEGEUS.                  I should like
You to have a name too, if only for something
To remember. Have you still some wine in your bowl?

DYNAMENE.  Not altogether.

TEGEUS.                         We haven't come to the end
By several inches. Did I splash you?

DYNAMENE.                         It doesn't matter.
Well, here's to my husband's name.

TEGEUS.                         Your husband's name.

DOTO.  The master.

DYNAMENE.        It was kind of you to come.

TEGEUS.  It was more than coming. I followed my future
here,
As we all do if we're sufficiently inattentive
And don't vex ourselves with questions; or do I mean
Attentive? If so, attentive to what? Do I sound
Incoherent?

DYNAMENE.    You're wrong. There isn't a future here,
Not here, not for you.

TEGEUS.                   Your name's Dynamene.

DYNAMENE. Who—Have I been utterly irreverent? Are
you—
Who made you say that? Forgive me the question,
But are you dark or light? I mean which shade
Of the supernatural? Or if neither, what prompted you?

TEGEUS.  Dynamene——

DYNAMENE.    No, but I'm sure you're the friend of nature,
It must be so, I think I see little Phoebuses
Rising and setting in your eyes.

DOTO.                         They're not little Phoebuses,
They're hookwinks, madam. Your name is on your
brooch.
No little Phoebuses tonight.

DYNAMENE.                   That's twice
You've played me a trick. Oh, I know practical jokes
Are common on Olympus, but haven't we at all
Developed since the gods were born? Are gods

And men both to remain immortal adolescents?
How tiresome it all is.
TEGEUS.          It was you, each time,
  Who said I was supernatural. When did I say so?
  You're making me into whatever you imagine
  And then you blame me because I can't live up to it.
DYNAMENE. I shall call you Chromis. It has a breadlike
    sound.
  I think of you as a crisp loaf.
TEGEUS.          And now
  You'll insult me because I'm not sliceable.
DYNAMENE. I think drinking is harmful to our tempers.
TEGEUS. If I seem to be frowning, that is only because
  I'm looking directly into your light: I must look
  Angrily, or shut my eyes.
DYNAMENE.        Shut them.—Oh,
  You have eyelashes! A new perspective of you.
  Is that how you look when you sleep?
TEGEUS.          My jaw drops down.
DYNAMENE. Show me how.
TEGEUS.       Like this.
DYNAMENE.        It makes an irresistible
  Moron of you. Will you waken now?
  It's morning; I see a thin dust of daylight
  Blowing on to the steps.
TEGEUS.       Already? Dynamene,
  You're tricked again. This time by the moon.
DYNAMENE.          Oh well,
  Moon's daylight, then. Doto is asleep.
TEGEUS.       Doto
  Is asleep . . .
DYNAMENE.    Chromis, what made you walk about
  In the night? What, I wonder, made you not stay
  Sleeping wherever you slept? Was it the friction

7

Of the world on your mind? Those two are difficult
To make agree. Chromis—now try to learn
To answer your name. I won't say Tegeus.
TEGEUS.                                          And I
Won't say Dynamene.
DYNAMENE.                    Not?
TEGEUS.                              It makes you real.
Forgive me, a terrible thing has happened. Shall I
Say it and perhaps destroy myself for you?
Forgive me first, or, more than that, forgive
Nature who winds her furtive stream all through
Our reason. Do you forgive me?
DYNAMENE.                                  I'll forgive
Anything, if it's the only way I can know
What you have to tell me.
TEGEUS.                              I felt us to be alone;
Here in a grave, separate from any life,
I and the only one of beauty, the only
Persuasive key to all my senses,
In spite of my having lain day after day
And pored upon the sepals, corolla, stamen, and bracts
Of the yellow bog-iris. Then my body ventured
A step towards interrupting your perfection of purpose
And my own renewed faith in human nature.
Would you have believed that possible?
DYNAMENE.                                  I have never
Been greatly moved by the yellow bog-iris. Alas,
It's as I said. This place is for none but the spider,
Raven and worms, not for a living man.
TEGEUS. It has been a place of blessing to me. It will always
Play in me, a fountain of confidence
When the world is arid. But I know it is true
I have to leave it, and though it withers my soul
I must let you make your journey.

DYNAMENE. No.

TEGEUS. Not true?

DYNAMENE. We can talk of something quite different.

TEGEUS. Yes, we can!
Oh yes, we will! Is it your opinion
That no one believes who hasn't learned to doubt?
Or, another thing, if we persuade ourselves
To one particular Persuasion, become Sophist,
Stoic, Platonist, anything whatever,
Would you say that there must be areas of soul
Lying unproductive therefore, or dishonoured
Or blind?

DYNAMENE. No, I don't know.

TEGEUS. No. It's impossible
To tell, Dynamene, if only I had
Two cakes of pearl-barley and hydromel
I could see you to Hades, leave you with your husband
And come back to the world.

DYNAMENE. Ambition, I suppose,
Is an appetite particular to man.
What is your definition?

TEGEUS. The desire to find
A reason for living.

DYNAMENE. But then, suppose it leads,
As often, one way or another, it does, to death.

TEGEUS. Then that may be life's reason. Oh, but how
Could I bear to return, Dynamene? The earth's
Daylight would be my grave if I had left you
In that unearthly night.

DYNAMENE. O Chromis——

TEGEUS. Tell me,
What is your opinion of Progress? Does it, for example,
Exist? Is there ever progression without retrogression?
Therefore is it not true that mankind

Can more justly be said increasingly to Gress?
As the material improves, the craftsmanship deteriorates
And honour and virtue remain the same. I love you,
Dynamene.

DYNAMENE. Would you consider we go round and round?

TEGEUS. We concertina, I think; taking each time
A larger breath, so that the farther we go out
The farther we have to go in.

DYNAMENE.                    There'll come a time
When it will be unbearable to continue.

TEGEUS. Unbearable.

DYNAMENE.          Perhaps we had better have something
To eat. The wine has made your eyes so quick
I am breathless beside them. It *is*
Your eyes, I think; or your intelligence
Holding my intelligence up above you
Between its hands. Or the cut of your uniform.

TEGEUS. Here's a new roll with honey. In the gods' names
Let's sober ourselves.

DYNAMENE.          As soon as possible.

TEGEUS.                              Have you
Any notion of algebra?

DYNAMENE.          We'll discuss you, Chromis.
We will discuss you, till you're nothing but words.

TEGEUS. I? There is nothing, of course, I would rather
discuss,
Except—if it would be no intrusion—you, Dynamene.

DYNAMENE. No, you couldn't want to. But your birthplace,
Chromis,
With the hills that placed themselves in you for ever
As you say, where was it?

TEGEUS.                    My father's farm at Pyxa.

DYNAMENE. There? Could it be there?

TEGEUS.                         I was born in the hills

Between showers, a quarter of an hour before milking
    time.
Do you know Pyxa? It stretches to the crossing of two
Troublesome roads, and buries its back in beechwood,
From which come the white owls of our nights
And the mulling and cradling of doves in the day.
I attribute my character to those shadows
And heavy roots; and my interest in music
To the sudden melodious escape of the young river
Where it breaks from nosing through the cresses and
    kingcups.
That's honestly so.

DYNAMENE.          You used to climb about
Among the windfallen tower of Phrasidemus
Looking for bees' nests.

TEGEUS.            What? When have I
Said so?

DYNAMENE.    Why, all the children did.

TEGEUS. Yes: but, in the name of light, how do you *know*
    that?

DYNAMENE. I played there once, on holiday.

TEGEUS.                 O Klotho,
Lachesis and Atropos!

DYNAMENE.        It's the strangest chance:
I may have seen, for a moment, your boyhood.

TEGEUS.                  I may
Have seen something like an early flower
Something like a girl. If I only could remember how I must
Have seen you. Were you after the short white violets?
Maybe I blundered past you, taking your look,
And scarcely acknowledged how a star
Ran through me, to live in the brooks of my blood for ever.
Or I saw you playing at hiding in the cave
Where the ferns are and the water drips.

DYNAMENE. I was quite plain and fat and I was usually
 Hitting someone. I wish I could remember you.
 I'm envious of the days and children who saw you
 Then. It is curiously a little painful
 Not to share your past.

TEGEUS.                    How did it come
 Our stars could mingle for an afternoon
 So long ago, and then forget us or tease us
 Or helplessly look on the dark high seas
 Of our separation, while time drank
 The golden hours? What hesitant fate is that?

DYNAMENE. Time? Time? Why—how old are we?

TEGEUS.                                        Young,
 Thank both our mothers, but still we're older than to-
   night
 And so older than we should be. Wasn't I born
 In love with what, only now, I have grown to meet?
 I'll tell you something else. I was born entirely
 For this reason, I was born to fill a gap
 In the world's experience, which had never known
 Chromis loving Dynamene.

DYNAMENE.                    You are so
 Excited, poor Chromis. What is it? Here you sit
 With a woman who has wept away all claims
 To appearance, unbecoming in her oldest clothes,
 With not a trace of liveliness, a drab
 Of melancholy, entirely shadow without
 A smear of sun. Forgive me if I tell you
 That you fall easily into superlatives.

TEGEUS. Very well. I'll say nothing, then. I'll fume
 With feeling.

DYNAMENE.      Now you go to the extreme. Certainly
 You must speak. You may have more to say. Besides
 You might let your silence run away with you

And not say something that you should. And how
Should I answer you then? Chromis, you boy,
I can't look away from you. You use
The lamplight and the moon so skilfully,
So arrestingly, in and around your furrows.
A humorous ploughman goes whistling to a team
Of sad sorrow, to and fro in your brow
And over your arable cheek. Laugh for me. Have you
Cried for women, ever?

TEGEUS                    In looking about for you.
But I have recognized them for what they were.

DYNAMENE. What were they?

TEGEUS.                    Never you: never, although
They could walk with bright distinction into all men's
Longest memories, never you, by a hint
Or a faint quality, or at least not more
Than reflectively, stars lost and uncertain
In the sea, compared with the shining salt, the shiners,
The galaxies, the clusters, the bright grain whirling
Over the black threshing-floor of space.
Will you make some effort to believe that?

DYNAMENE.                    No, no effort.
It lifts me and carries me. It may be wild
But it comes to me with a charm, like trust indeed,
And eats out of my heart, dear Chromis,
Absurd, discerning Chromis. You make me
Feel I wish I could look my best for you.
I wish, at least, that I could believe myself
To be showing some beauty for you, to put in the scales
Between us. But they dip to you, they sink
With masculine victory.

TEGEUS.                    Eros, no! No!
If this is less than your best, then never, in my presence,
Be more than your less: never! If you should bring

More to your mouth or to your eyes, a moisture
Or a flake of light, anything, anything fatally
More, perfection would fetch her unsparing rod
Out of pickle to flay me, and what would have been love
Will be the end of me. O Dynamene,
Let me unload something of my lips' longing
On to yours receiving. Oh, when I cross
Like this the hurt of the little space between us
I come a journey from the wrenching ice
To walk in the sun. That is the feeling.

DYNAMENE.                                    Chromis,
Where am I going? No, don't answer. It's death
I desire, not you.

TEGEUS.              Where is the difference? Call me
Death instead of Chromis. I'll answer to anything.
It's desire all the same, of death in me, or me
In death, but Chromis either way. Is it so?
Do you not love me, Dynamene?

DYNAMENE.                          How could it happen?
I'm going to my husband. I'm too far on the way
To admit myself to life again. Love's in Hades.

TEGEUS. Also here. And here are we, not there
In Hades. Is your husband expecting you?

DYNAMENE. Surely, surely?

TEGEUS.                Not necessarily. I,
If I had been your husband, would never dream
Of expecting you. I should remember your body
Descending stairs in the floating light, but not
Descending in Hades. I should say 'I have left
My wealth warm on the earth, and, hell, earth needs
    it.'
'Was all I taught her of love,' I should say, 'so poor
That she will leave her flesh and become shadow?'
'Wasn't our love for each other' (I should continue)

'Infused with life, and life infused with our love?
Very well; repeat me in love, repeat me in life,
And let me sing in your blood for ever.'

DYNAMENE. Stop, stop, I shall be dragged apart!
Why should the fates do everything to keep me
From dying honourably? They must have got
Tired of honour in Elysium. Chromis, it's terrible
To be susceptible to two conflicting norths.
I have the constitution of a whirlpool.
Am I actually twirling, or is it just sensation?

TEGEUS. You're still; still as the darkness.

DYNAMENE. What appears
Is so unlike what is. And what is madness
To those who only observe, is often wisdom
To those to whom it happens.

TEGEUS. Are we compelled
To go into all this?

DYNAMENE. Why, how could I return
To my friends? Am I to be an entertainment?

TEGEUS. That's for tomorrow. Tonight I need to kiss you,
Dynamene. Let's see what the whirlpool does
Between my arms; let it whirl on my breast. O love,
Come in.

DYNAMENE. I am there before I reach you; my body
Only follows to join my longing which
Is holding you already.—Now I am
All one again.

TEGEUS. I feel as the gods feel:
This is their sensation of life, not a man's:
Their suspension of immortality, to enrich
Themselves with time. O life, O death, O body,
O spirit, O Dynamene.

DYNAMENE. O all
In myself; it so covets all in you,

My care, my Chromis. Then I shall be
Creation.

TEGEUS. You have the skies already;
Out of them you are buffeting me with your gales
Of beauty. Can we be made of dust, as they tell us?
What! dust with dust releasing such a light
And such an apparition of the world
Within one body? A thread of your hair has stung me.
Why do you push me away?

DYNAMENE. There's so much metal
About you. Do I have to be imprisoned
In an armoury?

TEGEUS. Give your hand to the buckles and then
To me.

DYNAMENE. Don't help; I'll do them all myself.

TEGEUS. O time and patience! I want you back again.

DYNAMENE. We have a lifetime. O Chromis, think, think
Of that. And even unfastening a buckle
Is loving, and not easy. Very well,
You can help me. Chromis, what zone of miracle
Did you step into to direct you in the dark
To where I waited, not knowing I waited?

TEGEUS. I saw
The lamplight. That was only the appearance
Of some great gesture in the bed of fortune.
I saw the lamplight.

DYNAMENE. But here? So far from life?
What brought you near enough to see lamplight?

TEGEUS. Zeus,
That reminds me.

DYNAMENE. What is it, Chromis?

TEGEUS. I'm on duty.

DYNAMENE. Is it warm enough to do without your
greaves?

TEGEUS. Darling loom of magic, I must go back
  To take a look at those boys. The whole business
  Of guard had gone out of my mind.
DYNAMENE.                              What boys, my heart?
TEGEUS. My six bodies.
DYNAMENE.              Chromis, not that joke
  Again.
TEGEUS. No joke, sweet. Today our city
  Held a sextuple hanging. I'm minding the bodies
  Until five o'clock. Already I've been away
  For half an hour.
DYNAMENE.          What can they do, poor bodies,
  In half an hour, or half a century?
  You don't really mean to go?
TEGEUS.                          Only to make
  My conscience easy. Then, Dynamene,
  No cloud can rise on love, no hovering thought
  Fidget, and the night will be only to *us*.
DYNAMENE. But if every half-hour——
TEGEUS.                          Hush, smile of my soul,
  My sprig, my sovereign: this is to hold your eyes,
  I sign my lips on them both: this is to keep
  Your forehead—do you feel the claim of my kiss
  Falling into your thought? And now your throat
  Is a white branch and my lips two singing birds
  They are coming to rest. Throat, remember me
  Until I come back in five minutes. Over all
  Here is my parole: I give it to your mouth
  To give me again before it's dry. I promise:
  Before it's dry, or not long after.
DYNAMENE.                          Run,
  Run all the way. You needn't be afraid of stumbling.
  There's plenty of moon. The fields are blue. Oh, wait,
  Wait! My darling. No, not now: it will keep

Until I see you; I'll have it here at my lips.
Hurry.

TEGEUS. So long, my haven.

DYNAMENE. Hurry, hurry!

[*Exit* TEGEUS.

DOTO. Yes, madam, hurry; of course. Are we there
Already? How nice. Death doesn't take
Any doing at all. We were gulped into Hades
As easy as an oyster.

DYNAMENE. Doto!

DOTO. Hurry, hurry,
Yes, madam.—But they've taken out all my bones.
I haven't a bone left. I'm a Shadow: wonderfully shady
In the legs. We shall have to sit out eternity, madam,
If they've done the same to you.

DYNAMENE. You'd better wake up.
If you can't go to sleep again, you'd better wake up.
Oh dear.—We're still alive, Doto, do you hear me?

DOTO. You must speak for yourself, madam. I'm quite
dead.
I'll tell you how I know. I feel
Invisible. I'm a wraith, madam; I'm only
Waiting to be wafted.

DYNAMENE. If only you *would* be.
Do you see where you are? Look. Do you see?

DOTO. Yes. You're right, madam. We're still alive.
Isn't it enough to make you swear?
Here we are, dying to be dead,
And where does it get us?

DYNAMENE. Perhaps you should try to die
In some other place. Yes! Perhaps the air here
Suits you too well. You were sleeping very heavily.

DOTO. And all the time you alone and dying.

I shouldn't have. Has the corporal been long gone,
Madam?

DYNAMENE.     He came and went, came and went,
You know the way.

DOTO.                    Very well I do. And went
He should have, come he should never. Oh dear, he must
Have disturbed you, madam.

DYNAMENE.                    He could be said
To've disturbed me. Listen; I have something to say to
   you.

DOTO. I expect so, madam. Maybe I *could* have kept him out
But men are in before I wish they wasn't.
I think quickly enough, but I get behindhand
With what I ought to be saying. It's a kind of stammer
In my way of life, madam.

DYNAMENE.                    I have been unkind,
I have sinfully wronged you, Doto.

DOTO.                    Never, madam.

DYNAMENE. Oh yes, I was letting you die with me, Doto,
   without
Any fair reason. I was drowning you
In grief that wasn't yours. That was wrong, Doto.

DOTO. But I haven't got anything against dying, madam.
I may *like* the situation, as far as I like
Any situation, madam. Now if you'd said mangling,
A lot of mangling. I might have thought twice about
   staying.
We all have our dislikes, madam.

DYNAMENE.                    I'm asking you
To leave me, Doto, at once, as quickly as possible,
Now, before—now, Doto, and let me forget
My bad mind which confidently expected you
To companion me to Hades. Now good-bye,
Good-bye.

DOTO.          No, it's not good-bye at all.
I shouldn't know another night of sleep, wondering
How you got on, or what I was missing, come to that.
I should be anxious about you, too. When you belong
To an upper class, the netherworld might come strange.
Now I was born nether, madam, though not
As nether as some. No, it's not good-bye, madam.

DYNAMENE. Oh Doto, go; you must, you must! And if I
    seem
Without gratitude, forgive me. It isn't so,
It is far, far from so. But I can only
Regain my peace of mind if I know you're gone.

DOTO. Besides, look at the time, madam. Where should I go
At three in the morning? Even if I was to think
Of going; and think of it I never shall.

DYNAMENE. Think of the unmatchable world, Doto.

DOTO.                                             I do
Think of it, madam. And when I think of it, what
Have I thought? Well, it depends, madam.

DYNAMENE.                             I insist,
Obey me! At once! Doto!

DOTO.                    Here I sit.

DYNAMENE. What shall I do with you?

DOTO.                        Ignore me, madam.
I know my place. I shall die quite unobtrusive.
Oh look, the corporal's forgotten to take his equipment.

DYNAMENE. Could he be so careless?

DOTO.                    I shouldn't hardly have thought so.
Poor fellow. They'll go and deduct it off his credits.
I suppose, madam, I suppose he couldn't be thinking
Of coming back?

DYNAMENE.          He'll think of these. He will notice
He isn't wearing them. He'll come; he is sure to come.

DOTO. Oh.

DYNAMENE. I know he will.

DOTO.                    Oh, oh.
    Is that all for tonight, madam? May I go now, madam?

DYNAMENE. Doto! Will you?

DOTO.                    Just you try to stop me, madam.
    Sometimes going is a kind of instinct with me.
    I'll leave death to some other occasion.

DYNAMENE.                    Do,
    Doto. Any other time. Now you must hurry.
    I won't delay you from life another moment.
    Oh, Doto, good-bye.

DOTO.                Good-bye. Life is unusual,
    Isn't it, madam? Remember me to Cerberus.

[*Re-enter* TEGEUS. DOTO *passes him on the steps.*

DOTO (*as she goes*). You left something behind. Ye gods, what
        a moon!

DYNAMENE. Chromis, it's true; my lips are hardly dry.
    Time runs again; the void is space again;
    Space has life again; Dynamene has Chromis.

TEGEUS. It's over.

DYNAMENE.        Chromis, you're sick. As white as wool.
    Come, you covered the distance too quickly.
    Rest in my arms; get your breath again.

TEGEUS. I've breathed one night too many. Why did I see
        you,
    Why in the name of life did I see you?

DYNAMENE.                    Why?
    Weren't we gifted with each other? O heart,
    What do you mean?

TEGEUS.            I mean that joy is nothing
    But the parent of doom. Why should I have found
    Your constancy such balm to the world and yet
    Find, by the same vision, its destruction

A necessity? We're set upon by love
To make us incompetent to steer ourselves,
To make us docile to fate. I should have known:
Indulgences, not fulfilment, is what the world
Permits us.

DYNAMENE. Chromis, is this intelligible?
Help me to follow you. What did you meet in the fields
To bring about all this talk? Do you still love me?

TEGEUS. What good will it do us? I've lost a body.

DYNAMENE. A body?
One of the six? Well, it isn't with them you propose
To love me; and you couldn't keep it for ever.
Are we going to allow a body that isn't there
To come between us?

TEGEUS. But I'm responsible for it.
I have to account for it in the morning. Surely
You see, Dynamene, the horror we're faced with?
The relatives have had time to cut him down
And take him away for burial. It means
A court martial. No doubt about the sentence.
I shall take the place of the missing man.
To be hanged, Dynamene! Hanged, Dynamene!

DYNAMENE. No; it's monstrous! Your life is yours, Chromis.

TEGEUS. Anything but. That's why I have to take it.
At the best we live our lives on loan,
At the worst in chains. And I was never born
To have life. Then for what? To be had by it,
And so are we all. But I'll make it what it is,
By making it nothing.

DYNAMENE. Chromis, you're frightening me.
What are you meaning to do?

TEGEUS. I have to die,
Dance of my heart, I have to die, to die,
To part us, to go to my sword and let it part us.

I'll have my free will even if I'm compelled to it.
I'll kill myself.
DYNAMENE.          Oh, no! No, Chromis!
It's all unreasonable—no such horror
Can come of a pure accident. Have you hanged?
How can they hang you for simply not being some-
    where?
How can they hang you for losing a dead man?
They must have wanted to lose him, or they wouldn't
Have hanged him. No, you're scaring yourself for nothing
And making me frantic.
TEGEUS.                    It's section six, paragraph
Three in the Regulations. That's my doom.
I've read it for myself. And, by my doom,
Since I have to die, let me die here, in love,
Promoted by your kiss to tower, in dying,
High above my birth. For god's sake let me die
On a wave of life. Dynamene, with an action
I can take some pride in. How could I settle to death
Knowing that you last saw me stripped and strangled
On a holly tree? Demoted first and then hanged!
DYNAMENE. Am I supposed to love the corporal
Or you? It's you I love, from head to foot
And out to the ends of your spirit. What shall I do
If you die? How could I follow you? I should find you
Discussing me with my husband, comparing your feelings,
Exchanging reactions. Where should I put myself?
Or am I to live on alone, or find in life
Another source of love, in memory
Of Virilius and of you?
TEGEUS.                    Dynamene,
Not that! Since everything in the lives of men
Is brief to indifference, let our love at least
Echo and perpetuate itself uniquely

8

As long as time allows you. Though you go
To the limit of age, it won't be far to contain me.
DYNAMENE.  It will seem like eternity ground into days and
    days.
TEGEUS.  Can I be certain of you, for ever?
DYNAMENE.                          But, Chromis,
    Surely you said——
TEGEUS.              Surely we have sensed
    Our passion to be greater than mortal? Must I
    Die believing it is dying with me?
DYNAMENE.                          Chromis,
    You must never die, never! It would be
    An offence against truth.
TEGEUS.            I cannot live to be hanged,
    It would be an offence against life. Give me my sword,
    Dynamene. O Hades, when you look pale
    You take the heart out of me. I could die
    Without a sword by seeing you suffer. Quickly!
    Give me my heart back again with your lips
    And I'll live the rest of my ambitions
    In a last kiss.
DYNAMENE.    Oh, no, no, no!
    Give my blessing to your desertion of me?
    Never, Chromis, never. Kiss you and then
    Let you go? Love you, for death to have you?
    Am I to be made the fool of courts martial?
    Who are they who think they can discipline souls
    Right off the earth? What discipline is that?
    Chromis, love is the only discipline
    And we're the disciples of love. I hold you to that:
    Hold you, hold you.
TEGEUS.              We have no chance. It's determined
    In section six, paragraph three, of the Regulations.
    That has more power than love. It can snuff the great

Candles of creation. It makes me able
To do the impossible, to leave you, to go from the light
That keeps you.

DYNAMENE.          No!

TEGEUS.               O dark, it does. Good-bye,
My memory of earth, my dear most dear
Beyond every expectation. I was wrong
To want you to keep our vows existent
In the vacuum that's coming. It would make you
A heaviness to the world, when you should be,
As you are, a form of light. Dynamene, turn
Your head away. I'm going to let my sword
Solve all the riddles.

DYNAMENE.               Chromis, I have it! I know!
Virilius will help you.

TEGEUS.               Virilius?

DYNAMENE. My husband. He can be the other body.

TEGEUS. Your husband can?

DYNAMENE.               He has no further use
For what he left of himself to lie with us here.
Is there any reason why he shouldn't hang
On your holly tree? Better, far better, he,
Than you who are still alive, and surely better
Than *idling* into corruption?

TEGEUS.               Hang your husband?
Dynamene, it's terrible, horrible.

DYNAMENE. How little you can understand. I loved
His life not his death. And now we can give his death
The power of life. Not horrible: wonderful!
Isn't it so? That I should be able to feel
He moves again in the world, accomplishing
Our welfare? It's more than my grief could do.

TEGEUS. What can I say?

DYNAMENE.               That you love me; as I love him

And you. Let's celebrate your safety then.
Where's the bottle? There's some wine unfinished in this
bowl.
I'll share it with you. Now forget the fear
We were in; look at me, Chromis. Come away
From the pit you nearly dropped us in. My darling,
I give you Virilius.

TEGEUS. Virilius.
And all that follows.

DOTO (*on the steps, with the bottle*). The master. Both the
masters.


CURTAIN

# THE BESPOKE OVERCOAT
## by Wolf Mankowitz

## AUTHOR'S NOTE

Love is a luxury which very poor people can afford, and *The Bespoke Overcoat* is a story of this love. It is not a love which conquers all. FENDER does not get enough food or a tailor-made overcoat, in this life. In life he does not find satisfaction, except in so far as he is able to accept with humour and humility the deprivations forced upon him. It is because this humour and humility is shared with his friend that FENDER, in spite of everything, would prefer to go on living. To prefer to go on living is to love in the context of this story, and because this is loving at its most deprived the story is a sad one.

In producing *The Bespoke Overcoat* that remarkable artist Alec Clunes concentrated entirely upon this feeling which, by its intensity, animates a piece which is not well-constructed. The story was written without any directions for staging or the production of effects. The only stage, the only effects, the only theatre I had in mind were in the heart of a drunken tailor. There was no indication of time past or time present, because a twinge of conscience lasts a moment or a life-time, and *The Bespoke Overcoat* is about the unreasonable conscience felt by the poor who love the poorer with a love which conquers nothing.

So Alec Clunes's production, which was, in effect, the writing of the play for the practical stage, dispensed with sets, used the barest properties, used darkness broken by three constantly moving areas of light, to tell a simple story with great simplicity. He realized that FENDER was not a ghost and that this story was not a ghost-story; he understood that *The Bespoke Overcoat* was a sustained, typically over-long Jewish joke—than which there is no sadder and no funnier story. And I am deeply grateful to him for having understood so much, for having made it available to other people, and for having taught me in the process, as he has taught so many other artists, something of the meaning of theatre.

WOLF MANKOWITZ

# CHARACTERS

MORRY, a tailor
FENDER, a warehouse clerk
RANTING, his employer
A CLERK

# THE BESPOKE OVERCOAT

## SCENE I

*The action of the play is distributed among three separate areas permanently set and used in turn.*

*Area A, midstage R., is* RANTING'S *warehouse, which consists of a sizeable table, placed obliquely, with a chair or stool L. and to the* U.S. *end of it.* U.S. *of the table, and rather behind it, a large rack supports a selection of overcoats on hangers.*

*Area B is* D.S.C. *and has no furnishing.*

*Area C, midstage L., is* MORRY'S *room, which consists of a mattress lying obliquely on the floor, and beside it R., at the* U.S. *end, a chair.*

*These three areas are encompassed by a black surround with entrances* D.R., D.L., *and* U.C. *During the entire play, these are in total darkness, as are any two of the acting areas not being used. Throughout, the stage directions will be related to the three areas described.*

*When the* CURTAIN *rises* MORRY *is standing in the area B, with a navy blue overcoat over his arm. A barrel organ is playing, off, and fades out as the light at B fades in.*

MORRY. Fender dead. That old man Fender dead. Funny thing. You're a good tailor, he used to say. You're a good tailor. No, you're a good tailor. Look around. I don't care where you look, he says, you are a number one tailor. Look at this coat, he says. What, that old coat? A coat must be twenty years old. Mind you, I can tell straight-away by the cross-stitch it's my coat. It's your coat, he shouts. You made it. Twenty-two years ago I come to you

for a coat. This is him. I still got him. You got a good
point. I tell him, I'm a good tailor. It's only the truth. I'm
a good tailor. Straightaway, I see I made a mistake. I fell
in. How much, Fender says, will you take to mend a coat
like this? I ask you. It's falling to pieces on his back. I
told him straight, no nonsense. Look Fender, I told him,
I can run you up a pair of trousers from lining canvas you
can walk up Saville Road nobody can tell you from the
Prince of Wales. But, Fender, do me a favour. Take the
coat somewhere else. A new coat I can make, but the
Union says no miracles. A rag, that's all. I got my clients
to think about. Good afternoon. A lovely piece of worsted.
Mind you, I got a suit length here: in a hundred year you
wouldn't see nothing better. Clients. Fender dead. An old
man. (*Turns* u.s., *still speaking.*) He sits in that stone cold
warehouse all day long. (*Turns head round to audience.*)
Who could mend such a coat? (*Moves slowly* u.s. *to C exit.*)
That's enough. (*Light starts to fade.*) Leave me alone. All
this nagging, nagging. (*He has gone, and so has the light.*)

## SCENE II

*As the light fades in on C, sitting cross-legged and hunched on*
MORRY'S *mattress is* FENDER. *He rubs his hands.*

FENDER. Oi. How that Morry can thread a needle in this
cold, I don't know. Such a cold.

MORRY (*entering* u.s.c.). I got trouble of my own. After all,
I'm in Bond Street? I'm a merchant prince? I'm not even
a limited company.

FENDER. I thought you was a limited company.

MORRY (*turning*). Me? Never. What do I want with shares
and directors? So—what can I do for you? It's late,
but . . .

FENDER. To be managing director is not a nice thing? You got no ambition? Terrible cold in here. My old guvernor—managing director three companies. Chairman—six companies. But what a man! (*Rises.*) Look, Morry. I still got no overcoat. Put on the gas ring.

MORRY. Fender! You ain't dead?

FENDER. Sure I'm dead. Would I sit up half the night in the freezing cold if I wasn't dead? I can tell you, I won't be sorry to get back. They got central heating, constant hot water, room service. And the food—as much as you like. Kosher,[1] of course.

MORRY (*holding his head*). I won't touch the rotten brandy.

FENDER. Drinks? You can have what you like, any time, day or night, on the house.

MORRY. Go on. So tell me, Fender. Is is really you?

FENDER (*holding out his hand*). Feel my hand. Feel.

MORRY (*taking his hand*). Believe me, you are cold. That lousy brandy. It kills you. (*Sneezes.*)

FENDER (*sitting on chair*). Gesundheit.[2]

MORRY. Thank you.

FENDER. All I want is to get back. Listen, Morry. You know the first person I met down there?

MORRY. Down there?

FENDER. I tell you. Morry, a secret: everybody goes down there. You know who I met? Lennie.

MORRY. Lennie from Fournier Street?

FENDER. Who else? He's doing the same job. And *what* herrings! I tell you, Morry, I won't be sorry to get back.

MORRY (*kneeling on mattress*). Fender! You don't hold that overcoat against me, do you, Fender? Believe me, if I had known you would catched a cold and died I would give you my own coat.

---

[1] Food prepared in accordance with Jewish religious and dietary custom.
[2] Literally, health. Equivalent to the English 'bless you'.

FENDER. That blankety coat. For that coat I'm here and not at the hotel. Look, Morry. I got nothing against you.

MORRY (*rising to one knee*). You ain't going to haunt me, Fender? You wouldn't haunt an old friend?

FENDER. Don't talk silly, Morry. That haunting is a special job. They don't give it to new residents. For haunting you get a commission.

MORRY (*rising and moving behind* FENDER. *Crossing arms*). So listen, Fender. It goes without saying I am pleased to see you. I'm glad you enjoy being dead. But you won't think I am rude, if I ask what you want of my life?

FENDER. I'll tell you. But first light that gas-ring so at least I won't freeze—listen to me—to death, I nearly said. You don't know, Morry, (*The light begins to fade.*) what sort of life it was at that Ranting clothing company. No wonder I didn't lose any sleep about dying . . . (*The light has gone.*)

## SCENE III

*The light fades in on A.* FENDER *is sitting on the stool with his notebook and pencil on the table in front of him. The conversation continues from the previous* SCENE.

FENDER. After that warehouse for forty-three years, any change would be a pleasure. Forty-three years a shipping clerk.

MORRY (*off*). So long?

FENDER. Forty-three years next Purim,[1] if I didn't die before.

[RANTING *enters* D.R. *carrying a board with lists.*

RANTING (*to behind desk*). And sixty gross denim trousers.

FENDER (*writing*). Sixty gross denim trousers.

[1] A Jewish festival.

RANTING. And forty gross cellaloid collars.

FENDER. Cellaloid collars. Forty gross cellaloid.

RANTING (*tapping with pencil, impatiently*). Cellaloid makes with a C, no S.

FENDER. And what more?

RANTING. Eleven dozen raincoats, Prussian collar.

FENDER. Eleven dozen raincoats.

RANTING. Prussian collar.

FENDER. You know something, Mr. Ranting? It's cold in this warehouse. I said it's cold, Mr. Ranting. I feel the cold something terrible.

RANTING. Fender, I don't think you enjoy your work like in the olden days. (*Sits on table, head turned half* D.S. *towards* FENDER.)

FENDER. What an idea! I enjoy my work? Certainly I enjoy. I feel the cold, that's all.

RANTING. Naturally, you are getting on. The work is hard. Nobody is as young as he used to be.

FENDER. What are you talking, Mr. Ranting? Nobody is as young as he used to be? And how could he?

RANTING. I am saying, Fender, an old man is an old man.

FENDER (*rises*). Certainly. Of course. An old man is an old man. Mr. Ranting, I tell you something: my father, when he was seventy—no, over seventy—he can bend a horseshoe straight with his bare hands. And even he felt the cold.

RANTING (*getting off table*). All I am saying, Fender, is stop driving me mad with your crying 'it's so cold, it's so cold'. Get a new overcoat; you won't feel it.

FENDER. I make an arrangement with you, Mr. Ranting. I'll take one of the overcoats, the big ones with the sheepskin lining, and every week from my wages take off a certain sum. (*Holds out his hands.*) A proposition, Mr. Ranting?

RANTING. One of them coats, Fender? Leave me alone. (FENDER *moves as if to speak*.) Hup! A coat like this is worth twenty pounds anybody's money. What do you make? With all due respect, Fender, what do you make? You won't live so long to pay off such a coat.

FENDER (*sitting on stool, again*). That's true. So what can you do?

RANTING (*reading from list*). Seventeen dozen pair shooting breeches.

FENDER (*writing*). Seventeen dozen pair breeches.

RANTING. Shooting.

FENDER. Shooting, shooting. (*Indicates the entry in his book.*)

RANTING (*in disgust*). Ah! (*Exit* D.R.)

FENDER (*rising and taking off his coat*). Maybe Morry can mend the old coat again. (*Cross fade lights from A to C.*) After all he's a good tailor. (*Turns* U.S. *as the light goes.*)


## SCENE IV

*As the light fades in on C* FENDER *is standing* U.S. *of mattress.* MORRY *enters* D.L.

MORRY. Look, Fender, look. The seams is all rotten. Look, the lining is like ribbons. Look, the material is thread-bare.

FENDER. A tailor like you, Morry, to make such a fuss. You should be ashamed.

MORRY (*sitting on chair*). The padding is like an old horse blanket.

FENDER. Who asks for new padding? Only make the coat good. Who cares about the padding, so long as the coat is warm?

MORRY. It can't be done.

FENDER. Don't make jokes, Morry.

MORRY. If I say it can't be done, it can't be done.

FENDER. So, all right, charge a little more.

MORRY. Charge! What does charge matter? It can't be done.

FENDER. Why are you so hard for, Morry? After all, you can patch with off cuts. (MORRY *holds head in hands*.) I am not asking, after all, for West End style; I should look so smart. I don't care how smart. Only mend the coat, Morry.

MORRY. Fender, listen to me, Fender. A good coat like I make has got twenty years' wear. I double stitch the seams with best thread, no rubbish. Every stitch I test. (*Bites imaginary thread*.) so it's good and strong I use good material: crombie, tweed, what you like. The best. I use a lovely lining; someone else would make a wedding dress from it, such a lining I use.

FENDER. You use marvellous lining, Morry.

MORRY. I make the whole coat, the buttons holes, the pockets, everything.

FENDER. Don't I tell everybody? Morry—a needle like Paganini. I tell everybody.

MORRY. I would make you such a coat for cost, Fender.

FENDER. How much costs such a coat?

MORRY. Three yards, say.

FENDER. Say two and a half.

MORRY. And lining.

FENDER. Don't worry yourself with lining.

MORRY. I can make you a good coat for twelve pound.

FENDER. You can't mend the old coat?

MORRY. Please, Fender, do me a favour.

FENDER. I can ask? Twelve pound is money.

MORRY (*rises*). Listen, Fender. I break my neck: ten pound for the coat. You got ten pound?

FENDER. I look like a banker? I can save ten pound.

MORRY. So.

FENDER (*as he starts to put on his old coat*). So. So I'm going to have made a bespoke overcoat.

MORRY. Bespoke is good.

FENDER. Certainly bespoke. You think I would wear Ranting's rubbish? (*Sits on chair.*)

MORRY (*moving D.S.L. and reaching off-stage for patterns*). What material you like?

FENDER. I can choose material?

MORRY (*to* FENDER *with patterns*). Here, patterns.

FENDER. The grey is not nice for me. The blue is better?

MORRY (*fingering the blue material*). Blue is nice. You can wear blue for any occasion.

FENDER. Nigger brown is smart.

MORRY. For a young man.

FENDER. Black is always good.

MORRY. Black is good, but a nice, dark blue is nicer.

FENDER (*rising, and moving D.S. of mattress*). Believe me, Morry, I think you are right. The blue is good—and thick. What a material!

MORRY (*down to* FENDER). I should say. So you can save ten pounds?

FENDER. Save? Sure I can save. An old man like me, if I got an overcoat, what do I need? (*Moving D.S.C. to B.*) If I got a bespoke overcoat, what more can I need? (*Exit into darkness D.R.*)


SCENE V


MORRY *takes out black bread etc. from his pocket and moves to his chair.*

MORRY. With a piece of black bread and a herring you can't go wrong. You got in black bread vitamins, nutriment *and* a good flavour from herrings. In the old days, (*Sits.*)

sometimes six clients a week, all wanting coats, suits, a spare pair of trousers, something. The trade is not good any more. Believe me, if I had a boy I wouldn't let him see a needle and thread. It's a thing of the past. Things are so bad now, you know what I'm doing? I'm making a ten pound coat for Fender. For ten pounds, it's a wonderful coat. The material, the seams. No wind can blow through a coat like this. (*Rises and moves* D.S. *a few paces.*) Let it blow as much as it likes. I read an interesting thing somewhere. When it's cold, it's not really cold. You are hot; that's why you feel the cold. Also you pull in your muscles. That's bad. Fender: his trouble is he's pulled his muscles so far in they won't pull any more. (*Moving* D.L. *to exit, as light fades.*) I was always interested in science things like this. (*Cross fade to B.*)

## SCENE VI

RANTING *enters* D.R. *with a plate of chopped liver and a fork.*

RANTING. The chopped liver is tukke[1] good, Alf. You want some? Good boy. (*Stops* D.C. *B.*) Bring some more chopped liver, Maisie. So I was telling you, Alf: this exhibition they got such machines you wouldn't believe. They got a machine there, (I'm not telling you a word of a lie, Alf) they got a machine can add up how much you made last year, take away your overheads, knock off your income tax, and show you if you got anything left. By my life. It has a dictation machine, a suspended filing system, a place special for telephone directories, and a permutator for working out football pools so they should win. And I worry myself to nothing, worrying, worrying the whole

---

[1] Untranslatable. A word used for additional emphasis.

9

time over an old clerk's mistakes. What you say? Can a machine laugh like a man? Can it cry like a man? What difference? So long as a clerk clerks good, what difference he's laughing or crying? (*Exit* D.R. *in blackout as we hear* FENDER *laugh, off.*)

## SCENE VII

*The light fades in on* FENDER, *laughing quietly, as he enters* D.R. *and moves to A below table, with the baigel half eaten and wrapped in paper.*

FENDER. A marvellous story, I must tell it to Morry. I enjoy a good laugh. (*He sighs and looks at the baigel.*) A baigel[1] is enough. After all, bread and salt is food. It's the same dinner, only I leave out the soup. That woman, terrible, but what soup, I'm not saying it's not worth a sixpence. A bowl like that, where could you get it for sixpence? In a big restaurant they bring you half as much, and charge terrible prices. A woman cooks soup like that must make somebody a marvellous wife. Mind you, boss-eyed and what temper, a terrible woman. Still a baigel is plenty. Eat it slow, careful, every crumb does you good. Soup! who wants soup? (*Moves* U.S.) When I get the coat, I put it on. I walk up to a table. (*Sits.*) I sit down in the overcoat, blue, nice: a bowl of soup, missus, and a baigel. (*Rises and moves a few paces* D.S.) Be careful! You want the soup should drop on this new overcoat—a bespoke overcoat—ruined. (*He laughs as, lifting the flap of his torn coat, his hand slips through a hole.*) I don't think I got room for these bits. No, I'm full up. I couldn't eat another thing, not even a fresh lutka[2] or a piece of

---

[1] A round bread roll with a hole in it.
[2] Grated fried potato cake.

cheesecake. (*Turns to his accounts.*) Sixteen dozen flying jackets. (U.S. *to sit.*) With such jackets you can fly?

RANTING (*enters* D.R., *moves behind table from which he brushes crumbs*). How many times, Fender? Don't eat in the warehouse. It brings the mice. The mice eat the clothing.

FENDER. How many clothing can a little mouse eat?

RANTING (*reading*). Twenty-eight gross denim trousers. (*Fade out.*)

## SCENE VIII

*Area C. Fade in on* FENDER *entering breathlessly* U.C.

FENDER (*calls*). Morry, I come to see how the coat is coming, Morry.

MORRY (*footsteps, off*). The coat is all right.

FENDER. Which is the coat, Morry?

MORRY (*entering* D.L., *with half-made coat*). Here! Here!

FENDER. Should I try it on?

MORRY (*holding out coat*). Try it on. Don't be silly. What's a matter with you? You're a film starlet, you got to have a changing room else you can't take off the old coat. (FENDER *removes coat.*) So. That's right. Take it off.

[FENDER *gives his coat to* MORRY, *who puts it on chair, and puts on the new coat.*

FENDER. If I knew, I would put my other shirt on. You seen it, Morry? The drill shirt, with tabs on the shoulders, very smart.

MORRY. And why should you? Today is a bank holiday? Look. My own shirt. Everybody wears his old shirt for a working day. Nu. Try it.

FENDER (*as* MORRY *fits the coat*). In Clacton the sun is hot. This makes him the sun, you understand. What a hot! You got a nice deck chair, Mrs. Felderman. I can see. A comfortable deck chair. Certainly a new overcoat—a bespoke overcoat. (*Lifts the left arm with sleeve in it.*) Suits me? Under the arms is a bit tight.

MORRY (*feeling armhole*). It's fine. You got plenty room, look, look.

FENDER. A coat like this makes a difference.

MORRY (*kneeling in front to fit coat*). Fender, you like the coat? What about a couple of pound on account? I got expenses. (*Rising.*) Can you manage a couple?

[FENDER *takes out purse, sorts out notes and silver, and hands them over with great dignity.*

FENDER. Certainly. You know, Morry, twenty shillings, if you saved money like I do, thirty shillings, and didn't throw it away on that rotten brandy, thirty-five shillings, you would be a rich man. Forty shillings.

MORRY. And what would I do with my money?

FENDER. A question. What can you do with it?

MORRY. I can take an off-licence.

FENDER. An off-licence is a good idea. (*Taking off new coat.*)

MORRY. I use my knowledge. A special line in brandy. Old stuff—Napoleon—something good. (*Takes overcoat from* FENDER *and hands him his old one.*)

FENDER. How can you know it's good?

MORRY. I try every bottle, personal. I put up a smart notice, Morry's Napoleon Brandy; every bottle personal tasted. Thanks for the two pound. You can spare?

FENDER. Sure I can spare. The coat won't be long now, Morry?

MORRY. This week I make an exception. I have a drink tonight; that way tomorrow I take less.

FENDER. Tukke?

MORRY. Listen, Fender, drinking is by me not by you; it's my hobby so I shouldn't know? (*Exeunt. Cross fade to B.*)

## SCENE IX

*When the lights go up on B,* RANTING *is straphanging* D.S.C.

RANTING (*in a new coat*). On the Central Line is always hot. You like the coat? Yesterday I picked it up. America style. (*Lurches.*) Sorry, miss. Dear? I should say it's dear! You want me to wear one of me own coats? Twenty-five nicker—a pony, this coat—I beg your pardon. Knock off the booze and you'll be able to afford. My advice to you friend, is—knock off the demon drink.

[*He goes out* D.R. *Cross fade to* C.

## SCENE X

FENDER *is asleep on* MORRY'S *mattress, covered by the half-finished overcoat.* MORRY *enters drunkenly,* U.S.C. *singing and carrying a bottle.*

MORRY. It says on the label extra special reserve, cognac Napoleon brandy, old special reserve. A brandy like this is a brandy like this. This. (*Drinks.*) A brandy. (*Turns to mattress.*) I got company? So late? (U.S. *to put bottle on chair.*) Hey, wake up. I got company. You sit here a minute. Don't go way. I'll come back. (*Kneeling* U.S. *of mattress.*) Wake up, Fender, it's you? What an unexpected pleasure.

FENDER (*sitting up*). I was having a dream. A flying overcoat and inside the pockets bowls of soup. And do you know, the soup never upset in the coat.

MORRY. I got here a brandy; you never drank such a brandy in your life.

FENDER (*peering at the label*). Special reserve. Must be good.

MORRY. Take a little drop. Go on. Take.

FENDER (*trying it*). Ahh, like fire. (*Hands bottle back.*) A good one all right. Morry—Moishele.[1]

MORRY (*holding out bottle in front of him*). It's good brandy.

FENDER. I got bad news, Morry.

MORRY. Where can you find a brandy like this?

FENDER. That Ranting. He give me the sack.

MORRY (*as he sits back on his heels and puts bottle on floor with a thud*). He give you the sack?

FENDER. He give me the sack.

MORRY. After so long he give you the sack?

FENDER. He give me.

MORRY. He give it to *you*?

FENDER. The sack.

MORRY. Oi.

FENDER. I have with great regrets, Morry I must tell you, to cancel the coat. I came to tell you. Cancel the coat.

MORRY (*trying to give him the bottle*). Take another drop brandy. Good for your cough.

FENDER. I don't fancy.

MORRY. Take. Don't be shy. Take. (FENDER *drinks from bottle, and as he lifts his arm we see that the old coat is torn under the arm.*) If I could mend that coat, Fender, I would mend it, I want you to know. I defy any master tailor to make that coat good.

FENDER. What can you do? It's just an old coat, that's all.

MORRY (*rises*). You can't find the rest of the ten pounds? I'll finish the coat.

FENDER. How?

MORRY (*puts arm round* FENDER *and pats him on shoulder*). With a needle. How else?

[*The lights slowly fade.*

---

[1] Affectionate diminutive of Moses.

## SCENE XI

FENDER (*at B*, D.S.C.). I told him, polite, but strong. Mr.
Ranting, I been with this firm with your father and your
uncle so many years. All this time I done the same job;
nobody complains. Suddenly business is so bad you have
to turn me off? Let him answer me that. No good.
Excuses, anybody can find excuses. What I ask you, Mr.
Ranting, is, is it right? Let him answer me that. That's
what I should have said. I should have told him off, big
as he is. The governor, (*Turns* U.S. *and spits.*) I used to
give him a handkerchief he should wipe his nose. A little
boy crying round the warehouse with his stockings down
gives me the sack. Why didn't I tell him? Fender, he says,
you got something put by, an insurance policy, something? I got something put by, don't worry. You got no
family? Don't worry, I got plenty of family, I got friends.
He worries about me. I even got a niece with a boarding-
house in Clacton, and can she cook? Lovely weather the
whole time. (*Turns* U.S.C. *and then back to audience.*) Mind
you, Morry is a good friend. In the morning I put on
my new coat. I go to Ranting. I tell him. Give me that
coat with the sheepskin. (*Coughs.*) Funny thing, a cough
like this, comes right through you. Like a bowl of soup.
It flies up through you like a flying jacket. There he goes.
(*He traces the path of the imaginary jacket round the theatre.
It returns as the threatening celluloid collars.* FENDER *is
dying.*) Seventeen dozen cellaloid collars, cellaloid makes
with a C, no S—or S, no C. (*Weakly.*) Funny thing, I don't
seem to know nothing any more. (*Sinks down as the lights
slowly fade.*)

## SCENE XII

*The lights fade in on area A as a* CLERK, *followed by* RANTING, *enters* D.R. RANTING *goes* U.S. *to behind table.* CLERK *sits at table with notebook and pencil.*

RANTING. Thirty dozen pair shooting breeches.

CLERK. Thirty dozen pair shooting breeches.

RANTING. And a hundred dozen Balaclava helmets.

[MORRY *enters* U.S.C. *with finished overcoat over his arm.*

MORRY (*coming to* U.S. *of table*). Mr. Ranting. Excuse me, Mr. Ranting.

RANTING. And sixty various drill jackets. Can I help you, sir?

MORRY. I come for Fender. I finished him a coat.

RANTING. And two gross khaki drill shorts. He don't work here no more. I say work, but you should understand he was past it.

CLERK. Two gross shorts.

RANTING. Khaki drill.

CLERK. What?

MORRY. Khaki drill.

RANTING. Thank you. Fender lives by the arches in Flower and Dean Street. Or maybe with his niece at Clacton or somewhere. Pardon me. And twenty-eight pith helmets. (*Exit* D.S.R.) Ah!

CLERK. Twenty-eight pith helmets. (*Rests his arms and head on table.*)

[*Cross fade A to C.*

## SCENE XIII

*Area C, continuing as from* SCENE II; MORRY *is* U.S. *of mattress, level with* FENDER, *who sits in chair.*

MORRY. So I go to your lodging. I knock on the door. No answer. I knock again. An old woman comes. She's a bit deaf.

FENDER. She's stone deaf. A bit, he says.

MORRY. I shout in her ear, where is Fender? Fender—Fender! where should he be? He's dead. He didn't have my age, but he's dead. You can knock me over with a feather bed.

FENDER. She got her head screwed on, the old girl. I was dead all right. Mind you, she makes out she's older than she is. I don't like that sort of thing.

MORRY. But so sudden.

FENDER (*rising and crossing in front of* MORRY). Listen, Morry. You die when you are ready? You die when you have to, that's all. Still, I haven't done so bad. I can't complain. If only I kept my mouth shut I would be all right.

MORRY. I made the coat as quick as I can, Fender. (*Sits in chair.*)

FENDER. Look, Morry, I got nothing against you. You behave like a perfect gentleman. I told everybody at the hotel. Morry's a wonderful tailor. You think you look smart? Wait until Morry gets here. No. It was that Ranting. You see, Morry, I didn't take too long dying, but the whilst I am screaming and cursing, using terrible language, all against that Ranting. And when I get down there, it must have been on my mind. So the first couple of weeks, I am stopping the porter, the commissionaire, the chamber-maids, even the guests, telling them about the overcoat. At last, they can't stand it any more. The manager sends for me. Fender, he says, you like the hotel? It's a wonderful hotel, I tell him. Everything of the best. I am very satisfied. Look, Fender, he says, I am very glad if you are comfortable, but I have to tell you everyone has a headache with your overcoat. Do me a favour: go down to the cloakroom, pick yourself any coat. Thank you, I tell him. It's not the same. I can see he is upset. I can't have the place turned upside down, he says. (*Pointing upwards.*) You'll have to go back for a while. When you get it, (*Points downwards.*) come back. It's on my mind, I told him. Next thing I know, I'm here. And here I am.

MORRY (*half rises*). And I got your overcoat all wrapped up ready, Fender. Take it and good luck to you.

FENDER (*moving* D.S. *level with bottom of mattress*). It's no good, Morry. It wouldn't make me happy. Somehow, I got to have that sheepskin coat from Ranting. I am not saying your coat isn't wonderful. It is. But I must have from Ranting a coat. I give him forty-three years nearly. He must give me a coat.

MORRY (*moving down to* FENDER *with bottle.*) You know what?

FENDER. What?

MORRY. We go to Rantings and take the coat. That's what. (*Drinks.*)

FENDER (*as* MORRY *offers him the bottle*). Not a bad idea. (*Drinks and returns bottle. Exeunt* D.S.L. *with* MORRY'S *arm round* FENDER. *Cross fade to A.*)

## SCENE XIV

*As the light fades in on A,* RANTING *enters from* U.S.C., *singing. The* CLERK *is seated at the table, writing in his notebook.*

RANTING. That book you been making up for the past hour, what's the matter, you can't read?

CLERK. The old clerk had his own way of doing things. It takes a little while to work out. But I mastered it.

RANTING (*taking hat off*). You got your head screwed on right. You go to the dog tracks in the evening?

CLERK. Not for me, Mr. Ranting.

RANTING. Horses?

CLERK. No, horses, neither.

RANTING. You must spiel[1] something. Poker, shemmy?[2]

CLERK (*rising and moving behind his stool*). I'm developing myself, Mr. Ranting.

RANTING. Something new?

CLERK. The human frame has nine hundred seventy six individual muscles, each of whom can be developed up to peak power, give proper exercises and consideration.

RANTING. Nearly a thousand? So many?

CLERK. It has been proved by the best efficiency authorities that each of these muscular resources is vital to one. And what do we do? You sit cramped—like this. The muscles get slack and useless. You stand like this. The muscles suffer.

RANTING. Sit and stand you can't avoid.

CLERK (*taking off his overalls*). Look at this, Mr. Ranting. (*Rolls up sleeve and demonstrates muscle.*)

RANTING. Marvellous. Like Kid Berg. You should be a boxer.

CLERK. Worse thing you can do for the muscles, boxing. Fatal to the muscle tone.

RANTING. So what can you do with all them muscles?

CLERK. So far, I still have four hundred and eighty nine muscles undeveloped.

RANTING. And then?

CLERK. I hope to stand as Mr. Universe.

RANTING. A meshuggus.[3] Put back the coat.

---

[1] Play.         [2] Chemin-de-fer.
[3] Literally 'a craziness'. English equivalent, 'what a crazy thing to do.'

CLERK (*restoring coat and moving* D.S.R.). When I get these pecs up I'll take my first competition.

RANTING. Local? (*Picks up clerk's notebook.*)

CLERK. Down at the Roxy.

RANTING. Maybe I'll come.

CLERK. You'll enjoy it, Mr. Ranting. The body beautiful.

RANTING. So I'll enjoy it. The whilst Mr. Universe, go shut the door. (*Pushes* CLERK *out* D.R. *and follows him.*)

## SCENE XV

MORRY *and* FENDER *enter* D.L. *and move towards area B where the light now is. They come in arm in arm, singing and stumbling.* MORRY *carries an empty beer crate.*

MORRY. In your position, Fender, it's not professional to drink so much at once.

FENDER. You know I met Lennie?

MORRY. You were saying before. How is he doing?

FENDER. Very nice. They let him open a little stall outside the hotel, on the promenade. You can get any kind of herring from him.

MORRY (*puts crate down and stands on it*). I get in the window and give you a lift up. Just a minute. (*Gets down.*) See if you can walk through the wall.

FENDER (*crossing to* R. *of* MORRY, *pauses*). Don't talk silly, Morry.

MORRY. If you're a ghost you can walk through walls. And if you're not a ghost at least it's scientific experiment.

FENDER. It's true. I'll try. (*He tries.*) I feel silly. Get through the window, Morry. Just a minute. (*Takes key from pocket.*) A solution. I'll go round and open the door. (*Exit* D.R.)

MORRY (*gets on crate and tries to open window*). I can give

myself a stricture with this. Shift, you—it don't budge.
Get up.

FENDER (*off*). I done it. Come round. It's cold in here.

MORRY (*getting off crate and picking it up*). It would be nice
if he walked through the wall, like I told him. (*Moving* R.)
I even got to tell him how to be a ghost proper. (*Exit* D.R.
*Blackout*.)

## SCENE XVI

*Area A*. FENDER *enters* U.S.C. *with a torch and crosses* R. *to
switch on imaginary light*.

FENDER. It's easy. You should try. I'll just switch on the
light.

MORRY (*follows him in as the lights come on*). Right. Now, let's
see. You remember where the coat is?

FENDER (*moving* U.S. *of stool*). Wait a minute. Trousers over
there. Jackets here. (*Turns to audience*.) Would you believe it? I haven't been away five minutes and they shift
the jackets.

MORRY (*moving to* U.S. *of coat rack*). Here are the coats. What
about this? What a terrible cut. This one?

FENDER (*taking his old coat off and examining coat rack*). Not
for me.

MORRY. The blue is nice.

FENDER. No.

MORRY. It's a silk lining. A good lining.

FENDER. For what?

MORRY. This?

FENDER. Too short. (*Takes out coat with sheepskin lining*.)
Ah! Ah! This is different. This I'll take.

MORRY. It's a nice weight, Fender, (*Helping him on with it*.)
but the workmanship. Not nice.

FENDER (*moving* D.S.C.). How many times do I have to tell
you, Morry? It's not personal. Only I must have one of
Ranting's coats. That's all. He owes me. (*On these lines*
FENDER *becomes, it seems to us and to* MORRY, *less mobile,
more like a dead man.*)

MORRY (*moving* D.S. *to* R. *of* FENDER). Terrible cold in here.
So. Can you go?

FENDER. I can go.

MORRY. My work is better.

FENDER. Certainly your work is better.

MORRY. So now you're all right, heh?

FENDER. I feel all right.

MORRY. Fender, you know something. (*Hesitates.*) This
brandy is good.

FENDER. So—thank you, Morry.

MORRY. So, Fender, you're going now? You'll go back to
the hotel?

FENDER (*turning* U.S.). Where else have I got to go to?

MORRY. Fenderler—you should give to Lennie my best
regards.

FENDER (*turning back to* MORRY). He's selling herrings like
hot cakes, all day long. (*Moves* U.S.) He'll be pleased. A
long life to you, Morry. Pray for me. (*His voice fades on
this line and he has gone.*)

MORRY (*calls after him*). May you come to your place in
peace, Fender. (*Putting his hat on to pray.*) Yiskadal,
Veyiskaddish, . . .

[*The Hebrew Prayer for the dead is broken by barrel-organ
music, off, as* MORRY'S *head sinks upon his chest. Slow*
CURTAIN *as light fades.*

THE END

# THE PEN OF MY AUNT
## by Gordon Daviot

# CHARACTERS

MADAME
SIMONE
STRANGER
CORPORAL

# THE PEN OF MY AUNT

SCENE—*A French country house during the Occupation.*

*The lady of the house is seated in her drawing-room.*

SIMONE (*approaching*). Madame! Oh, madame! Madame, have you——

MADAME. Simone.

SIMONE. Madame, have you seen what——

MADAME. Simone!

SIMONE. But madame——

MADAME. Simone, this may be an age of barbarism, but I will have none of it inside the walls of this house.

SIMONE. But madame, there is a—there is a——

MADAME (*silencing her*). Simone. France may be an occupied country, a ruined nation, and a conquered race, but we will keep, if you please, the usages of civilization.

SIMONE. Yes, madame.

MADAME. One thing we still possess, thank God; and that is good manners. The enemy never had it; and it is not something they can take from *us*.

SIMONE. No, madame.

MADAME. Go out of the room again. Open the door——

SIMONE. Oh, *madame*! I wanted to tell you——

MADAME. —open the door, shut it behind you—quietly— take two paces into the room, and say what you came to say. (SIMONE *goes hastily out, shutting the door. She reappears, shuts the door behind her, takes two paces into the room, and waits.*) Yes, Simone?

SIMONE. I expect it is too late now; they will be here.

MADAME. Who will?

SIMONE. The soldiers who were coming up the avenue.

MADAME. After the last few months I should not have thought that soldiers coming up the avenue was a remarkable fact. It is no doubt a party with a billeting order.

SIMONE (*crossing to the window*). No, madame, it is two soldiers in one of their little cars, with a civilian between them.

MADAME. Which civilian?

SIMONE. A stranger, madame.

MADAME. A stranger? Are the soldiers from the Combatant branch?

SIMONE. No, they are those beasts of Administration. Look, they have stopped. They are getting out.

MADAME (*at the window*). Yes, it is a stranger. Do you know him, Simone?

SIMONE. I have never set eyes on him before, madame.

MADAME. You would know if he belonged to the district?

SIMONE. Oh, madame, I know every man between here and St. Estèphe.

MADAME (*dryly*). No doubt.

SIMONE. Oh, merciful God, they are coming up the steps.

MADAME. My good Simone, that is what the steps were put there for.

SIMONE. But they will ring the bell and I shall have to——

MADAME. And you will answer it and behave as if you had been trained by a butler and ten upper servants instead of being the charcoal-burner's daughter from over at Les Chênes. (*This is said encouragingly, not in unkindness.*) You will be very calm and correct——

SIMONE. Calm! Madame! With my inside turning over and over like a wheel at a fair!

MADAME. A good servant does not have an inside, merely an exterior. (*Comforting.*) Be assured, my child. You have your place here; that is more than those creatures on our doorstep have. Let that hearten you——

SIMONE. Madame! They are not going to ring. They are coming straight in.

MADAME (*bitterly*). Yes. They have forgotten long ago what bells are for.

[*Door opens.*

STRANGER (*in a bright, confident, casual tone*). Ah, there you are, my dear aunt. I am so glad. Come in, my friend, come in. My dear aunt, this gentleman wants you to identify me.

MADAME. Identify you?

CORPORAL. We found this man wandering in the woods——

STRANGER. The corporal found it inexplicable that anyone should wander in a wood.

CORPORAL. And he had no papers on him——

STRANGER. And I rightly pointed out that if I carry all the papers one is supposed to these days, I am no good to God or man. If I put them in a hip pocket, I can't bend forward; if I put them in a front pocket, I can't bend at all.

CORPORAL. He said that he was your nephew, madame, but that did not seem to us very likely, so we brought him here.

[*There is the slightest pause; just one moment of silence.*

MADAME. But of course this is my nephew.

CORPORAL. He is?

MADAME. Certainly.

CORPORAL. He lives here?

MADAME (*assenting*). My nephew lives here.

CORPORAL. So! (*Recovering.*) My apologies, madame. But you will admit that appearances were against the young gentleman.

MADAME. Alas, Corporal, my nephew belongs to a generation who delight in flouting appearances. It is what they call 'expressing their personality', I understand.

CORPORAL (*with contempt*). No doubt, madame.

MADAME. Convention is anathema to them, and there is no sin like conformity. Even a collar is an offence against their liberty, and a discipline not to be borne by free necks.

CORPORAL. Ah yes, madame. A little more discipline among your nephew's generation, and we might not be occupying your country today.

STRANGER. You think it was that collar of yours that conquered my country? You flatter yourself, Corporal. The only result of wearing a collar like that is varicose veins in the head.

MADAME (*repressive*). Please! My dear boy. Let us not descend to personalities.

STRANGER. The matter is not personal, my good aunt, but scientific. Wearing a collar like that retards the flow of fresh blood to the head, with the most disastrous consequences to the grey matter of the brain. The hypothetical grey matter. In fact, I have a theory——

CORPORAL. Monsieur, your theories do not interest me.

STRANGER. No? You do not find speculation interesting?

CORPORAL. In this world one judges by results.

STRANGER (*after a slight pause of reflection*). I see. The collared conqueror sits in the high places, while the collarless conquered lies about in the woods. And who comes best out of that, would you say? Tell me, Corporal, as man to man, do you never have a mad, secret desire to lie unbuttoned in a wood?

CORPORAL. I have only one desire, monsieur, and that is to see your papers.

STRANGER (*taken off-guard and filling in time*). My papers?

MADAME. But is that necessary, Corporal? I have already told you that——

CORPORAL. I know that madame is a very good collaborator and in good standing——

MADAME. In that case——

CORPORAL. But when we begin an affair we like to finish it. I have asked to see monsieur's papers, and the matter will not be finished until I have seen them.

MADAME. You acknowledge that I am in 'good standing', Corporal?

CORPORAL. So I have heard, madame.

MADAME. Then I must consider it a discourtesy on your part to demand my nephew's credentials.

CORPORAL. It is no reflection on madame. It is a matter of routine, nothing more.

STRANGER (*murmuring*). The great god Routine.

MADAME. To ask for his papers was routine; to insist on their production is discourtesy. I shall say so to your Commanding Officer.

CORPORAL. Very good, madame. In the meantime, I shall inspect your nephew's papers.

MADAME. And what if I——

STRANGER (*quietly*). You may as well give it up, my dear. You could as easily turn a steamroller. They have only one idea at a time. If the Corporal's heart is set on seeing my papers, he shall see them. (*Moving towards the door.*) I left them in the pocket of my coat.

SIMONE (*unexpectedly, from the background*). Not in your *linen* coat?

STRANGER (*pausing*). Yes. Why?

SIMONE (*with apparently growing anxiety*). Your *cream* linen coat? The one you were wearing yesterday?

STRANGER. Certainly.

SIMONE. Merciful Heaven! I sent it to the laundry!

STRANGER. To the laundry!

SIMONE. Yes, monsieur; this morning; in the basket.

STRANGER (*in incredulous anger*). You sent my coat, *with my papers in the pocket*, to the laundry!

SIMONE (*defensive and combatant*). I didn't know monsieur's papers were in the pocket.

STRANGER. You didn't know! You didn't know that a packet of documents weighing half a ton were in the pocket. An identity card, a *laisser passer*, a food card, a drink card, an army discharge, a permission to wear civilian clothes, a permission to go farther than ten miles to the east, a permission to go more than ten miles to the west, a permission to——

SIMONE (*breaking in with spirit*). How was I to know the coat was heavy! I picked it up with the rest of the bundle that was lying on the floor.

STRANGER (*snapping her head off*). My coat was on the back of the chair.

SIMONE. It was on the floor.

STRANGER. On the back of the chair!

SIMONE. It was on the floor with your dirty shirt and your pyjamas, and a towel and what not. I put my arms round the whole thing and then—woof! into the basket with them.

STRANGER. I tell you that coat was on the back of the chair. It was quite clean and was not going to the laundry for two weeks yet—if then. I hung it there myself, and——

MADAME. My dear boy, what does it matter? The damage is done now. In any case, they will find the papers when they unpack the basket, and return them tomorrow.

STRANGER. If someone doesn't steal them. There are a lot of people who would like to lay hold of a complete set of papers, believe me.

MADAME (*reassuring*). Oh, no. Old Fleureau is the soul of

honesty. You have no need to worry about them. They will be back first thing tomorrow, you shall see; and then we shall have much pleasure in sending them to the Administration Office for the Corporal's inspection. Unless, of course, the Corporal insists on your personal appearance at the office.

CORPORAL (*cold and indignant*). I have seen monsieur. All that I want now is to see his papers.

STRANGER. You shall see them, Corporal, you shall see them. The whole half-ton of them. You may inspect them at your leisure. Provided, that is, that they come back from the laundry to which this idiot has consigned them.

MADAME (*again reassuring*). They will come back, never fear. And you must not blame Simone. She is a good child, and does her best.

SIMONE (*with an air of belated virtue*). I am not one to pry into pockets.

MADAME. Simone, show the Corporal out, if you please.

SIMONE (*natural feeling overcoming her for a moment*). He knows the way out. (*Recovering.*) Yes, madame.

MADAME. And Corporal, try to take your duties a little less literally in future. My countrymen appreciate the spirit rather than the letter.

CORPORAL. I have my instructions, madame, and I obey them. Good day, madame. Monsieur.

[*He goes, followed by* SIMONE—*door closes. There is a moment of silence.*

STRANGER. For a good collaborator, that was a remarkably quick adoption.

MADAME. Sit down, young man. I will give you something to drink. I expect your knees are none too well.

STRANGER. My knees, madame, are pure gelatine. As for my stomach, it seems to have disappeared.

MADAME (*offering him the drink she has poured out*). This will recall it, I hope.

STRANGER. You are not drinking, madame.

MADAME. Thank you, no.

STRANGER. Not with strangers. It is certainly no time to drink with strangers. Nevertheless, I drink the health of a collaborator. (*He drinks.*) Tell me, madame, what will happen tomorrow when they find that you have no nephew?

MADAME (*surprised*). But of course I have a nephew. I tell lies, my friend; but not *silly* lies. My charming nephew has gone to Bonneval for the day. He finds country life dull.

STRANGER. Dull? This—this heaven?

MADAME (*dryly*). He likes to talk and here there is no audience. At Headquarters in Bonneval he finds the audience sympathetic.

STRANGER (*understanding the implication*). Ah.

MADAME. He believes in the Brotherhood of Man—if you can credit it.

STRANGER. After the last six months?

MADAME. His mother was American, so he has half the Balkans in his blood. To say nothing of Italy, Russia, and the Levant.

STRANGER (*half-amused*). I see.

MADAME. A silly and worthless creature, but useful.

STRANGER. Useful?

MADAME. I—borrow his cloak.

STRANGER. I see.

MADAME. Tonight I shall borrow his identity papers, and tomorrow they will go to the office in St. Estèphe.

STRANGER. But—he will have to know.

MADAME (*placidly*). Oh, yes, he will know, of course.

STRANGER. And how will you persuade such an enthusiastic collaborator to deceive his friends?

MADAME. Oh, that is easy. He is my heir.

STRANGER (*amused*). Ah.

MADAME. He is, also, by the mercy of God, not too unlike you, so that his photograph will not startle the Corporal too much tomorrow. Now tell me what you were doing in my wood.

STRANGER. Resting my feet—I am practically walking on my bones. And waiting for tonight.

MADAME. Where are you making for? (*As he does not answer immediately*). The coast? (*He nods.*) That is four days away—five if your feet are bad.

STRANGER. I know it.

MADAME. Have you friends on the way?

STRANGER. I have friends at the coast, who will get me a boat. But no one between here and the sea.

MADAME (*rising*). I must consult my list of addresses. (*Pausing.*) What was your service?

STRANGER. Army.

MADAME. Which Regiment?

STRANGER. The 79th.

MADAME (*after the faintest pause*). And your Colonel's name?

STRANGER. Delavault was killed in the first week, and Martin took over.

MADAME (*going to her desk*). A 'good collaborator' cannot be too careful. Now I can consult my notebook. A charming colour, is it not? A lovely shade of red.

STRANGER. Yes—but what has a red quill pen to do with your notebook?—Ah, you write with it of course—stupid of me.

MADAME. Certainly I write with it—but it is also my note-book—look—I only need a hairpin—and then—so—out of my quill pen comes my notebook—a tiny piece of paper—but enough for a list of names.

STRANGER. You mean that you keep that list on your desk?
(*He sounds disapproving.*)

MADAME. Where did you expect me to keep it, young man?
In my corset? Did you ever try to get something out of
your corset in a hurry? What would you advise as the
ideal quality in a hiding-place for a list of names?

STRANGER. That the thing should be difficult to find, of course.

MADAME. Not at all. That it should be easily destroyed in
emergency. It is too big for me to swallow—I suspect they
do that only in books—and we have no fires to consume
it, so I had to think of some other way. I did try to
memorize the list, but what I could not be sure of remembering were those that—that had to be scored off. It
would be fatal to send someone to an address that—that
was no longer available. So I had to keep a written
record.

STRANGER. And if you neither eat it nor burn it when the
moment comes, how do you get rid of it?

MADAME. I could, of course, put a match to it, but scraps of
freshly-burned paper on a desk take a great deal of
explaining. If I ceased to be looked on with approval my
usefulness would end. It is important therefore that there
should be no sign of anxiety on my part: no burned paper,
no excuses to leave the room, no nods and becks and
winks. I just sit here at my desk and go on with my letters.
I tilt my nice big inkwell sideways for a moment and dip
the pen into the deep ink at the side. The ink flows into
the hollow of the quill, and all is blotted out. (*Consulting
the list.*) Let me see. It would be good if you could rest
your feet for a day or so.

STRANGER (*ruefully*). It would.

MADAME. There is a farm just beyond the Marnay cross-
roads on the way to St. Estèphe—— (*She pauses to consider.*)

STRANGER. St. Estèphe is the home of the single-minded Corporal. I don't want to run into him again.

MADAME. No, that might be awkward; but that farm of the Cherfils would be ideal. A good hiding-place, and food to spare, and fine people——

STRANGER. If your nephew is so friendly with the invader, how is it that the Corporal doesn't know him by sight?

MADAME (*absently*). The unit at St. Estèphe is a non-commissioned one.

STRANGER. Does the Brotherhood of Man exclude sergeants, then?

MADAME. Oh, definitely. Brotherhood does not really begin under field rank, I understand.

STRANGER. But the Corporal may still meet your nephew somewhere.

MADAME. That is a risk one must take. It is not a very grave one. They change the personnel every few weeks, to prevent them becoming too acclimatized. And even if he met my nephew, he is unlikely to ask for the papers of so obviously well-to-do a citizen. If you could bear to go *back* a little——

STRANGER. Not a step! It would be like—like denying God. I have got so far, against all the odds, and I am not going a yard back. Not even to rest my feet!

MADAME. I understand; but it is a pity. It is a long way to the Cherfils farm—two miles east of the Marnay crossroads it is, on a little hill.

STRANGER. I'll get there; don't worry. If not tonight then tomorrow night. I am used to sleeping in the open by now.

MADAME. I wish we could have you here, but it is too dangerous. We are liable to be billeted on at any moment, without notice. However, we can give you a good meal, and a bath. We have no coal, so it will be one of those flat-tin-saucer baths. And if you want to be very kind to Simone you might have it somewhere in the kitchen regions and so save her carrying water upstairs.

STRANGER. But of course.

MADAME. Before the war I had a staff of twelve. Now I have Simone. I dust and Simone sweeps, and between us we keep the dirt at bay. She has no manners but a great heart, the child.

STRANGER. The heart of a lion.

MADAME. Before I put this back you might memorize these: Forty Avenue Foch, in Crest, the back entrance.

STRANGER. Forty Avenue Foch, the back entrance.

MADAME. You may find it difficult to get into Crest, by the way. It is a closed area. The pot boy at the Red Lion in Mans.

STRANGER. The pot boy.

MADAME. Denis the blacksmith at Laloupe. And the next night should take you to the sea and your friends. Are they safely in your mind?

STRANGER. Forty Avenue Foch in Crest; the pot boy at the Red Lion in Mans: and Denis the blacksmith at Laloupe. And to be careful getting into Crest.

MADAME. Good. Then I can close my notebook—or roll it up, I should say—then—it fits neatly, does it not? Now let us see about some food for you. Perhaps I could find you other clothes. Are these all you——

> [*The* CORPORAL's *voice is heard mingled in fury with the still more furious tones of* SIMONE. *She is yelling:* 'Nothing of the sort, I tell you, nothing of the sort', *but no words are clearly distinguishable in the angry row.*

> [*The door is flung open, and the* CORPORAL *bursts in dragging a struggling* SIMONE *by the arm.*

SIMONE (*screaming with rage and terror*). Let me go, you foul fiend, you murdering foreign bastard, let me go. (*She tries to kick him.*)

CORPORAL (*at the same time*). Stop struggling, you lying deceitful little bit of no-good.

MADAME. Will someone explain this extraordinary——

CORPORAL. This creature——

MADAME. Take your hand from my servant's arm, Corporal. She is not going to run away.

CORPORAL (*reacting to the voice of authority and automatically complying*). Your precious servant was overheard telling the gardener that she had never set eyes on this man.

SIMONE. I did not! Why should I say anything like that?

CORPORAL. With my own ears I heard her, my own two ears. Will you kindly explain that to me if you can.

MADAME. You speak our language very well, Corporal, but perhaps you are not so quick to understand.

CORPORAL. I understand perfectly.

MADAME. What Simone was saying to the gardener, was no doubt what she was announcing to all and sundry at the pitch of her voice this morning.

CORPORAL (*unbelieving*). And what was that?

MADAME. That she *wished* she had never set eyes on my nephew.

CORPORAL. And why should she say that?

MADAME. My nephew, Corporal, has many charms, but tidiness is not one of them. As you may have deduced from the episode of the coat. He is apt to leave his room——

SIMONE (*on her cue; in a burst of scornful rage*). Cigarette ends, pyjamas, towels, bedclothes, books, papers—all over the floor like a *flood*. Every morning I tidy up, and in two hours it is as if a bomb had burst in the room.

STRANGER (*testily*). I told you already that I was sor——

SIMONE (*interrupting*). As if I had nothing else to do in this enormous house but wait on you.

STRANGER. Haven't I said that I——

SIMONE. And when I have climbed all the way up from the kitchen with your shaving water, you let it get cold; but will you shave in cold? Oh, no! I have to bring up another——

STRANGER. I didn't ask you to climb the damned stairs, did I?

SIMONE. And do I get a word of thanks for bringing it? Do I indeed? You say: '*Must* you bring it in that hideous jug; it offends my eyes.'

STRANGER. So it does offend my eyes!

MADAME. Enough, enough! We had enough of that this morning. You see, Corporal?

CORPORAL. I could have sworn——

MADAME. A natural mistake, perhaps. But I think you might have used a little more common sense in the matter. (*Coldly.*) And a great deal more dignity. I don't like having my servants manhandled.

CORPORAL. She refused to come.

SIMONE. Accusing me of things I never said!

MADAME. However, now that you are here again you can make yourself useful. My nephew wants to go into Crest the day after tomorrow, and that requires a special pass. Perhaps you would make one out for him.

CORPORAL. But I——

MADAME. You have a little book of permits in your pocket, haven't you?

CORPORAL. Yes. I——

MADAME. Very well. Better make it valid for two days. He is always changing his mind.

CORPORAL. But it is not for me to grant a pass.

MADAME. You sign them, don't you?

CORPORAL. Yes, but only when someone tells me to.

MADAME. Very well, if it will help you, I tell you to.

CORPORAL. I mean, permission must be granted before a pass is issued.

MADAME. And have you any doubt that a permission will be granted to my nephew?

CORPORAL. No, of course not, madame.

MADAME. Then don't be absurd, Corporal. To be absurd twice in five minutes is too often. You may use my desk —and my own special pen. Isn't it a beautiful quill, Corporal?

CORPORAL. Thank you, madame, no. *We* Germans have come a long way from the geese.

MADAME. Yes?

CORPORAL. I prefer my fountain-pen. It is a more efficient implement. (*He writes.*) For the 15th and the 16th. 'Holder of identity card number'—What is the number of your identity, monsieur?

STRANGER. I have not the faintest idea.

CORPORAL. You do not know?

STRANGER. No. The only numbers I take an interest in are lottery numbers.

SIMONE. I know the number of monsieur's card.

MADAME (*afraid that she is going to invent one*). I don't think that likely, Simone.

SIMONE (*aware of what is in her mistress's mind, and reassuring her*). But I really *do* know, madame. It is the year I was born, with two 'ones' after it. Many a time I have seen it on the outside of the card.

CORPORAL. It is good that someone knows.

SIMONE. It is—192411.

CORPORAL. 192411. (*He fills in the dates.*)

MADAME (*as he nears the end*). Are you going back to St. Estèphe now, Corporal?

CORPORAL. Yes, madame.

MADAME. Then perhaps you will give my nephew a lift as far as the Marnay cross-roads.

CORPORAL. It is not permitted to take civilians as passengers.

STRANGER. But you took me here as a passenger.

CORPORAL. That was different.

MADAME. You mean that when you thought he was a miscreant you took him in your car, but now that you know he is my nephew you refuse?

CORPORAL. When I brought him here it was on service business.

MADAME (*gently reasonable*). Corporal, I think you owe me something for your general lack of tact this afternoon. Would it to be too much to ask you to consider my nephew a miscreant for the next hour while you drive him as far as the Marnay cross-roads?

CORPORAL. But——

MADAME. Take him to the cross-roads with you and I shall agree to forget your—your lack of efficiency. I am sure you are actually a very efficient person, and likely to be a sergeant any day now. We won't let a blunder or two stand in your way.

CORPORAL. If I am caught giving a lift to a civilian, I shall *never* be a sergeant.

MADAME (*still gentle*). If I report on your conduct this afternoon, tomorrow you will be a private.

CORPORAL (*after a long pause*). Is monsieur ready to come now?

STRANGER. Quite ready.

CORPORAL. You will need a coat.

MADAME. Simone, get monsieur's coat from the cupboard in the hall. And when you have seen him off, come back here.

SIMONE. Yes, madame.

[*Exit* SIMONE.

CORPORAL. Madame.

MADAME. Good day to you, Corporal.

[*Exit* CORPORAL.

STRANGER. Your talent for blackmail is remarkable.

MADAME. The place has a yellow barn. You had better wait somewhere till evening, when the dogs are chained up.

STRANGER. I wish I had an aunt of your calibre. All mine are authorities on crochet.

MADAME. I could wish you were my nephew. Good luck, and be careful. Perhaps one day, you will come back, and dine with me, and tell me the rest of the tale.

[*The sound of a running engine comes from outside.*

STRANGER. Two years today, perhaps?

MADAME. One year today.

STRANGER (*softly*). Who knows? (*He lifts her hand to his lips.*) Thank you, and *au revoir*. (*Turning at the door.*) Being sped on my way by the enemy is a happiness I had not anticipated. I shall never be able to repay you for that. (*He goes out.*) (*Off.*) Ah, my coat—thank you, Simone.

[*Sound of car driving off.*

[MADAME *pours out two glasses. As she finishes,* SIMONE *comes in, shutting the door correctly behind her and taking two paces into the room.*

SIMONE. You wanted me, madame?

MADAME. You will drink a glass of wine with me, Simone.

SIMONE. With you, madame!

MADAME. You are a good daughter of France and a good servant to me. We shall drink a toast together.

SIMONE. Yes, madame.

MADAME (*quietly*). To Freedom.

SIMONE (*repeating*). To Freedom. May I add a bit of my own, madame?

MADAME. Certainly.

SIMONE (*with immense satisfaction*). And a very bad end to that Corporal!

CURTAIN

# MOTHER'S DAY
## by J. B. Priestley

## CHARACTERS

MRS. ANNIE PEARSON
GEORGE PEARSON
DORIS PEARSON
CYRIL PEARSON
MRS. FITZGERALD

The action takes place in the living-room of the
Pearsons' house in a London suburb

Time: the present

# MOTHER'S DAY

SCENE—*The living-room of the Pearson family. Afternoon.*

*It is a comfortably furnished, much lived-in room in a small suburban semi-detached villa. If necessary only one door need be used, but it is better with two—one up* L. *leading to the front door and the stairs and the other in the* R. *wall leading to the kitchen and the back door. There can be a muslin-covered window in the* L. *wall and possibly one in the* R. *wall, too. The fireplace is assumed to be in the fourth wall. There is a settee up* R., *an armchair down* L. *and one down* R. *A small table with two chairs either side of it stands* C.

*When the* CURTAIN *rises it is an afternoon in early autumn and the stage can be well lit.* MRS. PEARSON *at* R., *and* MRS. FITZGERALD *at* L., *are sitting opposite each other at the small table, on which are two teacups and saucers and the cards with which Mrs. Fitzgerald has been telling Mrs. Pearson's fortune. Mrs. Pearson is a pleasant but worried-looking woman in her forties. Mrs. Fitzgerald is older, heavier and a strong and sinister personality. She is smoking. It is very important that these two should have sharply contrasting voices—*MRS. PEARSON *speaking in a light, flurried sort of tone, with a touch of suburban Cockney perhaps; and* MRS. FITZGERALD *with a deep voice, rather Irish perhaps.*

MRS. FITZGERALD (*collecting up the cards*). And that's all I can tell you, Mrs. Pearson. Could be a good fortune. Could be a bad one. All depends on yourself now. Make up your mind—and there it is.

MRS. PEARSON. Yes, thank you, Mrs. Fitzgerald. I'm much obliged, I'm sure. It's wonderful having a real fortune-teller living next door. Did you learn that out East, too?

MRS. FITZGERALD. I did. Twelve years I had of it, with my old man rising to be Lieutenant Quartermaster. He learnt a lot, and I learnt a lot more. But will you make up your mind now, Mrs. Pearson dear? Put your foot down, once an' for all, an' be the mistress of your own house an' the boss of your own family.

MRS. PEARSON (*smiling apologetically*). That's easier said than done. Besides I'm so fond of them even if they are so thoughtless and selfish. They don't mean to be . . .

MRS. FITZGERALD (*cutting in*). Maybe not. But it'ud be better for them if they learnt to treat you properly . . .

MRS. PEARSON. Yes, I suppose it would, in a way.

MRS. FITZGERALD. No doubt about it at all. Who's the better for being spoilt—grown man, lad or girl? Nobody. You think it does 'em good when you run after them all the time, take their orders as if you were the servant in the house, stay at home every night while they go out enjoying themselves? Never in all your life. It's the ruin of them as well as you. Husbands, sons, daughters should be taking notice of wives an' mothers, not giving 'em orders an' treating 'em like dirt. An' don't tell me you don't know what I mean, for I know more than you've told me.

MRS. PEARSON (*dubiously*). I—keep dropping a hint . . .

MRS. FITZGERALD. Hint? It's more than hints your family needs, Mrs. Pearson.

MRS. PEARSON (*dubiously*). I suppose it is. But I do hate any unpleasantness. And it's so hard to know where to start. I keep making up my mind to have it out with them— but somehow I don't know how to begin. (*She glances at her watch or at a clock*.) Oh—good gracious! Look at the time. Nothing ready and they'll be home any minute—and probably all in a hurry to go out again . . .

[*As she is about to rise*, MRS. FITZGERALD *reaches out across the table and pulls her down.*

MRS. FITZGERALD. Let 'em wait or look after themselves for once. This is where your foot goes down. Start now. (*She lights a cigarette from the one she has just finished.*)

MRS. PEARSON (*embarrassed*). Mrs. Fitzgerald—I know you mean well—in fact, I agree with you—but I just can't—and it's no use you trying to make me. If I promise you I'd really have it out with them, I know I wouldn't be able to keep my promise.

MRS. FITZGERALD. Then let me do it.

MRS. PEARSON (*flustered*). Oh no—thank you very much, Mrs. Fitzgerald—but that wouldn't do at all. It couldn't possibly be somebody else—they'd resent it at once and wouldn't listen—and really I couldn't blame them. I know I ought to do it—but you see how it is? (*She looks apologetically across the table, smiling rather miserably.*)

MRS. FITZGERALD (*coolly*). You haven't got the idea.

MRS. PEARSON (*bewildered*). Oh—I'm sorry—I thought you asked me to let you do it.

MRS. FITZGERALD. I did. But not as me—as *you*.

MRS. PEARSON. But—I don't understand. You couldn't be me.

MRS. FITZGERALD (*coolly*). We change places. Or—really—bodies. You look like me. I look like you.

MRS. PEARSON. But that's impossible.

MRS. FITZGERALD. How do you *know*? Ever tried it?

MRS. PEARSON. No, of course not . . .

MRS. FITZGERALD (*coolly*). I have. Not for some time, but it still ought to work. Won't last long, but long enough for what we want to do. Learnt it out East, of course, where they're up to all these tricks. (*She holds her hand out across the table, keeping the cigarette in her mouth*.) Gimme your hands, dear.

MRS. PEARSON (*dubiously*). Well—I don't know—is it right?

MRS. FITZGERALD. It's your only chance. Give me your hands an' keep quiet a minute. Just don't think about anything. (*Taking her hands*.) Now look at me.

[*They stare at each other.*

(*Muttering*). *Arshtatta dum—arshtatta lam—arshtatta lam-dumbona . . .*

[*This little scene should be acted very carefully. We are to assume that the personalities change bodies. After the spell has been spoken, both women, still grasping hands, go lax, as if the life were out of them. Then both come to life, but with the personality of the other. Each must try to adopt the voice and mannerisms of the other. So now* MRS. PEARSON *is bold and dominating and* MRS. FITZGERALD *is nervous and fluttering.*

MRS. PEARSON (*now with Mrs. Fitzgerald's personality*). See what I mean, dear? (*She notices the cigarette.*) Here—you don't want that. (*She snatches it and puts it in her own mouth, puffing contentedly.*)

[MRS. FITZGERALD, *now with Mrs. Pearson's personality, looks down at herself and sees that her body has changed and gives a scream of fright.*

MRS. FITZGERALD (*with Mrs. Pearson's personality*). Oh—it's happened.

MRS. PEARSON (*complacently*). Of course it's happened. Very neat. Didn't know I had it in me.

MRS. FITZGERALD (*alarmed*). But whatever shall I do, Mrs. Fitzgerald? George and the children can't see me like this.

MRS. PEARSON (*grimly*). They aren't going to—that's the point. They'll have me to deal with—only they won't know it.

MRS. FITZGERALD (*still alarmed*). But what if we can't change back? It'ud be *terrible*.

MRS. PEARSON. Here—steady, Mrs. Pearson—if you had to live my life it wouldn't be so bad. You'd have more fun as me than you've had as you . . .

MRS. FITZGERALD. Yes—but I don't want to be anybody else . . .

MRS. PEARSON. Now—stop worrying. It's easier changing back—I can do it any time we want . . .

MRS. FITZGERALD. Well—do it now . . .

MRS. PEARSON. Not likely. I've got to deal with your family first. That's the idea, isn't it? Didn't know how to begin with 'em, you said. Well. I'll show you.

MRS. FITZGERALD. But what am I going to do?

MRS. PEARSON. Go into my house for a bit—there's nobody there—then pop back and see how we're doing. You ought to enjoy it. Better get off now before one of 'em comes.

MRS. FITZGERALD (*nervously rising*). Yes—I suppose that's best. You're sure it'll be all right?

MRS. PEARSON (*chuckling*). It'll be *wonderful*. Now off you go, dear.

[MRS. FITZGERALD *crosses and hurries out through the door* R. *Left to herself,* MRS. PEARSON *smokes away—lighting another cigarette—and begins laying out the cards for patience on the table.*

*After a few moments* DORIS PEARSON *comes bursting in* L. *She is a pretty girl in her early twenties, who would be pleasant enough if she had not been spoilt.*

DORIS (*before she has taken anything in*). Mum—you'll have to iron my yellow silk. I must wear it tonight. (*She now sees what is happening, and is astounded.*) What are you doing? (*She moves down* L.C.)

[MRS. PEARSON *now uses her ordinary voice, but her manner is not fluttering and apologetic but cool and incisive.*

MRS. PEARSON (*not even looking up*). What d'you think I'm doing—whitewashing the ceiling?

DORIS (*still astounded*). But you're *smoking*!

MRS. PEARSON. That's right, dear. No law against it, is there?

DORIS. But I thought you didn't smoke.

MRS. PEARSON. Then you thought wrong.

DORIS. Are we having tea in the kitchen?

MRS. PEARSON. Have it where you like, dear.

DORIS (*angrily*). Do you mean it isn't ready?

MRS. PEARSON. Yours isn't. I've had all I want. Might go out later and get a square meal at the *Clarendon*.

DORIS (*hardly believing her ears*). Who might?

MRS. PEARSON. I might. Who d'you think?

DORIS (*staring at her*). Mum—what's the matter with you?

MRS. PEARSON. Don't be silly.

DORIS (*indignantly*). It's not me that's being silly—and I must say it's a bit much when I've been working hard all day and you can't even bother to get my tea ready. Did you hear what I said about my yellow silk?

MRS. PEARSON. No. Don't you like it now? I never did.

DORIS (*indignantly*). Of course I like it. And I'm going to wear it tonight. So I want it ironing.

MRS. PEARSON. Want it ironing? What d'you think it's going to do—iron itself?

DORIS. No, you're going to iron it for me—you always do.

MRS. PEARSON. Well, this time I don't. And don't talk rubbish to me about working hard, I've a good idea how much you do, Doris Pearson. I put in twice the hours you do, and get no wages nor thanks for it. Why are you going to wear your yellow silk? Where are you going?

DORIS (*sulkily*). Out with Charlie Spence.

MRS. PEARSON. Why?

DORIS (*wildly*). Why? Why? What's the matter with you? Why shouldn't I go out with Charlie Spence if he asks me and I want to? Any objections? Go on—you might as well tell me . . .

MRS. PEARSON (*severely*). Can't you find anybody better? I wouldn't be seen dead with Charlie Spence. Buck teeth and half-witted. . . .

DORIS. He isn't . . .

MRS. PEARSON. When I was your age I'd have found somebody better than Charlie Spence—or given myself up as a bad job.

DORIS (*nearly in tears*). Oh—shut up!

[DORIS *runs out* L. MRS. PEARSON *chuckles and begins putting the cards together.*

*After a moment* CYRIL PEARSON *enters* L. *He is the masculine counterpart of Doris.*

CYRIL (*briskly*). Hello—Mum. Tea ready?

MRS. PEARSON. No.

CYRIL (*moving to the table; annoyed*). Why not?

MRS. PEARSON (*coolly*). I couldn't bother.

CYRIL. Feeling off-colour or something?

MRS. PEARSON. Never felt better in my life.

CYRIL (*aggressively*). What's the idea then?

MRS. PEARSON. Just a change.

CYRIL (*briskly*). Well, snap out of it, Ma—and get cracking. Haven't too much time.

[CYRIL *is about to go when* MRS. PEARSON'S *voice checks him.*

MRS. PEARSON. *I've* plenty of time.

CYRIL. Yes, but I haven't. Got a busy night tonight. (*Moving* L. *to the door.*) Did you put my things out?

MRS. PEARSON (*coolly*). Can't remember. But I doubt it.

CYRIL (*moving to the table; protesting*). Now—look. When I asked you this morning, you promised. You said you'd have to look through 'em first in case there was any mending.

MRS. PEARSON. Yes—well now I've decided I don't like mending.

CYRIL. That's a nice way to talk—what would happen if we all talked like that?

MRS. PEARSON. You all do talk like that. If there's something at home you don't want to do, you don't do it. If it's something at your work, you get the Union to bar it. Now all that's happened is that *I've* joined the movement.

CYRIL (*staggered*). I don't get this, Mum. What's going on?

MRS. PEARSON (*laconic and sinister*). Changes.

[DORIS *enters* L. *She is in the process of dressing and is now wearing a wrap. She looks pale and red-eyed.*

MRS. PEARSON. You look terrible. I wouldn't wear that face even for Charlie Spence.

DORIS (*moving above the table; angrily*). Oh—shut up about Charlie Spence. And anyhow I'm not ready yet—just dressing. And if I do look terrible, it's your fault—you made me cry.

CYRIL (*curious*). Why—what did she do?

DORIS. Never you mind.

MRS. PEARSON (*rising and preparing to move to the kitchen*). Have we any stout left? I can't remember.

CYRIL. Bottle or two. I think. But you don't want stout now.

MRS. PEARSON (*moving* L. *slowly*). I do.

CYRIL. What for?

MRS. PEARSON (*turning at the door*). To drink—you clot!

[MRS. PEARSON *exits* R. *Instantly* CYRIL *and* DORIS *are in a huddle, close together at* L.C., *rapidly whispering.*

DORIS. Has she been like that with you, too?

CYRIL. Yes—no tea ready—couldn't care less . . .

DORIS. Well, I'm glad it's both of us. I thought I'd done something wrong.

CYRIL. So did I. But it's her of course . . .

DORIS. She was smoking and playing cards when I came in. I couldn't believe my eyes.

CYRIL. I asked her if she was feeling off-colour and she said she wasn't.

DORIS. Well, she's suddenly all different. An' that's what made me cry. It wasn't what she said but the way she said it—an' the way she *looked*.

CYRIL. Haven't noticed that. She looks just the same to me.

DORIS. She doesn't to me. Do you think she could have hit her head or something—y'know—an' got—what is it?— y'know . . .

CYRIL (*staggered*). Do you mean she's barmy?

DORIS. No, you fathead. Y'know—concussion. She might have.

CYRIL. Sounds far-fetched.

DORIS. Well, she's far-fetched, if you ask me. (*She suddenly begins to giggle.*)

CYRIL. Now then—what is it?

DORIS. If she's going to be like this when Dad comes home . . . (*She giggles again.*)

CYRIL (*beginning to guffaw*). I'm staying in for that—two front dress circles for the first house . . .

[MRS. PEARSON *enters* R., *carrying a bottle of stout and a half-filled glass.* CYRIL *and* DORIS *try to stop their*

*guffawing and giggling, but they are not quick enough.*
MRS. PEARSON *regards them with contempt.*

MRS. PEARSON (*coldly*). You two are always talking about being grown-up—why don't you both try for once to be your age? (*She moves to the settee and sits.*)

CYRIL. Can't we laugh now?

MRS. PEARSON. Yes, if it's funny. Go on, tell me. Make me laugh. I could do with it.

DORIS. Y'know you never understand our jokes, Mum . . .

MRS. PEARSON. I was yawning at your jokes before you were born, Doris.

DORIS (*almost tearful again*). What's making you talk like this? What have we done?

MRS. PEARSON (*promptly*). Nothing but come in, ask for something, go out again, then come back when there's nowhere else to go.

CYRIL (*aggressively*). Look—if you won't get tea ready, then I'll find something to eat myself . . .

MRS. PEARSON. Why not? Help yourself. (*She takes a sip of stout.*)

CYRIL (*turning on his way to the kitchen*). Mind you, I think it's a bit thick. I've been working all day.

DORIS. Same here.

MRS. PEARSON (*calmly*). Eight hour day?

CYRIL. Yes—eight hour day—an' don't forget it.

MRS. PEARSON. I've done my eight hours.

CYRIL. That's different.

DORIS. Of course it is.

MRS. PEARSON (*calmly*). It *was*. Now it isn't. Forty-hour week for all now. Just watch it at the week-end when I have my two days off.

[DORIS *and* CYRIL *exchange alarmed glances. Then they stare at* MRS. PEARSON *who returns their look calmly.*

CYRIL. Must grab something to eat. Looks as if I'll need to keep my strength up.

[CYRIL *exits to the kitchen.*

DORIS (*moving to the settee; anxiously*). Mummie, you don't mean you're not going to do *anything* on Saturday and Sunday?

MRS. PEARSON (*airily*). No, I wouldn't go that far. I might make a bed or two and do a bit of cooking *as a favour*. Which means, of course, I'll have to be asked very nicely and thanked for everything and generally made a fuss of. But any of you forty-hour-a-weekers who expect to be waited on hand and foot on Saturday and Sunday, with no thanks for it, are in for a nasty disappointment. Might go off for the week-end perhaps.

DORIS (*aghast*). Go off for the week-end?

MRS. PEARSON. Why not? I could do with a change. Stuck here day after day, week after week. If I don't need a change, who does?

DORIS. But where would you go, who would you go with?

MRS. PEARSON. That's my business. You don't ask me where you should go and who you should go with, do you?

DORIS. That's different.

MRS. PEARSON. The only difference is that I'm a lot older and better able to look after myself, so it's you who should do the asking.

DORIS. Did you fall or hit yourself with something?

MRS. PEARSON (*coldly*). No. But I'll hit you with something, girl, if you don't stop asking silly questions.

[DORIS *stares at her open-mouthed, ready to cry.*

DORIS. Oh—this is awful . . . (*She begins to cry, not passionately.*)

MRS. PEARSON (*coldly*). Stop blubbering. You're not a baby.

If you're old enough to go out with Charlie Spence, you're old enough to behave properly. Now stop it.

[GEORGE PEARSON *enters* L. *He is about fifty, fundamentally decent but solemn, self-important, pompous. Preferably he should be a heavy, slow-moving type. He notices* DORIS'S *tears.*]

GEORGE. Hello—what's this? Can't be anything to cry about.

DORIS (*through sobs*). You'll see.

[DORIS *runs out* L. *with a sob or two on the way.* GEORGE *stares after her a moment, then looks at* MRS. PEARSON.]

GEORGE. Did she say 'You'll see' . . . ?

MRS. PEARSON. Yes.

GEORGE. What did she mean?

MRS. PEARSON. Better ask her.

[GEORGE *looks slowly again at the door then at* MRS. PEARSON. *Then he notices the stout that* MRS. PEARSON *raises for another sip. His eyes almost bulge.*]

GEORGE. Stout?

MRS. PEARSON. Yes.

GEORGE (*amazed*). What are you drinking stout for?

MRS. PEARSON. Because I fancied some.

GEORGE. At this time of day?

MRS. PEARSON. Yes—what's wrong with it at this time of day?

GEORGE (*bewildered*). Nothing, I suppose, Annie—but I've never seen you do it before . . .

MRS. PEARSON. Well, you're seeing me now.

GEORGE (*with heavy distaste*). Yes, an' I don't like it. It doesn't look right. I'm surprised at you.

MRS. PEARSON. Well, that ought to be a nice change for you.

GEORGE. What do you mean?

MRS. PEARSON. It must be some time since you were surprised at me, George.

GEORGE. I don't like surprises—I'm all for a steady going on—you ought to know that by this time. By the way, I forgot to tell you this morning I wouldn't want any tea. Special snooker match night at the club tonight—an' a bit of supper going. So no tea.

MRS. PEARSON. That's all right. There isn't any.

GEORGE (*astonished*). You mean you didn't get any ready?

MRS. PEARSON. Yes. And a good thing, too, as it's turned out.

GEORGE (*aggrieved*). That's all very well, but suppose I'd wanted some?

MRS. PEARSON. My goodness! Listen to the man! Annoyed because I don't get a tea for him that he doesn't even want. Ever tried that at the club?

GEORGE. Tried what at the club?

MRS. PEARSON. Going up to the bar and telling 'em you don't want a glass of beer but you're annoyed because they haven't already poured it out. Try that on them and see what you get.

GEORGE. I don't know what you're talking about.

MRS. PEARSON. They'd laugh at you even more than they do now.

GEORGE (*indignantly*). Laugh at me? They don't laugh at me.

MRS. PEARSON. Of course they do. You ought to have found that out by this time. Anybody else would have done. You're one of their standing jokes. Famous. They call you Pompy-ompy Pearson because they think you're so slow and pompous.

GEORGE (*horrified*). Never!

MRS. PEARSON. It's always beaten me why you should want to spend so much time at a place where they're always

12

laughing at you behind your back and calling you names. Leaving your wife at home, night after night. Instead of going out with her, who doesn't make you look a fool . . .

[CYRIL *enters* R., *with a glass of milk in one hand and a thick slice of cake in the other.* GEORGE, *almost dazed, turns to him appealingly.*

GEORGE. Here, Cyril, you've been with me to the club once or twice. They don't laugh at me and call me Pompy-ompy Pearson, do they?

[CYRIL, *embarrassed, hesitates.*

(*Angrily.*) Go on—tell me. Do they?
CYRIL (*embarrassed*). Well—yes, Dad. I'm afraid they do.

[GEORGE *slowly looks from one to the other, staggered.*

GEORGE (*slowly*). Well—I'll be—damned!

[GEORGE *exits* L. *slowly, almost as if somebody had hit him over the head.* CYRIL, *after watching him go, turns indignantly to* MRS. PEARSON.

CYRIL. Now you shouldn't have told him that, Mum. That's not fair. You've hurt his feelings. Mine, too.
MRS. PEARSON. Sometimes it does people good to have their feelings hurt. The truth oughtn't to hurt anybody for long. If your father didn't go to the club so often, perhaps they'd stop laughing at him.
CYRIL (*gloomily*). I doubt it.
MRS. PEARSON (*severely*). Possibly you do, but what I doubt is whether your opinion's worth having. What do you know? Nothing. You spend too much time and good money at greyhound races and dirt tracks and ice shows . . .

CYRIL (*sulkily*). Well, what if I do? I've got to enjoy myself somehow, haven't I?

MRS. PEARSON. I wouldn't mind so much if you were really enjoying yourself. But are you? And where's it getting you?

[*There is a sharp hurried knocking heard off* L.

CYRIL. Might be for me. I'll see.

[CYRIL *hurries out* L. *In a moment he re-enters, closing the door behind him.*

It's that silly old bag from next door—Mrs. Fitzgerald. You don't want her here, do you?

MRS. PEARSON (*sharply*). Certainly I do. Ask her in. And don't call her a silly old bag neither. She's a very nice woman, with a lot more sense than you'll ever have.

[CYRIL *exits* L. MRS. PEARSON *finishes her stout, smacking her lips.*

    CYRIL *re-enters* L., *ushering in* MRS. FITZGERALD, *who hesitates in the doorway.*

Come in, come in, Mrs. Fitzgerald.

MRS. FITZGERALD (*moving to* L.C.; *anxiously*). I—just wondered—if everything's—all right . . .

CYRIL (*sulkily*). No, it isn't.

MRS. PEARSON (*sharply*). Of course it is. You be quiet.

CYRIL (*indignantly and loudly*). Why should I be quiet?

MRS. PEARSON (*shouting*). Because I tell you to—you silly, spoilt, young piecan.

MRS. FITZGERALD (*protesting nervously*). Oh—no—surely . . .

MRS. PEARSON (*severely*). Now, Mrs. Fitzgerald, just let me manage my family in my own way—*please*!

MRS. FITZGERALD. Yes—but Cyril . . .

CYRIL (*sulky and glowering*). Mr. Cyril Pearson to you, please, Mrs. Fitzgerald.

[CYRIL *stalks off into the kitchen.*

MRS. FITZGERALD (*moving to the settee; whispering*). Oh—dear—what's happening?

MRS. PEARSON (*calmly*). Nothing much. Just putting 'em in their places, that's all. Doing what you ought to have done long since.

MRS. FITZGERALD. Is George home? (*She sits beside* MRS. PEARSON *on the settee.*)

MRS. PEARSON. Yes. I've been telling him what they think of him at the club.

MRS. FITZGERALD. Well, they think a lot of him, don't they?

MRS. PEARSON. No, they don't. And now he knows it.

MRS. FITZGERALD (*nervously*). Oh—dear—I wish you hadn't, Mrs. Fitzgerald . . .

MRS. PEARSON. Nonsense! Doing 'em all a world of good. And they'll be eating out of your hand soon—you'll see . . .

MRS. FITZGERALD. I don't think I want them eating out of my hand . . .

MRS. PEARSON (*impatiently*). Well, whatever you want, they'll be doing it—all three of 'em. Mark my words, Mrs. Pearson.

[GEORGE *enters* L. *glumly. He is unpleasantly surprised when he sees the visitor. He moves to the armchair* L., *sits down heavily and glumly lights his pipe. Then he looks from* MRS. PEARSON *to* MRS. FITZGERALD, *who is regarding him anxiously.*

GEORGE. Just looked in for a minute, I suppose, Mrs. Fitzgerald?

MRS. FITZGERALD (*who doesn't know what she is saying*). Well—yes—I suppose so, George.

GEORGE (*aghast*). George!

MRS. FITZGERALD (*nervously*). Oh—I'm sorry . . .

MRS. PEARSON (*impatiently*). What does it matter? Your name's George, isn't it? Who d'you think you are—Duke of Edinburgh?

GEORGE (*angrily*). What's he got to do with it? Just tell me that. And isn't it bad enough without her calling me George? No tea. Pompy-ompy Pearson. And poor Doris has been crying her eyes out upstairs—yes, crying her eyes out.

MRS. FITZGERALD (*wailing*). Oh—dear—I ought to have known . . .

GEORGE (*staring at her, annoyed*). *You* ought to have known! Why ought you to have known? Nothing to do with you, Mrs. Fitzgerald. Look—we're at sixes and sevens here just now—so perhaps you'll excuse us . . .

MRS. PEARSON (*before* MRS. FITZGERALD *can reply*). I won't excuse you, George Pearson. Next time a friend and neighbour comes to see me, just say something when you see her—Good evening or How d'you do? or something—an' don't just march in an' sit down without a word. It's bad manners . . .

MRS. FITZGERALD (*nervously*). No—it's all right . . .

MRS. PEARSON. No, it isn't all right. We'll have some decent manners in this house—or I'll know the reason why. (*Glaring at* GEORGE.) Well?

GEORGE (*intimidated*). Well what?

MRS. PEARSON (*taunting him*). Why don't you get off to your club? Special night tonight, isn't it? They'll be waiting for you—wanting to have a good laugh. Go on then. Don't disappoint 'em.

GEORGE (*bitterly*). That's right. Make me look silly in front of her now! Go on—don't mind me. Sixes and sevens! Poor Doris been crying her eyes out! Getting the neighbours in to see the fun! (*Suddenly losing his temper, glaring at* MRS. PEARSON, *and shouting.*) All right—let her hear it. What's the matter with you? Have you gone barmy—or what?

MRS. PEARSON (*jumping up; savagely*). If you shout at me again like that, George Pearson, I'll slap your big fat silly face . . .

MRS. FITZGERALD (*moaning*). Oh—no—no—no—please, Mrs. Fitzgerald . . .

[MRS. PEARSON *sits.*

GEORGE (*staring at her, bewildered*). Either I'm off my chump or you two are. How d'you mean—'No—no, please, Mrs. Fitzgerald'? Look—*you're* Mrs. Fitzgerald. So why are you telling yourself to stop when you're not doing anything? Tell *her* to stop—then there'd be some sense in it. (*Staring at Mrs. Pearson.*) I think you must be tiddly.

MRS. PEARSON (*starting up; savagely*). Say that again, George Pearson.

GEORGE (*intimidated*). All right—all right—all right . . .

[DORIS *enters* L. *slowly, looking miserable. She is still wearing the wrap.* MRS. PEARSON *sits on the settee.*

MRS. FITZGERALD. Hello—Doris dear!

DORIS (*miserably*). Hello—Mrs. Fitzgerald!

MRS. FITZGERALD. I thought you were going out with Charlie Spence tonight.

DORIS (*annoyed*). What's that to do with you?

MRS. PEARSON (*sharply*). Stop that!

MRS. FITZGERALD (*nervously*). No—it's all right . . .

MRS. PEARSON (*severely*). It isn't all right. I won't have a daughter of mine talking to anybody like that. Now answer Mrs. Fitzgerald properly, Doris—or go upstairs again . . .

[DORIS *looks wonderingly at her father*.

GEORGE (*in despair*). Don't look at me. I give it up. I just give it up.

MRS. PEARSON (*fiercely*). Well? Answer her.

DORIS (*sulkily*). I was going out with Charlie Spence tonight—but now I've called it off . . .

MRS. FITZGERALD. Oh—what a pity, dear! Why have you?

DORIS (*with a flash of temper*). Because—if you must know—my mother's been going on at me—making me feel miserable—an' saying he's got buck-teeth and is half-witted . . .

MRS. FITZGERALD (*rather bolder; to* MRS. PEARSON). Oh—you shouldn't have said that . . .

MRS. PEARSON (*sharply*). Mrs. Fitzgerald, I'll manage my family—you manage yours.

GEORGE (*grimly*). Ticking *her* off now, are you, Annie?

MRS. PEARSON (*even more grimly*). They're waiting for you at the club, George, don't forget. And don't you start crying again, Doris . . .

MRS. FITZGERALD (*getting up; with sudden decision*). That's enough—quite enough.

[GEORGE *and* DORIS *stare at her bewildered*.

(*To* GEORGE *and* DORIS.) Now listen, you two. I want to have a private little talk with Mrs. Fitz—(*she corrects herself hastily*) with Mrs. Pearson, so I'll be obliged if you'll leave us alone for a few minutes. I'll let you know when we've finished. Go on, please. I promise you that you won't regret it. There's something here that only I can deal with.

GEORGE (*rising*). I'm glad somebody can—'cos I can't. Come on, Doris.

[GEORGE *and* DORIS *exit* L. *As they go* MRS. FITZGERALD

*moves to* L. *of the small table and sits. She eagerly beckons* MRS. PEARSON *to do the same thing.*

MRS. FITZGERALD. Mrs. Fitzgerald, we must change back now—we really must . . .

MRS. PEARSON (*rising*). Why?

MRS. FITZGERALD. Because this has gone far enough. I can see they're all miserable—and I can't bear it . . .

MRS. PEARSON. A bit more of the same would do 'em good. Making a great difference already . . . (*She moves to* R. *of the table and sits.*)

MRS. FITZGERALD. No, I can't stand any more of it—I really can't. We must change back. Hurry up, please, Mrs. Fitzgerald.

MRS. PEARSON. Well—if you insist . . .

MRS. FITZGERALD. Yes—I do—please—*please.*

[*She stretches her hands across the table eagerly.* MRS. PEARSON *takes them.*

MRS. PEARSON. Quiet now. Relax.

[MRS. PEARSON *and* MRS. FITZGERALD *stare at each other.* (*Muttering; exactly as before.*) *Arshtatta dum—arshtatta lam—arshtatta lamdumbona* . . .

[*They carry out the same action as before, going lax and then coming to life. But this time, of course, they become their proper personalities.*

MRS. FITZGERALD. Ah well—I enjoyed that.

MRS. PEARSON. I didn't.

MRS. FITZGERALD. Well, you ought to have done. Now—listen, Mrs. Pearson. Don't go soft on 'em again, else it'll all have been wasted . . .

MRS. PEARSON. I'll try not to, Mrs. Fitzgerald.

MRS. FITZGERALD. They've not had as long as I'd like to

have given 'em—another hour or two's rough treatment might have made it certain . . .

MRS. PEARSON. I'm sure they'll do better now—though I don't know how I'm going to explain . . .

MRS. FITZGERALD (*severely*). Don't you start any explaining or apologizing—or you're done for.

MRS. PEARSON (*with spirit*). It's all right for you, Mrs. Fitzgerald. After all, they aren't your husband and children . . .

MRS. FITZGERALD (*impressively*). Now you listen to me. You admitted yourself you were spoiling 'em—and they didn't appreciate you. Any apologies—any explanations—an' you'll be straight back where you were. I'm warning you, dear. Just give 'em a look—a tone of voice—now an' again, to suggest you might be tough with 'em if you wanted to be—an' it ought to work. Anyhow, we can test it.

MRS. PEARSON. How?

MRS. FITZGERALD. Well, what is it you'd like 'em to do that they don't do? Stop at home for once?

MRS. PEARSON. Yes—and give me a hand with supper . . .

MRS. FITZGERALD. Anything you'd like 'em to do—that you enjoy whether they do or not?

MRS. PEARSON (*hesitating*). Well—yes. I—like a nice game of rummy—but, of course, I hardly ever have one—except at Christmas . . .

MRS. FITZGERALD (*getting up*). That'll do then. (*She moves towards the door* L. *then turns.*) But remember—keep firm—or you've had it. (*She opens the door. Calling.*) Hoy! You can come in now. (*Coming away from the door, and moving* R. *slightly. Quietly.*) But remember—remember—a firm hand.

[GEORGE, DORIS *and* CYRIL *file in through the doorway, looking apprehensively at* MRS. PEARSON.

I'm just off. To let you enjoy yourself.

[*The family look anxiously at* MRS. PEARSON, *who smiles. Much relieved, they smile back at her.*

DORIS (*anxiously*). Yes, Mother?

MRS. PEARSON (*smiling*). Seeing that you don't want to go out, I tell you what I thought we'd do . . .

MRS. FITZGERALD (*giving a final warning*). Remember!

MRS. PEARSON (*nodding, then looking sharply at the family*). No objections, I hope?

GEORGE (*humbly*). No, Mother—whatever you say . . .

MRS. PEARSON (*smiling*). I thought we'd have a nice family game of rummy—and then you children could get the supper ready while I have a talk with your father . . .

GEORGE (*firmly*). Suits me. (*He looks challengingly at the children.*) What about you two?

CYRIL (*hastily*). Yes—that's all right.

DORIS (*hesitating*). Well—I . . .

MRS. PEARSON (*sharply*). What? Speak up!

DORIS (*hastily*). Oh—I think it would be lovely . . .

MRS. PEARSON (*smiling*). Good-bye, Mrs. Fitzgerald. Come again soon.

MRS. FITZGERALD. Yes, dear. 'Night all—have a nice time.

[MRS. FITZGERALD *exits* L. *and the family cluster round Mother as—*

*the* CURTAIN *falls.*

# TRIFLES
by Susan Glaspell

## CHARACTERS

HENRY PETERS
*(Sheriff)*

GEORGE HENDERSON
*(County Attorney)*

LEWIS HALE

MRS. PETERS

MRS. HALE


*Scene*

A Gloomy Kitchen

# TRIFLES

SCENE—*The Kitchen in the now abandoned farm-house of* JOHN WRIGHT.

*It is a gloomy room, and left without having been put in order. There are unwashed pans under the sink, a loaf of bread outside the bread-box, a dish-towel on the table and other signs of incompleted work.*

*The door to the outside world is in the rear wall. To the right of this, under the window, there is a sink, and to the left there is a form with a hat-rack on the wall. The fireplace is in the centre of the Left wall with an armchair Downstage of it and a rocking-chair Upstage of it. Upstage of the fireplace there is a side-table also set against the wall. There is a kitchen table approximately in the centre of the stage with a chair at either end of it. The door leading to the other part of the house is in the wall up Right. Below this, set against the wall, is a cupboard with a chair Upstage and slightly to the left of it. Downstage of the cupboard is a bread-box.*

*As the* CURTAIN *rises the outer door* C. *opens and the* SHERIFF *comes in followed by the* COUNTY ATTORNEY *and* HALE. *The* SHERIFF *and* HALE *are men in middle life, the* COUNTY ATTORNEY *is a young man. After the men there enter two women—the* SHERIFF'S *wife—she is a slight wiry woman with a thin nervous face—and* MRS. HALE. *The latter is larger and would ordinarily be called more comfortable looking, but she is disturbed now and looks fearfully about as she enters. They take up their positions from* R. *to* L. *as follows: The* SHERIFF, MRS. HALE, MRS. PETERS *(the* SHERIFF'S *wife), the* COUNTY ATTORNEY *and* HALE. *The latter two are round the fire* L.

COUNTY ATTORNEY (*rubbing his hands*). This feels good. Come up to the fire, ladies.

MRS. PETERS (*after taking a step forward*). I'm not—cold. (*She steps* L., *then back again.*)

SHERIFF (*unbuttoning his overcoat and stepping away from the group as if to mark the beginning of official business*). Now, Mr. Hale, before we move things about, you explain to Mr. Henderson just what you saw when you came here yesterday morning.

[*He moves up to the table.*

COUNTY ATTORNEY (L.). By the way, has anything been moved? Are things just as you left them yesterday?

SHERIFF (*looking about*). It's just the same. When it dropped below zero last night I thought I'd better send Frank out this morning to make a fire for us—no use getting pneumonia with a big case on, but I told him not to touch anything except the fire—and you know Frank. (*He turns away* R.)

COUNTY ATTORNEY. Somebody should have been left here yesterday. (*He moves to the table.*)

SHERIFF (R.). Oh—yesterday. When I had to send Frank to Morris Centre for that man who went crazy—I want you to know I had my hands full yesterday. I knew you could get back from Omaha by today, and as long as I went over everything here myself——

COUNTY ATTORNEY (*taking out a note book*). Well, Mr. Hale, tell just what happened when you came here yesterday morning. (*He sits* L. *of the table.*)

HALE (L.). Well, Harry and I had started to town with a load of potatoes. We came along the road from my place and as I got here I said, 'I'm going to see if I can't get John Wright to go in with me on a party telephone.' I spoke to Wright about it once before and he put me off,

saying folks talked too much anyway, and all he asked
was peace and quiet—I guess you know about how much
he talked himself; but I thought maybe if I went to the
house and talked about it before his wife, though I said
to Harry that I didn't know as what his wife wanted
made much difference to John——

COUNTY ATTORNEY. Yes, yes; let's talk about that later, Mr.
Hale. I do want to talk about that, but tell now just what
happened when you got to the house.

HALE (*taking a step* c.). I didn't hear or see anything; I
knocked at the door, and still it was all quiet inside. I
knew they must be up, it was past eight o'clock. So I
knocked again, and I thought I heard somebody say,
'Come in.' I wasn't sure, I'm not sure yet, but I opened
the door—this door (*indicating the door by which the two
women are still standing*) and there in that rocker—
(*pointing to it*) sat Mrs. Wright.

[*They all look at the rocker.*

COUNTY ATTORNEY. What—was she doing?

HALE. She was rockin' back and forth. She had her apron in
her hand and was kind of—pleating it.

COUNTY ATTORNEY. And how did she—look?

HALE. Well, she looked queer.

COUNTY ATTORNEY. How do you mean—queer?

HALE (L.C.). Well, as if she didn't know what she was going
to do next. And kind of done up.

COUNTY ATTORNEY. How did she seem to feel about your
coming?

HALE. Why, I don't think she minded—one way or other.
She didn't pay much attention. I said, 'How do, Mrs.
Wright, it's cold, ain't it?' And she said, 'Is it?'—and went
on kind of pleating at her apron. Well, I was surprised;
she didn't ask me to come up to the fire, or to sit down,

but just sat there, not even looking at me, so I said, 'I want to see John.' And then she—laughed. I guess you would call it a laugh. I thought of Harry and the team outside, so I said a little sharp: 'Can't I see John?' 'No,' she says, kind o' dull like. 'Ain't he home?' says I. 'Yes,' says she, 'he's home.' 'Then why can't I see him?' I asked her, out of patience. ' 'Cause he's dead,' says she. '*Dead?*' says I. She just nodded her head, not getting a bit excited, but rockin' back and forth. 'Why—where is he?' says I, not knowing what to say. She just pointed upstairs— (*himself pointing to the room above*) like that. I got up, with the idea of going up there. I walked from there to here—then I says, 'Why, what did he die of?' 'He died of a rope round his neck,' says she, and just went on pleatin' at her apron. Well, I went out and called Harry. I thought I might—need help. We went upstairs and there he was lyin'—with his neck——

COUNTY ATTORNEY. I think I'd rather have you go into that upstairs, where you can point it all out. Just go on now with the rest of the story.

HALE. Well, my first thought was to get that rope off. It looked . . . (*He stops, his face twitches.*) . . . but Harry, he went up to him, and he said, 'No, he's dead all right, and we'd better not touch anything.' So we went back downstairs. She was still sitting that same way. 'Has anybody been notified?' I asked. 'No,' says she, unconcerned. 'Who did this, Mrs. Wright?' said Harry. He said it business-like—and she stopped pleatin' of her apron. 'I don't know,' she says. 'You don't *know*?' says Harry. 'No,' says she. 'Weren't you sleepin' in the bed with him?' says Harry. 'Yes,' says she, 'but I was on the inside.' 'Somebody slipped a rope round his neck and strangled him and you *didn't wake up*?' says Harry. 'I didn't wake up,' she said after him. We must a' looked as if we didn't see how that could be, for after a minute she said, 'I sleep sound.' Harry was going to ask her more questions but I said maybe we ought to let her tell her story first to the coroner, or the sheriff, so Harry went fast as he could to Rivers's place, where there's a telephone.

COUNTY ATTORNEY. And what did Mrs. Wright do when she knew that you had gone for the coroner?

HALE. She moved from that chair to this one over here (*pointing to a small chair in the corner*) and just sat there with her hands held together and looking down. I got a feeling that I ought to make some conversation, so I said I had come in to see if John wanted to put in a telephone, and at that she started to laugh, and then she stopped and looked at me—scared.

[*The* COUNTY ATTORNEY *makes a note.*

I dunno, maybe it wasn't scared. I wouldn't like to say it was. Soon Harry got back, and then Dr. Lloyd came, and you, Mr. Peters, and so I guess that's all I know that you don't. (*He moves* L. *to the fire.*)

COUNTY ATTORNEY (*rising and crossing below table to* R.). I guess we'll go upstairs first—and then out to the barn and around there. (*To the* SHERIFF.) You're convinced that there was nothing important here—nothing that would point to any motive?

SHERIFF. Nothing here but kitchen things. (*He moves above table to* L.)

[*The* COUNTY ATTORNEY, *after again looking around the kitchen, opens the door of a cupboard* R. *and looks on a shelf. He pulls his hand away, sticky.*

COUNTY ATTORNEY. Here's a nice mess.

[*The women draw nearer.*

MRS. PETERS (*to the other woman*). Oh, her fruit; it did freeze. (*To the* ATTORNEY.) She worried about that when it turned so cold. She said the fire'd go out and her jars would break.

SHERIFF (L.). Well, can you beat the women! Held for murder and worryin' about her preserves.

COUNTY ATTORNEY (*up* R.). I guess before we're through she may have something more serious than preserves to worry about.

HALE (L.). Well, women are used to worrying over *trifles*.

[*The two women move a little closer together.*

COUNTY ATTORNEY (*with the gallantry of a young politician*). And yet, for all their worries, what would we do without the ladies? (*The women do not unbend. He goes to the sink, takes a dipperful of water from the pail and pouring it into a basin, washes his hands. He starts to wipe them on the roller towel, then turns it for a cleaner place.*) Dirty towels! (*He kicks his foot against the pans under the sink.*) Not much of a housekeeper, would you say, ladies?

MRS. HALE (*stiffly*). There's a great deal of work to be done on a farm.

COUNTY ATTORNEY. To be sure. And yet (*with a little bow to her*) I know there are some Dickson county farm-houses which do not have such roller towels. (*He gives it a pull to expose its full length again.*)

MRS. HALE. Those towels get dirty awful quick. Men's hands aren't always as clean as they might be.

COUNTY ATTORNEY (R.). Ah, loyal to your sex, I see. But you and Mrs. Wright were neighbours. I suppose you were friends, too.

MRS. HALE (*shaking her head*). I've not seen much of her of late years. I've not been in the house—it's more than a year.

COUNTY ATTORNEY. And why was that? You didn't like her?

MRS. HALE. I liked her well enough. Farmers' wives have their hands full, Mr. Henderson. And then——

COUNTY ATTORNEY. Yes——?

MRS. HALE (*looking about*). It never seemed a very cheerful place.

COUNTY ATTORNEY. No—it's not cheerful. I shouldn't say she had the homemaking instinct.

MRS. HALE. Well, I don't know as Wright had, either.

COUNTY ATTORNEY. Oh! You mean that they didn't get on very well?

MRS. HALE (*up* C.). No, I don't mean anything. But I don't think a place'd be any cheerfuller for John Wright's being in it.

COUNTY ATTORNEY (R.C.). I'd like to talk more of that a little later. I want to get the lay of things upstairs now. (*He goes* R. *to where three steps lead to a stair door.*)

SHERIFF (*crossing above table to* R.). I suppose anything Mrs. Peters does'll be all right. She was to take in some clothes for her, you know, and a few little things. We left in such a hurry yesterday.

COUNTY ATTORNEY. Yes, but I would like to see what you take, Mrs. Peters, and keep an eye out for anything that might be of use to us. Come on, Hale!

MRS. PETERS. Yes, Mr. Henderson.

[*The three men exit* R.

   *The women listen to their steps on the stairs, then look about the kitchen.*

MRS. HALE (*up* R.C.). I'd hate to have men coming into my kitchen, snooping around and criticizing. (*She arranges the pans under the sink which the* ATTORNEY *had shoved out of place, and pours the dirty water into a pail.*)

MRS. PETERS. Of course it's no more than their duty.

MRS. HALE. Duty's all right, but I guess that deputy sheriff that came out to make the fire didn't make this any cleaner. (*She gives the roller towel a pull.*) Wish I'd thought of that sooner. Seems mean to talk about her for not having things slicked up when she had to come away in such a hurry.

MRS. PETERS (*who has gone to a small table up* L. *in the corner of the room, and lifted one end of a towel that covers a pan*). She had bread set. (*She stands still.*)

[MRS. HALE *has her eyes fixed on a loaf of bread beside the bread-box, which is on a low shelf at the other side of the room.*

MRS. HALE (*moving slowly towards it*). She was going to put this in there. (*She picks up loaf, then abruptly drops it— then in a manner of returning to familiar things.*) It's a shame about her fruit. I wonder if it's all gone. (*She looks into the cupboard.*) I think there's some here that's all right, Mrs. Peters. Yes—here; (*holding it up*) this is cherries, too. (*Looking again.*) I declare I believe that's the only one. (*She gets down, bottle in her hand, and goes to the sink and wipes it on the outside.*) She'll feel awful sorry after all her hard work in the hot weather. I remember the afternoon I put up my cherries last summer.

[*She puts the bottle on the big kitchen table* C., *and with a sigh, is about to sit down in the rocking-chair. Before she is seated she realizes what chair it is, and with a slow look at it, steps back. The chair which she had touched rocks to and fro.*

MRS. PETERS (*crossing to* R.C.). Well, I must get those things from the front room closet. (*She goes to the door* R., *but after looking into the other room, steps back.*) You coming with me, Mrs. Hale? You could help me carry them.

[*They go into the other room and their voices can be heard off* R. *Then they reappear,* MRS. PETERS *carrying a dress and skirt,* MRS. HALE *following with a pair of shoes.*

My, it's cold in there. (*She puts the clothes on the big table, and hurries to the fire* L.

MRS. HALE (*above table* C. *examining the skirt*). Wright was close. (*Making up a parcel.*) I think maybe that's why she kept so much to herself. She didn't even belong to the Ladies' Aid. I suppose she felt she couldn't do her part, and then you don't enjoy things when you feel shabby. She used to wear pretty clothes and be lively, when she was Minnie Foster, one of the town girls singing in the choir. But that—oh, that was thirty years ago. This all you was to take in?

MRS. PETERS. She said she wanted an apron. (*She moves* C.) Funny thing to want, for there isn't much to get you dirty in jail, goodness knows. But I suppose just to make her feel more natural. (*Crossing* R.) She said they was in the top drawer in this cupboard. Yes, here. And then her little shawl, that always hung behind the door. (*She opens stair door* R. *and looks.*) Yes, here it is. (*She quickly shuts the door leading upstairs.*)

MRS. HALE (*abruptly moving towards her*). Mrs. Peters!

MRS. PETERS (R.C.). Yes, Mrs. Hale?

MRS. HALE (L.C.). Do you think, she did it?

MRS. PETERS (*in a frightened voice*). Oh, I don't know.

MRS. HALE (*taking the shawl and apron from her*). Well, I don't think she did. Asking for an apron and her little shawl. Worrying about her fruit.

[*The men's voices are heard off* R.

MRS. PETERS (*starting to speak, then in a low voice*). Mr. Peters says it looks bad for her. Mr. Henderson is awful sarcastic in a speech and he'll make fun of her sayin' she didn't wake up.

MRS. HALE. Well, I guess John Wright didn't wake when they was slipping that rope under his neck.

MRS. PETERS. No, it's strange. It must have been done awful crafty and still. They say it was such a—funny way to kill a man, rigging it all up like that.

MRS. HALE. That's just what Mr. Hale said. There was a gun in the house. He says that's what he can't understand.

MRS. PETERS. Mr. Henderson said coming out that what was needed for the case was a motive; something to show anger, or—sudden feeling.

MRS. HALE (*who is standing by the table*). Well, I don't see any signs of anger around here. (*She puts her hand on the dish towel which lies on the table, and stands looking down at table, one half of which is clean, the other half messy.*) It's wiped to here. (*She makes a move as if to finish work, then turns and looks at loaf of bread outside the bread-box. She drops the towel. Then in that voice of coming back to familiar things.*) Wonder how they are finding things upstairs. I hope she had it a little more tidy up there. (*She moves L.*) You know it seems kind of *sneaking*. Locking her up in town and then coming out here and trying to get her own house to turn against her!

MRS. PETERS. But, Mrs. Hale, the law is the law. (*She goes C. above table.*)

MRS. HALE (*crossing R.*). I s'pose 'tis. (*Unbuttoning her coat.*) Better loosen up your things, Mrs. Peters. You won't feel them when you go out.

[MRS. PETERS *takes off her fur tippet, goes to hang it on*

*hook at back of room* L.C., *then stands looking at the small corner table up* L.

MRS. PETERS (*moving* L.). She was piecing a quilt. (*She brings a large sewing-basket from the table up* L., *and puts it on the table* C., *and they look at the bright pieces.*)

MRS. HALE. It's a log cabin pattern. Pretty, isn't it? I wonder if she was goin' to quilt it or just knot it?

[*Voices have been heard coming down the stairs. The* SHERIFF *enters, followed by* HALE *and the* COUNTY ATTORNEY.

SHERIFF. They wonder if she was going to quilt it or just knot it! (*He crosses up* C. *and opens the door.*)

[*The men laugh; the women look abashed.*

COUNTY ATTORNEY (*rubbing his hands over the fire*). Frank's fire didn't do much up there, did it? Well, let's go out to the barn and get that cleared up.

[*The men exit* C.

MRS. HALE (*resentfully*). I don't know as there's anything so strange, our takin' up our time with little things while we're waiting for them to get the evidence. (*She sits* R. *of the big table, smoothing out a block with decision.*) I don't see as it's anything to laugh about.

MRS. PETERS (*apologetically*). Of course they've got awful important things on their minds. (*She takes the chair from* L. *of table to above table and sits.*)

MRS. HALE (*examining another block*). Mrs. Peters, look at this one. Here, this is the one she was working on, and look at the sewing! All the rest of it has been so nice and even. And look at this! It's all over the place! Why, it looks as if she didn't know what she was about!

[*After she has said this they look at each other, then start to glance back at the door. After an instant* MRS. HALE *has pulled at a knot and ripped the sewing.*

MRS. PETERS. Oh, what are you doing, Mrs. Hale?

MRS. HALE (*mildly*). Just pulling out a stitch or two that's not sewed very good. (*Threading a needle.*) Bad sewing always made me fidgety.

MRS. PETERS (*nervously*). I don't think we ought to touch things.

MRS. HALE. I'll just finish up this end. (*Suddenly stopping and leaning forward.*) Mrs. Peters!

MRS. PETERS. Yes, Mrs. Hale?

MRS. HALE. What do you suppose she was so nervous about?

MRS. PETERS. Oh—I don't know. I don't know as she was nervous. I sometimes sew awful queer when I'm just tired.

[MRS. HALE *starts to say something, looks at* MRS. PETERS, *then goes on sewing.*

Well, I must get these things wrapped up. They may be through sooner than we think. (*Putting apron and other things together.*) I wonder where I can find a piece of paper, and string. (*She rises and crosses to* R.)

MRS. HALE. In that cupboard, maybe.

MRS. PETERS (*looking at the cupboard*). Why, here's a bird-cage. (*She holds it up.*) Did she have a bird, Mrs. Hale? (*She moves back* C.)

MRS. HALE. Why, I don't know whether she did or not—I've not been here for so long. There was a man around last year selling canaries cheap, but I don't know as she took one; maybe she did. She used to sing real pretty herself.

MRS. PETERS (*glancing around*). Seems funny to think of a bird here. But she must have had one, or why would she have a cage? I wonder what happened to it? (*She moves up above table.*)

MRS. HALE. I s'pose maybe the cat got it.

MRS. PETERS. No, she didn't have a cat. She's got that feeling some people have about cats—being afraid of them. My cat got in her room and she was real upset and asked me to take it out.

MRS. HALE. My sister Bessie was like that. Queer, ain't it?

MRS. PETERS (*examining the cage*). Why, look at this door. It's broke. One hinge is pulled apart.

MRS. HALE (*also looking*). Looks as if someone must have been rough with it.

MRS. PETERS. Why, yes. (*She brings the cage forward and puts it on the table.*)

MRS. HALE. I wish if they're going to find any evidence they'd be about it. I don't like this place. (*She rises and crosses below table to the fire* L.)

MRS. PETERS. But I'm awful glad you came with me, Mrs. Hale. It would be lonesome for me sitting here alone. (*She sits above the table.*)

MRS. HALE. It would, wouldn't it? But I tell you what I do wish, Mrs. Peters. (*Stepping* C.) I wish I had come over sometimes when *she* was here. I—(*Looking round the room.*)—wish I had.

MRS. PETERS. But of course you were awful busy, Mrs. Hale—your house and your children.

MRS. HALE. I could've come. I stayed away because it weren't cheerful, and that's why I ought to have come. (*Moving* L., *then above table to* R.) I—I've never liked this place. Maybe because it's down in a hollow and you don't see the road. I dunno what it is, but it's a lonesome place and always was. I wish I had come over to see Minnie Foster sometimes. I can see now—— (*She shakes her head and sits* R. *of the table.*)

MRS. PETERS. Well, you mustn't reproach yourself, Mrs. Hale. Somehow we just don't see how it is with other folks until something turns up.

MRS. HALE. Not having children makes less work—but it makes a quiet house, and Wright out to work all day, and no company when he did come in. Did you know John Wright, Mrs. Peters?

MRS. PETERS. Not to know him; I've seen him in town. They say he was a good man.

MRS. HALE. Yes—good; he didn't drink, and kept his word as well as most, I guess, and paid his debts. But he was a hard man, Mrs. Peters. Just to pass the time of day with him—— (*She shivers.*) Like a raw wind that gets to the bone. (*She pauses, her eye falling on the cage.*) I should think she would 'a' wanted a bird. But what do you suppose happened to it?

MRS. PETERS. I don't know, unless it got sick and died. (*She reaches over and swings the broken door, then swings it again. Both women watch it.*)

MRS. HALE. You weren't raised round here, were you? (MRS. PETERS *shakes her head.*) You didn't know—her?

MRS. PETERS. Not till they brought her yesterday.

MRS. HALE. She—come to think of it, she was kind of like a bird herself—real sweet and pretty, but kind of timid and —fluttery. How—she—did—change. (*She pauses; then as if struck by a happy thought and relieved to get back to everyday things.*) Tell you what, Mrs. Peters, why don't you take the quilt in with you? It might take up her mind.

MRS. PETERS. Why, I think that's a real nice idea, Mrs. Hale. There couldn't possibly be any objection to it, could there? Now, just what would I take? I wonder if her patches are in here—and her things.

[*They look in the sewing basket.*

MRS. HALE. Here's some red. I expect this has got sewing things in it. (*She brings out a fancy box.*) What a pretty box. Looks like something somebody would give you. Maybe her scissors are in here. (*She opens box.*) Why——

[MRS. PETERS *bends nearer, then turns her face away.*

There's something wrapped up in this piece of silk.
MRS. PETERS. Why, this isn't her scissors.
MRS. HALE (*lifting the silk*). Oh, Mrs. Peters—it's——

[MRS. PETERS *bends closer.*

MRS. PETERS (*rising*). It's the bird.
MRS. HALE (*jumping up*). But, Mrs. Peters—look at it! Its neck! Look at its neck! It's all—other side to.
MRS. PETERS. Somebody wrung—its—neck.

[*Their eyes meet. A look of growing comprehension, of horror. Voices are heard outside.* MRS. HALE *slips box under quilt pieces, and sinks into her chair. Enter* SHERIFF *and* COUNTY ATTORNEY C.

COUNTY ATTORNEY (*as one turning from serious things to little pleasantries*). Well, ladies, have you decided whether she was going to quilt it or knot it? (*He crosses down* L.)
MRS. PETERS. We think she was going to—knot it. (*She reseats herself.*)
COUNTY ATTORNEY. Well, that's interesting. I'm sure. (*Seeing the bird-cage.*) Has the bird flown? (*He moves above table to* R.C.)
MRS. HALE (*putting more quilt pieces over the box*). We think the—cat got it.
COUNTY ATTORNEY (*preoccupied*). Is there a cat? (*He moves down* R.)

[MRS. HALE *glances in a quick covert way at* MRS. PETERS.

MRS. PETERS. Well, not now. They're superstitious, you know. They leave.

COUNTY ATTORNEY (*to the* SHERIFF, *continuing an interrupted conversation*). No sign at all of anyone having come from outside. Their own rope. Now let's go up again and go over it piece by piece. (*They start upstairs.*) It would have to have been someone who knew just the——

[*The two women sit there not looking at one another, but as if peering into something and at the same time holding back. When they talk now it is in the manner of feeling their way over strange ground, as if afraid of what they are saying, but as if they cannot help saying it.*

MRS. HALE. She liked the bird. She was going to bury it in that pretty box.

MRS. PETERS (*in a whisper*). When I was a girl—my kitten—there was a boy took a hatchet, and before my eyes—and before I could get there—— (*She covers her face an instant.*) If they hadn't held me back I would have—(*she catches herself, and looks where voices are heard off* R., *then falters weakly*)—hurt him.

MRS. HALE (*with a slow look round her*). I wonder how it would seem never to have had any children around. (*Pause.*) No, Wright wouldn't like the bird—(*she picks up the bird-cage*)—a thing that sang. She used to sing. He killed that, too.

MRS. PETERS (*moving uneasily*). We don't know who killed the bird.

MRS. HALE. I knew John Wright.

MRS. PETERS. It was an awful thing was done in this house that night, Mrs. Hale. Killing a man while he slept, slipping a rope around his neck that choked the life out of him.

MRS. HALE. His neck. Choked the life out of him.

MRS. PETERS (*with rising voice*). We don't know who killed him. We don't know.

MRS. HALE (*her own feeling not interrupted*). If there'd been years and years of nothing, then a bird to sing to you, it would be awful—still, after the bird was still.

MRS. PETERS (*something within her speaking*). *I know* what stillness is. When we homesteaded in Dakota, and my first baby died—after he was two years old, and me with no other then——

MRS. HALE (*moving*). How soon do you suppose they'll be through looking for the evidence?

MRS. PETERS. I know what stillness is. (*Pulling herself together.*) The law has got to punish crime, Mrs. Hale.

MRS. HALE (*not as if answering that*). I wish you'd seen Minnie Foster when she wore a white dress with blue ribbons and stood up there in the choir and sang. (*She rises and moves above the table, looking around the room.*) Oh, I *wish* I'd come over here once in a while! That was a crime! That was a crime! Who's going to punish that?

MRS. PETERS (*looking upstairs*). We mustn't—take on.

MRS. HALE. I might have known she needed help! I know how things can be—for women. I tell you, it's queer, Mrs. Peters. We live close together and we live far apart. We all go through the same things—it's all just a different kind of the same thing. (*Brushes her eyes, noticing the bottle of fruit, reaches out for it.*) If I was you I wouldn't tell her her fruit was gone. Tell her it *ain't*. Tell her it's all right. Take this in to prove it to her. She—she may never know whether it was broke or not. (*She sits* R. *of table.*)

[MRS. PETERS *rises, takes the bottle, looks about for something to wrap it in; takes petticoat from the clothes brought from the other room, and very nervously begins winding this about the bottle.*

MRS. PETERS (*in a false voice*). My, it's a good thing the men couldn't hear us. Wouldn't they just laugh! Getting all stirred up over a little thing like a—dead canary. As if that could have anything to do with—with—wouldn't they *laugh*! (*She crosses to the fire and sits.*)

[*The men are heard coming downstairs.*

MRS. HALE (*under her breath*). Maybe they would—maybe they wouldn't.

COUNTY ATTORNEY (*crossing* L. *above table*). No, Peters, it's all perfectly clear except a reason for doing it. But you know juries when it comes to women. If there was some definite thing. Something to show—something to make a story about—a thing that would connect up with this strange way of doing it——

[*The women's eyes meet for an instant. Enter* HALE *from outer door* C.

HALE (*up* C.). Well, I've got the team around. Pretty cold out there.

COUNTY ATTORNEY (L.). I'm going to stay here a while by myself. (*To the* SHERIFF.) You can send Frank out for me, can't you? I want to go over everything. I'm not satisfied that we can't do better.

SHERIFF (*up* R.). Do you want to see what Mrs. Peters is going to take in?

[*The* ATTORNEY *goes to the table, picks up the apron, and laughs.*

COUNTY ATTORNEY. Oh, I guess they're not very dangerous things the ladies have picked out. (*He moves a few things about, disturbing the quilt pieces which cover the box. He then steps back.*) No, Mrs. Peters doesn't need supervising.

For that matter, a sheriff's wife is married to the law. Ever think of it that way, Mrs. Peters?

MRS. PETERS. Not—just that way.

SHERIFF (*chuckling*). Married to the law. (*He moves towards the other room.*) I just want you to come in here a minute, George. We ought to take a look at these windows.

COUNTY ATTORNEY (*scoffingly*). Oh, windows! (*He crosses R. above the table.*)

[MRS. PETERS *rises and goes to above table* C.

SHERIFF. We'll be right out. Mr. Hale.

[HALE *goes out* C. *The* SHERIFF *follows the* COUNTY ATTORNEY *out* R. *Then* MRS. HALE *rises, hands tight together, looking intensely at* MRS. PETERS, *whose eyes make a slow turn, finally meeting* MRS. HALE'S. *A moment* MRS. HALE *holds her, then her own eyes point the way to where the box is concealed. Suddenly* MRS. PETERS *throws back the quilt pieces and tries to put the box in the bag she is carrying. It is too big. She opens the box and starts to take the bird out, but it goes to pieces and she stands there helpless. Suddenly there is a sound of voices in the other room.* MRS. HALE *snatches the box and puts it in the pocket of her big coat. The* COUNTY ATTORNEY *and* SHERIFF *enter* R.

COUNTY ATTORNEY (*down* R.—*facetiously*). Well, Henry, at least we found out that she was not going to quilt it. She was going to—what is it you call it, ladies?

MRS. HALE (*her hand against her pocket*). We call it—knot it, Mr. Henderson.

CURTAIN

# THE DOCK BRIEF
## by John Mortimer

## CHARACTERS

MORGENHALL, an unsuccessful barrister
FOWLE, an unsuccessful criminal


The action of the Play is in two Scenes
and passes in a prison cell

Time—the present

# THE DOCK BRIEF

## SCENE I

SCENE—*A prison cell.*

*The walls are grey and fade upwards into the shadows, so that the ceiling is not seen, and it might even be possible to escape upwards. The door, up one step, is L. of the back wall, and there is a small barred window high up in the wall R., through which the sky looks very blue. There is a bed, with a pillow and two dark blankets, against the wall L. A small table stands R. of the door, with a Bible on it, and an enamel bucket under it. R. of the table is a towel-rail with a towel. Under the window there is a chair with a stool on top of it.*

*When the* CURTAIN *rises,* FOWLE, *a small, fat man, is standing on the stool on tip-toes, his hands in his pockets. He is peering out of the window at the sky. The bolts of the door shoot back and the door opens.* MORGENHALL *strides in. He is an aged barrister with the appearance of a dusty vulture, dressed in a black gown and bands. He carries a brief-case and his legal wig. He stands by the door and speaks to an unseen warder off.*

MORGENHALL. Is this where—you keep Mr. Fowle? Good, excellent. (*He turns to the table, puts down his brief-case and wig, moves* C. *and looks towards the door.*) Then leave us alone like a kind fellow. Would you mind closing the door? These old places are so draughty.

[*The door closes. The bolts shoot back.*

(*He looks around.*) Mr. Fowle—where are you, Mr. Fowle? Not escaped, I pray. (*He looks around and sees Fowle.*)

Good Heavens, man, come down. Come down, Mr. Fowle.

[MORGENHALL *darts at Fowle and there is a struggle as he pulls the bewildered* FOWLE *down.*

I haven't hurt you? (*He takes the stool from the chair and sets it on the floor* L.C.)

[FOWLE *makes a negative-sounding noise.*

I was suddenly anxious. A man in your unfortunate position. Desperate measures. And I couldn't bear to lose you. No, don't stand up. It's difficult for you without braces, or a belt, I can see. And no tie, no shoe-laces. I'm so glad they're looking after you. You must forgive me if I frightened you just a little, Mr. Fowle. It was when I saw you up by that window . . .

FOWLE (*in a hoarse and sad voice*). Epping Forest.

MORGENHALL (*turning to him*). What did you say?

FOWLE. I think you can see Epping Forest.

MORGENHALL. No doubt you can. But why, my dear chap, why should you want to?

FOWLE. It's the home stretch.

MORGENHALL. Very well.

FOWLE. I thought I could get a glimpse of the green. Between the chimneys and that shed . . . (*He climbs on to the chair.*)

[MORGENHALL *crosses to* FOWLE *and there is a brief renewed struggle.*

MORGENHALL. No, get down. It's not wise to be up there, forever trying to look out. There's a draughty, sneeping wind. Treacherous. (*He draws* FOWLE C.)

FOWLE. Treacherous?

MORGENHALL. I'm afraid so. You never know what a mean,

sneeping wind can do. Catch you by the throat, start a sneeze, then a dry tickle on the chest. I don't want anything to catch you like that before . . .

FOWLE. Before what?

MORGENHALL. You're much better sitting quietly down there in the warm.

[FOWLE *crosses and sits on the bed.*

Just sit quietly and I'll introduce myself. (*He takes off his gown and puts it on the upstage end of the bed.*)

FOWLE. I am tired.

MORGENHALL. I'm Morgenhall. (*He sits on the stool.*)

FOWLE. Morgenhall?

MORGENHALL. Morgenhall. The barrister.

FOWLE. The barrister?

MORGENHALL. Perfectly so.

FOWLE. I'm sorry.

MORGENHALL. Why?

FOWLE. A barrister. That's very bad.

MORGENHALL. I don't know. Why's it so bad?

FOWLE. When a gentleman of your stamp goes wrong. A long fall.

MORGENHALL. What can you mean?

FOWLE. Different for an individual like me. I only kept a small seed shop.

MORGENHALL. Seed shop? My poor fellow. We mustn't let this unfortunate little case confuse us. We're going to remain very calm, very lucid. We're going to come to important decisions. Now, do me a favour, Mr. Fowle, no more seed shops.

FOWLE. Bird-seed, of course. Individuals down our way kept birds mostly. Canaries and budgies. The budgies talked. Lot of lonely people down our way. They kept them for the talk.

MORGENHALL. Mr. Fowle. I'm a barrister.

FOWLE. Tragic.

MORGENHALL. I know the law.

FOWLE. It's trapped you.

MORGENHALL. I'm here to help you.

FOWLE. We'll help each other.

[*There is a pause then* MORGENHALL *laughs uncontrollably.*

MORGENHALL. I see. Mr. Fowle, I see where you've been bewildered. You think I'm in trouble as well. Then I've got good news for you at last. I'm free. Oh, yes, I can leave here when I like.

FOWLE. Can you?

MORGENHALL. The police are my friends.

FOWLE. They are?

MORGENHALL. And I've never felt better in my life. There now. That's relieved you, hasn't it? I'm not in any trouble. (*He takes his spectacle case from his pocket and puts on his spectacles.*)

FOWLE. Family all well?

MORGENHALL. I never married.

FOWLE. Rent paid up?

MORGENHALL. A week or two owing, perhaps. Temporary lull in business. This case will end all that.

FOWLE. Which case?

MORGENHALL. Your case.

FOWLE. My . . . ?

MORGENHALL. Case.

FOWLE. Oh, that—it's not important.

MORGENHALL. Not?

FOWLE (*rising*). I don't care about it to any large extent. Not as at present advised.

MORGENHALL. Mr. Fowle. How could you say that?

FOWLE. The flavour's gone out of it.

MORGENHALL. But we're only at the beginning.

FOWLE (*crossing to* C.). I can't believe it's me concerned.

MORGENHALL. But it is you, Mr. Fowle. You mustn't let yourself forget that. You see, that's why you're here.

FOWLE. I can't seem to bother with it. (*He moves up* C.)

MORGENHALL. Can you be so busy?

FOWLE. Slopping in, slopping out. (*He moves down* R.C.) Peering at the old forest. It fills in the day.

MORGENHALL. You seem, if I may say so—(*he rises*) to have adopted an unpleasantly selfish attitude.

FOWLE. Selfish?

MORGENHALL. Dog in the manger. (*He moves* C.)

FOWLE. In the . . .?

MORGENHALL. Unenthusiastic.

FOWLE. You're speaking quite frankly, I well appreciate . . .

MORGENHALL. I'm sorry, Fowle. You made me say it. There's so much of this about, nowadays. There's so much ready-made entertainment. Free billiards, National Health, Television. There's not the spirit abroad there used to be.

FOWLE. You feel that?

MORGENHALL. Whatever I've done, I've always been mustard keen on my work. I've never lost the vision, Fowle. In all my disappointments I've never lost the love of the job.

FOWLE. The position in life you've obtained to.

MORGENHALL. Years of study I had to put in. It didn't just drop in my lap.

FOWLE. I've never studied. (*He sits on the chair* R.)

MORGENHALL. Year after year, Fowle, my window at college was alight until two a.m. There I sat among my books. I fed mainly on herrings . . .

FOWLE. Lean years?

MORGENHALL. And black tea. No subsidized biscuits, then, Fowle, no County Council tobacco, just work.

FOWLE. Bookwork, almost entirely? I'm only assuming that, of course.

MORGENHALL. Want to hear some Latin?

FOWLE. Only if you have time.

MORGENHALL. *Actus non sit reus nisi mens sit rea. Filius Nullius. In flagrante delicto.* Understand it? (*He removes his spectacles.*)

FOWLE. I'm no scholar.

MORGENHALL. You most certainly are not. But I had to be, we all had to be in my day. Then we'd sit for the examinations; mods, smalls, greats, tripos, little goes—rowing men fainting, Indian students vomiting with fear, and no creeping out for a peep at the book under the pretext of a pump ship or getting a glance at the other fellow's celluloid cuff.

FOWLE. That would be very unheard of?

MORGENHALL. Then weeks, months of waiting. (*He crosses to L.*) Nerve racking. Go up to the Lake District. Pace the mountains, play draughts—(*he crosses to C.*) forget to huff. (*He moves up R.C.*) Then comes the fatal postcard.

FOWLE. What's it say?

MORGENHALL. Satisfied the examiners.

FOWLE. Well done!

MORGENHALL. Don't rejoice so soon. True enough, I felt I'd turned a corner, got a fur hood, bumped on the head with a Bible. Told the only lady in my life that in five years' time, perhaps . . .

FOWLE. You'd arrived.

MORGENHALL. That's what I thought when they painted my name up on my London chambers. I sat down to fill in the time until they sent my first brief in a real case. I sat down to do the crossword puzzle while I waited. Five years later, Fowle, what was I doing?

FOWLE. A little charge of High Treason?

MORGENHALL. I was still doing the crossword puzzle.

FOWLE. But better at it?

MORGENHALL. Not much. Not very much. As the years pass there come to be clues you no longer understand.

FOWLE. So all that training?

MORGENHALL. Wasted. The talents rust.

FOWLE. And the lady?

MORGENHALL. Drove an ambulance, in the nineteen-fourteen. A stray piece of shrapnel took her. (*He picks up his brief-case.*) I don't care to talk of it.

FOWLE. Tragic.

MORGENHALL. It was.

FOWLE. Tragic my wife was never called up.

MORGENHALL (*moving down* c.). You mustn't talk like that, Fowle, your poor wife.

FOWLE. Don't let's carry on about me.

MORGENHALL. But we must carry on about you. That's what I'm here for.

FOWLE. You're here to . . . ?

MORGENHALL. To defend you. (*He crosses to* L.C. *and puts the brief-case on the stool.*)

FOWLE. Can't be done.

MORGENHALL. Why ever not?

FOWLE. I know who killed her.

MORGENHALL. Who?

FOWLE. Me.

[*There is a pause.* MORGENHALL *swings round up* L., *and after considerable thought, giggles.*

MORGENHALL. Really, Mr. Fowle, I have all the respect in the world for your opinions, but we must face this. You're a man of very little education.

FOWLE. That's true.

MORGENHALL. One has only to glance at you to see that

you're a person of very limited intelligence. (*He crosses to* FOWLE.)

FOWLE. Agreed, quite frankly.

MORGENHALL. You think you killed your wife.

FOWLE. Seems so to me.

MORGENHALL. Mr. Fowle. Look at yourself objectively. On questions of bird-seed I have no doubt you may be infallible—but on a vital point like this might you not be mistaken? Don't answer . . .

FOWLE. Why not, sir?

MORGENHALL. Before you drop the bomb of a reply, consider who will be wounded. Are the innocent to suffer?

FOWLE. I only want to be honest.

MORGENHALL. But you're a criminal, Mr. Fowle. You've broken through the narrow fabric of honesty. You are free to be kind, human, to do good.

FOWLE. But what I did to her . . .

MORGENHALL. She's passed, you know, out of your life. You've set up new relationships. You've picked out me.

FOWLE. Picked out?

MORGENHALL. Selected.

FOWLE. But I didn't know . . . (*He rises.*)

MORGENHALL. No, Mr. Fowle. That's the whole beauty of it. You didn't know me. You came to me under a system of chance, invented, like the football pools, to even out the harsh inequality of a world where you have to deserve success. You, Mr. Fowle, are my first Dock Brief.

FOWLE. Your Dock . . . ?

MORGENHALL. Brief.

FOWLE. You couldn't explain?

MORGENHALL. Yes, yes, of course.

[*They both cross to* L.C.

Criminals with no money and no friends exist. Luckily,

you're one of them. They're entitled to choose any
barrister sitting in court to defend them. The barrister,
however old, gets a brief—(*he moves up* c.) and is re-
munerated on a modest scale. Busy lawyers, wealthy
lawyers, men with other interests, creep out of court bent
double when the Dock Brief is chosen. (*He moves down* c.)
We regulars who are not busy sit on. I've been a regular
for years. It's not etiquette, you see, even if you want the
work, to wave at the prisoner, or whistle, or try to catch
his eye by hoisting any sort of little flag.

FOWLE. Didn't know.

MORGENHALL. But you *can* choose the most advantageous
seat. The seat any criminal would naturally point at. It's
the seat under the window, and for ten years my old
friend Tuppy Morgan, bagged it each day at ten. He sat
there, reading *Horace*, and writing to his innumerable
aunts, and almost once a year, a criminal pointed him
out. Oh, Mr. Fowle, Tuppy was a limpet on that seat. But
this morning, something, possibly a cold, perhaps death,
kept him indoors. So I had his place. And you spotted me,
no doubt.

FOWLE. Spotted you?

MORGENHALL. My glasses polished. My profile drawn and
learned in front of the great window.

FOWLE. I never noticed.

MORGENHALL. But when they asked you to choose a
lawyer?

FOWLE. I shut my eyes and pointed—I've picked horses
that way, and football teams. Never did me any good,
though, by any stretch of the imagination.

MORGENHALL. So even you, Mr. Fowle, didn't choose me?

FOWLE. Not altogether.

MORGENHALL. The law's a haphazard business.

FOWLE. It does seem chancy.

MORGENHALL. Years of training, and then to be picked out like a football pool.

FOWLE. Don't take it badly, sir.

MORGENHALL. Of course, you've been fortunate.

FOWLE. So unusual. (*He crosses to the bed.*) I was never one to draw the free bird at Christmas, or guess the weight of the cake. Now, I'm sorry I told you.

MORGENHALL. Never mind. You hurt me, temporarily, Fowle, I must confess.

[FOWLE *sits on the bed, leans back and puts his feet up.*

(*He moves the stool to* c.) It might have been kinder to have kept me in ignorance. (*He moves to the table, picks it up and sets it between the stool and the bed.*) But now it's done. Let's get down to business. And, Fowle——

FOWLE. Yes, sir?

MORGENHALL. —remember you're dealing with a fellow man. A man no longer young. Remember the hopes I've pinned on you and try——

FOWLE. Try...?

MORGENHALL. —try to spare me more pain.

FOWLE. I will, sir. Of course I will.

MORGENHALL (*picking up his brief-case*). Now. (*He sits on the stool.*) Let's get our minds in order. (*He takes some newspapers, a bottle of medicine, a paper-backed book and an old envelope from his brief-case, puts them on the table, then takes a pencil stub from his pocket, puts the brief-case on the floor and puts on his spectacles.*)

FOWLE. Sort things out.

MORGENHALL. Exactly. Now, this wife of yours.

FOWLE. Doris?

MORGENHALL. Doris. (*He makes notes on the envelope.*) A bitter, unsympathetic woman?

FOWLE. She was always cheerful. She loved jokes.

MORGENHALL. Oh, Fowle. Do be very careful.

FOWLE. I will, sir. But if you'd known Doris . . . She laughed all day and all night. 'Thank God,' she'd say, 'for my old English sense of fun.'

MORGENHALL. What sort of jokes, Fowle, did this Doris appreciate?

FOWLE. All sorts.

[MORGENHALL *writes.*

Pictures in the paper. Jokes on the wireless set. Laughs out of crackers, she'd keep them from Christmas to Christmas and trot them out in August.

[MORGENHALL *stops writing and looks up.*

MORGENHALL. You couldn't share it?

FOWLE. Not to that extent. I often missed the funny point.

MORGENHALL. Then you'd quarrel?

FOWLE. 'Don't look so miserable, it may never happen.' She said that every night when I came home. 'Where'd you get that miserable expression from?'

MORGENHALL. I can see it now. There is a kind of Sunday evening appearance to you.

FOWLE. I was quite happy. But it was always, 'Cat got your tongue?' 'Where's the funeral?' 'Play us a tune on that old fiddle face of yours.' Then we had to have our tea with the wireless on, so that she'd pick up the phrases.

MORGENHALL. You're not a wireless lover?

FOWLE. I couldn't always laugh. And she'd be doubled up across the table, gasping as if her lungs were full of water. 'Laugh,' she'd call. 'Laugh, damn you. What've you got to be so miserable about?' Then she'd go under, bubbling like a drowning woman.

MORGENHALL (*taking off his spectacles*). Made meals difficult?

FOWLE. Indigestible. I would have laughed, but the jokes never tickled me.

MORGENHALL. They tickled her?

FOWLE. Anything did.

[MORGENHALL *puts on his spectacles and resumes writing.*

Anything a little comic. Our names were misfortunate.

MORGENHALL. Your names?

FOWLE. Fowle. Going down the aisle she said: 'Now we're cock and hen, aren't we, old bird?' She laughed so hard we couldn't get her straightened up for the photograph.

MORGENHALL. Fond of puns, I gather you're trying to say.

FOWLE. Of any sort of joke. I had a little aviary at the bottom of my garden. As she got funnier so I spent more time with my birds. Budgerigars are small parrots. Circles round their eyes give them a sad, tired look.

MORGENHALL (*looking up*). You found them sympathetic?

FOWLE. Restful.

[MORGENHALL *writes.*

Until one of them spoke out at me.

MORGENHALL. Spoke—what words?

FOWLE. 'Don't look so miserable, it may never happen.'

MORGENHALL. The bird said that?

FOWLE. She taught it during the day when I was out at work. It didn't mean to irritate.

MORGENHALL. It was wrong of her, of course. To lead on your bird like that.

FOWLE (*rising and crossing to* R.). But it wasn't him that brought me to it. It was Bateson, the lodger.

MORGENHALL (*turning on his stool to face* FOWLE). Another man?

FOWLE. At long last.

MORGENHALL. I can see it now. A crime of passion. An unfaithful wife. *In flagrante* . . . Of course, you don't know what that means. We'll reduce it to manslaughter right away. A wronged husband and there's never a dry eye in the jury-box. You came in and caught them.

FOWLE. Always laughing together.

MORGENHALL. Maddening.

FOWLE. He knew more jokes than she did.

MORGENHALL. Stealing her before your eyes?

FOWLE. That's what I thought. He was a big man. Ex-police. Said he'd been the scream of the station. I picked him for her specially. In the chitty I put up in the local sweetshop, I wrote: 'Humorous type of lodger wanted.'

MORGENHALL. But wasn't that a risk?

FOWLE. Slight, perhaps. But it went all right. Two days after he came he poised a bag of flour to fall on her in the kitchen. Then she sewed up the legs of his pyjamas. They had to hold on to each other so as not to fall over laughing. 'Look at old misery standing there,' she said, 'he can never see anything subtle.'

MORGENHALL. Galling for you. Terribly galling.

FOWLE. I thought all was well. (*He moves* c.) I spent more time with the birds. I'd come home late and always be careful to scrunch the gravel at the front door. I went to bed early and left them with the Light Programme. On Sunday mornings I fed the budgies and suggested he took her tea in bed. 'Laughter,' she read out from her horoscope, 'leads to love, even for those born under the sign of the virgin.'

MORGENHALL. You trusted them. They deceived you.

FOWLE. They deceived me all right. (*He moves to the chair* R. *and sits.*) And I trusted them to do the right thing. Especially after I'd seen her on his knee and them both looking at the cartoons from one wrapping of chips.

MORGENHALL. Mr. Fowle. I'm not quite getting the drift of your evidence. My hope is—your thought may not prove a shade too involved for our literal-minded judge. (*He*

*takes off his spectacles and puts them in the case.*) Old
Tommy Banter was a rugger blue in ninety-eight. He
never rose to chess and his draughts had a brutal un-
intelligent quality.

FOWLE. When he'd first put his knee under her I thought
he'd do the decent thing. I thought I'd have peace in
my little house at last. The wireless set dead silent. The
end of all that happy laughter. No sound but the twitter
from the end of the garden and the squeak of my own
foot on the linoleum.

MORGENHALL (*pointing at* FOWLE *with his spectacle case*).
You wanted . . .

FOWLE. I heard them whispering together and my hopes
raised high. Then I came back and he was gone.

MORGENHALL. She'd . . .

FOWLE. Turned him out. Because he was getting over
familiar. 'I couldn't have that,' she said. 'I may like my
laugh, but, thank God, I'm still respectable. No, thank
you, there's safety in marriage.' She'd sent him away, my
last hope.

MORGENHALL. So you . . . ? (*He looks at* FOWLE *and makes a
gesture with his spectacle case.*)

FOWLE (*nodding*). I realize I did wrong.

MORGENHALL. You could have left.

FOWLE. Who'd have fed the birds? That thought was
uppermost.

MORGENHALL. So it's not a crime of passion?

FOWLE. Not if you put it like that.

MORGENHALL (*putting his spectacle case in his pocket*). Mr.
Fowle. (*He rises.*) I've worked and waited for you. (*He
moves up* C.) Now, you're the only case I've got, *and* the
most difficult.

FOWLE. I'm sorry.

MORGENHALL (*moving down* R.C.). A man could crack his

head against a case like you and still be far from a solution. Can't you see how twelve honest hearts will snap like steel when they learn you ended up your wife because she *wouldn't* leave you?

FOWLE. If she had left, there wouldn't have been the need.

MORGENHALL. There's no doubt about it. As I look at you, now, I see you're an unsympathetic figure.

FOWLE. There it is.

MORGENHALL. It'll need a brilliant stroke to save you. (*He moves up* L.) An unexpected move—something pulled out of a hat. (*He turns and thumps the table.*) I've got it. Something really exciting. The surprise witness.

FOWLE. Witness?

MORGENHALL. Picture the scene, Mr. Fowle. The court-room silent. The jury about to sink you. The prosecution flushed with victory. And then I rise, my voice a hoarse whisper, exhausted by that long trial. (*He picks up his wig and puts it on.*) 'My Lord. If your Lordship pleases.'

FOWLE (*rising and moving* C.). What are you saying?

MORGENHALL. Good Heavens, man, you don't expect me to do this off the cuff, without any sort of rehearsal?

FOWLE. No . . .

MORGENHALL (*leading* FOWLE *to the table*). Well, come along, man, sit down.

[FOWLE *sits on the table, with his feet on the stool.*

(*He takes the towel from the rail.*) Now, this towel over your head, please, to simulate the dirty grey wig. (*He drapes the towel over* FOWLE'S *head.*) Already you appear anonymous and vaguely alarming. Now, Fowle, forget your personality. You're Sir Tommy Banter, living with a widowed sister in a draughty great morgue on Wimbledon Common. Digestion, bad. Politics, an independent moral Conservative. Diversions, snooker in the basement of the morgue, peeping at the lovers on the Common and money being given away on the television. In love with capital punishment, corporal punishment, and a younger brother who is accomplished at embroidery. A small, alarmed man. Served with distinction in the Great War at sentencing soldiers to long terms of imprisonment. (*He crosses* R. *and stands behind the chair.*) A man without friends, unexpectedly adored by a great-niece, three years old.

FOWLE. I am?

MORGENHALL. Him.

FOWLE. It feels strange.

MORGENHALL. Now, my Lord. I ask your Lordship's leave to call the surprise witness.

FOWLE. Certainly.

MORGENHALL. What?

FOWLE. Certainly.

MORGENHALL (*crossing to* L.C.). For Heaven's sake, Fowle, this is like practising bullfights with a kitten. Here's an irregular application by the defence, something that might twist the trial in the prisoner's favour and prevent you catching the connection at Charing Cross. Your breakfast's like a lead weight on your stomach. The dog bit your ankle on the way downstairs. No, blind yourself with rage and terrible justice. (*He crosses to* R. *and stands behind the chair.*)

FOWLE. No. You can't call the surprise witness.

MORGENHALL. That's better. Oh, my Lord. (*He raises his left arm, facing* L.) If your Lordship would listen to me.

FOWLE. Certainly not. You've had your chance. Let's get on with it.

MORGENHALL. My Lord. Justice must not only be done, but must clearly be seen to be done. (*He lowers his arm and faces front.*) No one knows, as yet, what my surprise

witness will say. (*He faces* L.) Perhaps he'll say the
prisoner is guilty in his black heart as your Lordship
thinks. (*He faces front.*) But perhaps, gentlemen of the
jury, we have trapped an innocent. If so, shall we deny
him the one door through which he might walk to freedom? The public outcry would never die down.

FOWLE (*snatching off the towel and rising angrily to his feet*).
Hear, hear!

MORGENHALL. What's that?

FOWLE. The public outcry.

MORGENHALL. Excellent. Now, towel back on.

[FOWLE *resumes his seat and puts the towel on his head.*

You're the judge.

FOWLE (*as the judge*). Silence! I'll have all those noisy people
put out. Very well. Call the witness. But keep it short.

MORGENHALL. Deathly silence as the witness walks through
the breathless crowds. Let's see the surprise witness.

[MORGENHALL *slowly looks from* L. *to* R. FOWLE *follows
the look.* MORGENHALL *looks at the door.* FOWLE *does the
same.*

(*He crosses to* FOWLE). Take the towel off.

[FOWLE *rises, moves up* C., *stands on the step and takes off
the towel.* MORGENHALL *moves behind the chair.*

FOWLE (*standing very straight*). I swear to tell the truth . . .

MORGENHALL. You've got a real feeling for the Law. A pity
you came to it so late in life.

FOWLE. The whole truth . . .

MORGENHALL. Now, what's your name?

FOWLE (*absent-mindedly*). Herbert Fowle.

MORGENHALL (*facing* L. *and clapping his hands in annoyance*).
The witness.

FOWLE. Martin Jones.

MORGENHALL. Good, good, yes, very good. (*He faces front.*) Now, you knew Herbert Fowle?

FOWLE. All my life.

MORGENHALL. Always found him respectable?

FOWLE. Very quiet-spoken man, and clean living.

MORGENHALL. Where was he when this crime took place?

FOWLE. He was . . .

MORGENHALL (*turning to* FOWLE). Just a moment. (*He faces* L.) My Lord, will you sharpen a pencil and note this down.

FOWLE (*moving* R.C.). You dare to say that? To him?

MORGENHALL. Fearlessness, Mr. Fowle. The first essential in an advocate.

[FOWLE *moves to the table, sits and puts on the towel.*

Is your Lordship's pencil poised?

FOWLE (*as the judge*). Yes, yes. Get on with it.

MORGENHALL. Where was he?

[FOWLE *rises, goes to the step and takes off the towel.*

FOWLE (*as the witness*). In my house.

MORGENHALL. All the evening?

FOWLE. Playing whist. I went to collect him and we left Mrs. Fowle well and happy. I returned with him and she'd been removed to the Country and General.

MORGENHALL (*crossing to* FOWLE). Panic stirs the prosecution benches. The prosecutor tries a few fumbling questions. But you stand your ground, don't you?

FOWLE. Certainly.

MORGENHALL (*moving behind the chair*). My Lord. I demand the prisoner be released.

[FOWLE *goes to the table, sits and puts on the towel.*

FOWLE (*as the judge*). Certainly. Can't think what all this fuss has been about. Release the prisoner and reduce all police officers in court to the rank of P.C. (*He takes off the towel, rises, goes to the foot of the bed and sits.*)

[*There is a pause.* MORGENHALL *takes off his wig and crosses to the table.*

MORGENHALL. Fowle.

FOWLE. Yes, sir?

MORGENHALL. Aren't you going to thank me?

FOWLE. I don't know what I can say.

MORGENHALL. Words don't come easily to you, do they?

FOWLE. Very hard.

MORGENHALL. You could just stand and stammer in a touching way, and offer me that old gold watch of your father's.

FOWLE (*rising*). But . . .

MORGENHALL. Well, I think we've pulled your chestnut out of the fire. We'll just have to make sure of this fellow Jones.

FOWLE (*moving* L.C.). But . . .

MORGENHALL. Fowle, you're a good chap, but don't interrupt my thinking.

FOWLE. I was only reminding you . . .

MORGENHALL. Well, what?

FOWLE. We have no Jones.

MORGENHALL. Carried off in a cold spell? Then we can get his statement in under the Evidence Act?

FOWLE. He never lived. We made him up.

MORGENHALL (*after a pause*). Fowle. (*He moves* R.C.)

FOWLE. Yes, sir?

MORGENHALL. It's a remarkable thing—(*he moves* C.) but with no legal training, I think you've put your finger on a fatal weakness in our defence.

FOWLE. I was afraid it might be so.

MORGENHALL. It is so.

FOWLE (*moving to the downstage end of the bed*). Then we'd better just give in.

MORGENHALL. Give in? (*He crosses to* FOWLE). We do not give in. When my life depends on this case.

FOWLE. I forgot. Then we must try.

MORGENHALL. Yes. Brain. Brain. (*He moves up* c.) Go to work. It'll come to me, you know, in an illuminating flash. Hard, relentless brainwork. This is the way I go at the crosswords and I never give up. I have it. (*He moves down* c.) Bateson.

FOWLE. The lodger?

MORGENHALL. Bateson, the lodger. I never liked him. Under a ruthless cross-examination, you know, he might confess that it was he. Do you see a flash?

FOWLE. You look much happier.

MORGENHALL. I am much happier. And when I begin my ruthless cross-examination . . .

FOWLE. Would you care to try it?

MORGENHALL. Mr. Fowle, you and I are learning to muck in splendidly together over this. (*He moves behind the chair and puts on his wig.*)

[FOWLE *goes on to the doorstep and leans against the right wall of the doorway-arch, with his hands in his pockets.*

Mr. Bateson.

FOWLE (*as Bateson*). Yes, sir?

MORGENHALL. Perhaps you'd be good enough to take your hands out of your pockets when you address the Court. Not you, Mr. Fowle, of course. You became on very friendly terms with the prisoner's wife?

FOWLE. We had one or two good old laughs together. Ha, ha, ha!

MORGENHALL. The association was entirely innocent?

FOWLE. Innocent laughs. Jokes without offence. The cracker or Christmas card variety. No jokes that would have shamed a postcard.

MORGENHALL. And to tell those jokes, did you have to sit very close to Mrs. Fowle?

FOWLE. How do you mean?

MORGENHALL. Did you have to sit beneath her?

FOWLE. I don't understand.

MORGENHALL. Did she perch upon your knee?

[FOWLE *gives a horrified intake of breath.*

What was that?

FOWLE. Shocked breathing from the jury, sir.

MORGENHALL. Having its effect, eh? Bateson, will you kindly answer my question.

FOWLE. You're trying to trap me.

MORGENHALL. Not trying, Bateson, succeeding.

FOWLE. Well, she may have rested on my knee. Once or twice.

MORGENHALL. And you loved her, guiltily?

FOWLE. I may have done.

MORGENHALL. And planned to take her away with you?

FOWLE. I did ask her.

MORGENHALL. And when she refused . . .

FOWLE. Just a moment. (*He moves to the table, sits and puts on his towel. As the judge.*) Where's all this leading?

MORGENHALL. Your Lordship asks me. My Lord, it is our case that it was this man, Bateson, enraged by the refusal of the prisoner's wife to go away with him, who struck . . . (*He crosses to* c.) You see where we've got to?

FOWLE (*removing the towel*). I do.

MORGENHALL. Masterly. I think you'll have to agree with me?

FOWLE. Of course.

MORGENHALL. No flaws in this one?

FOWLE. Not really a flaw, sir. Perhaps a little hitch.

MORGENHALL. A hitch. Go on. Break it down.

FOWLE. No, sir, really. (*He rises and moves up* L.) Not after you've been so kind.

MORGENHALL. Never mind. All my life I've stood against the winds of criticism and neglect. I am used to hardship. Speak on, Mr. Fowle.

FOWLE. Soon as he left my house, Bateson was stopped by an officer. He'd lifted an alarm clock off of me, and the remains of a bottle of port. They booked him in straight away.

MORGENHALL. You mean—(*he faces front*) there wasn't time?

FOWLE. Hardly. Two hours later the next door observed Mrs. Fowle at the washing. Then I came home.

MORGENHALL (*turning to* FOWLE). Fowle, do you want to help me?

FOWLE. Of course. Haven't I shown it?

MORGENHALL. But you will go on putting all these difficulties in my way.

FOWLE. I knew you'd be upset. (*He sits on the bed.*)

MORGENHALL. Not really. After all, I'm a grown-up, even an old man. At my age one expects little gratitude. Oh, I'm not bitter. But a little help, just a very little encouragement . . .

FOWLE. But you'll win this case. A brilliant mind like yours.

MORGENHALL (*moving* R.C.). Yes. Thank God. It's very brilliant.

FOWLE. And all that training.

MORGENHALL. Years of it. (*He moves to the chair.*) Hard, hard training.

FOWLE. You'll solve it, sir.

[*There is a pause.* MORGENHALL *crosses to the upstage end of the bed, puts a foot up on it and leans over to* FOWLE.

MORGENHALL. Fowle. Do you know what I've heard Tuppy Morgan say? After all, he's sat here in court year in, year out, waiting for the Dock Brief himself. 'Wilfred,' he's frequently told me, 'if they ever give you a brief, old fellow, attack the medical evidence. Remember, the jury's full of rheumatism and arthritis and shocking gastric troubles. They love to see a medical man put through it. Always go for a doctor.'

FOWLE (*eagerly*). You'd like to try?

MORGENHALL (*straightening up*). Shall we?

FOWLE. I'd enjoy it. (*He rises and gets on to the step.*)

[MORGENHALL *crosses to the chair* R. *and leans over the back of it, with one foot on the chair.*

MORGENHALL. Doctor, did you say the lady died of heart failure?

FOWLE (*as the doctor*). No.

MORGENHALL. Come, Doctor, don't fence with me. Her heart wasn't normal when you examined her, was it?

FOWLE. She was dead.

MORGENHALL. So it had stopped.

FOWLE. Yes.

MORGENHALL. Then her heart had failed. (*He takes his foot off the chair.*)

FOWLE. Well . . .

MORGENHALL. So she died of heart failure?

FOWLE. But . . .

MORGENHALL. And heart failure might have been brought on by a fit. I say a fit of laughter at a curiously rich joke on the wireless?

[FOWLE *claps his hands, then comes off the step.*

FOWLE. Whew!

MORGENHALL (*after a pause*). Thank you, Fowle. (*He takes off his wig.*) It was kind, but, I thought, hollow. (*He crosses to the stool.*) I don't believe my attack on the doctor was convincing. (*He picks up his brief-case, puts it on the table, then sits on the stool.*)

FOWLE. Perhaps a bit unlikely. But clever.

MORGENHALL. Too clever. No. We're not going to win this on science, Fowle. Science must be thrown away. As I asked those questions, I saw I wasn't even convincing you of your own innocence. But you respond to emotion, Fowle, as I do, the magic of oratory, the wonderful power of words.

FOWLE. Now you're talking.

MORGENHALL. And I shall talk.

FOWLE. I wish I could hear some of it. Words as grand as print.

MORGENHALL. A golden tongue. A voice like a lyre to charm you out of hell.

FOWLE. Now you've commenced to wander away from all I've understood.

MORGENHALL. I was drawing on the riches of my classical education, which comforts me on buses, waiting at surgeries, or in prison cells. (*He rises.*) But I shall speak to the jury simply, without classical allusions. I shall say . . .

FOWLE. Yes?

MORGENHALL. I shall say . . .

FOWLE. What?

MORGENHALL. I had it on the tip of my tongue.

FOWLE. Oh.

MORGENHALL. I shan't disappoint you. I shall speak for a day, perhaps two days. At the end I shall say . . .

FOWLE. Yes. Just the closing words.

MORGENHALL. The closing words.

FOWLE. To clinch the argument.

MORGENHALL. Yes. The final, irrefutable argument.

FOWLE. If I could only hear.

MORGENHALL. You shall, Fowle. You shall hear it. (*He sits on the stool and takes out his handkerchief.*) In court. It'll come out in court, and when I sink back in my seat, exhausted, and wipe the real tears off my glasses . . . (*He replaces his handkerchief in his pocket.*)

FOWLE. The judge's summing-up.

MORGENHALL. What will Tommy say?

FOWLE (*as the judge*). Members of the jury . . .

MORGENHALL. Struggling with emotion, as well.

FOWLE. Members of the jury, I can't add anything to the words of the barrister. Go out and consider your verdict.

MORGENHALL. Have they left the box?

FOWLE. Just a formality.

MORGENHALL. I see. I wonder how long they'll be out. (*He pauses.*) They're out a long time.

FOWLE. Of course, it must seem long to you. The suspense.

MORGENHALL. I hope they won't disagree.

FOWLE. I don't see how they can. Look, they're coming back, sir.

[*There is a pause.* FOWLE *moves above the table.*

MORGENHALL (*as clerk of the court*). Members of the jury, have you considered your verdict?

FOWLE. We have.

MORGENHALL. And do you find the prisoner guilty or not guilty?

FOWLE. Not guilty, my Lord. (*He rushes to the table, sits on it and puts the towel on his head.*)

MORGENHALL (*rising and waving his wig*). Hooray!

FOWLE (*as the judge*). Now, if there's any sort of Mafeking around, I'll have the court closed.

MORGENHALL. So I'm surrounded, mobbed. Tuppy Morgan wrings my hand and says it was lucky he left the seat. The judge sends me a letter of congratulation. The journalists dart off to their little telephones. And what now? 'Of course, they'd make you a judge but you're probably too busy . . .' There's a queue of solicitors on the stairs. My old clerk writes on my next brief, 'A thousand guineas to divorce a duchess.' There are questions of new clothes, laying down the port. Oh, Mr. Fowle, the change in life you've brought me.

FOWLE (*rising*). It will be your greatest day. (*He removes the towel and crosses to* C.)

MORGENHALL. Yes, Mr. Fowle. (*He crosses to* FOWLE.) My greatest day.

[*The bolts shoot back and the door slowly opens.*

(*He moves up* C.) What's that? I said we weren't to be interrupted. It's draughty in here with that door open. (*He calls.*) Close it, there's a good chap, do. (*He moves down* C. *to* L. *of* FOWLE.)

FOWLE. I think, you know, they must want us for the trial. (*He moves up* R.C., *takes his jacket off the peg, goes to the chair, and sits and puts on his jacket.*)

[MORGENHALL *puts on his wig, puts the papers, medicine bottle, etc. in his brief-case, leaves the brief-case on the table, moves to the bed, picks up his gown and struggles to put it on.* FOWLE *rises, crosses to* MORGENHALL *and assists him.* MORGENHALL *goes to the door, remembers his brief-case, returns and picks it up.* FOWLE *does a 'thumbs-up' sign.*

MORGENHALL *nods, and with a dramatic sweep of his*

*gown, exits.* FOWLE *follows him off, and the lights* **dim to**
BLACK-OUT *as—*

*the,* CURTAIN *falls.*

## SCENE II

SCENE—*The same.*

*When the* CURTAIN *rises, the sky through the window shows
that it is late afternoon. The table has been replaced under the
window and the stool is* L.C. *The cell is empty. The door opens.*
MORGENHALL *enters. He is without his wig and gown and is
more agitated than ever. He stands by the open door and speaks
to an unseen warder off.*

MORGENHALL. He's not here at the moment—he's not . . . ?
Oh, I'm so glad. Just out temporarily? With the
Governor? Then, I'll wait for him. Poor soul. How's he
taking it? Well, I'll just sit down here and wait for Mr.
Fowle.

[*The door closes.*

(*He whistles for a few moments.*) 'May it please you, my
Lord—*members* of the jury . . .' I should have said, 'May
it please you, my *Lord*—members of the jury . . .' (*He
moves in to the stool and sits.*) I should have said—'Members of the jury. Is there one of you who doesn't crave for
peace—crave for peace. The silence of an undisturbed
life, the dignity of an existence without dependants—
without jokes. Have you never been tempted?' I should
have said, 'Members of the *jury*. You and I are men of
the world . . .' 'If your Lordship would kindly not
interrupt my speech to the jury.' 'I'm obliged.' 'Members

of the jury, before I was so rudely interrupted . . .' I might have said, 'Look at the prisoner, members of the jury. Has he hurt you, done you the slightest harm? Is he not the mildest of men? He merely took it upon himself to regulate his domestic affairs. An Englishman's home is his castle. Do any of you feel a primitive urge, members of the jury, to be revenged on this gentle bird-fancier? Members of the jury, I see I'm affecting your emotions, but let us consider the weight of the evidence.' Might have said that. (*He rises and paces* L. *and* R.) I might have said —(*with distress*) I might have said something . . .

> [*The door opens.*
>
> FOWLE *enters. He is smiling to himself, but as soon as he sees* MORGENHALL *he looks serious and solicitous. The door closes.*

FOWLE. I was hoping you'd find time to drop in, sir. I'm afraid you're upset.

MORGENHALL. No, no, my dear chap. (*He moves down* L.) Not at all upset.

FOWLE. The result of the trial's upset you.

MORGENHALL. I feel a little dashed. A little out of sorts.

FOWLE. It was disappointing for you.

MORGENHALL. A touch of disappointment. But there'll be other cases. There may be other cases.

FOWLE. But you'd built such high hopes on this particular one.

MORGENHALL. Well, there it is, Fowle. (*He moves to the stool and sits.*)

FOWLE. It doesn't do to expect too much of a particular thing.

MORGENHALL. You're right, of course.

FOWLE (*crossing below* MORGENHALL *to the bed*). Year after year, I used to look forward keenly to the Feathered

Friends Fanciers' annual do. (*He sits on the downstage end of the bed.*) Invariably it took the form of a dinner.

MORGENHALL. Your yearly treat?

FOWLE. Exactly. All I had in the enjoyment line. Each year I built high hopes on it. 'June thirteenth,' I'd say, 'now there's an evening to look forward to.'

MORGENHALL. Something to live for?

FOWLE. In a way. But when it came, you know, it was never up to it. Your collar was always too tight, or the food was inadequate, or someone had a nasty scene with the fancier in the chair. So, on June fourteenth, I always said to myself: 'Thank God for a night at home.'

MORGENHALL. It came and went and your life didn't change?

FOWLE. No, quite frankly.

MORGENHALL. And this case has left me just as I was before.

FOWLE. Don't say that.

MORGENHALL. Tuppy Morgan's back in his old seat under the window. The judge never congratulated me. No one's rung up to offer me a brief. I thought my old clerk looked coldly at me, and there was a titter in the luncheon-room when I ordered my usual roll and tomato soup.

FOWLE. But, I . . .

MORGENHALL (*rising and moving up* R.). And you're not left in a very favourable position.

FOWLE. Well, it's not so bad for me. After all, I had no education.

MORGENHALL (*turning to face* FOWLE). So many years before I could master the Roman Law relating to the ownership of chariots . . .

FOWLE. Wasted, you think?

MORGENHALL. I feel so.

FOWLE. But without that rich background, would an individual have been able to sway the Court as you did?

MORGENHALL. Sway?

FOWLE. The Court?

MORGENHALL. Did I do that?

FOWLE. It struck me you did.

MORGENHALL. Indeed . . .

FOWLE. It's turned out masterly.

MORGENHALL. Mr. Fowle, you're trying to be kind. (*He moves down* L.C.) When I was a child, I played French cricket with an uncle who deliberately allowed the ball to strike his legs. At the age of seven that irked me. At my age I can face the difficulties of accurate batting . . .

FOWLE. But, no, sir. (*He rises and moves to* L. *of* MORGENHALL.) I owe it all to you. Where I am.

MORGENHALL. I'm afraid near the end.

FOWLE. Just commencing.

MORGENHALL. I lost, Mr. Fowle. You may not be aware of it. It may not have been hammered home to you, yet. (*He crosses below* FOWLE *to the bed.*) But your case is lost. (*He sits on the downstage end of the bed.*)

FOWLE. But there are ways and ways of losing.

MORGENHALL. That's true, of course.

FOWLE (*moving to the bed and sitting beside* MORGENHALL). I noticed your artfulness right at the start, when the policeman gave evidence. You pulled out that red handkerchief, slowly and deliberately, like a conjuring trick.

MORGENHALL. And blew?

FOWLE. A sad, terrible trumpet.

MORGENHALL. Unnerved him, I thought.

FOWLE. He never recovered. There was no call to ask questions after that.

MORGENHALL. And then they called that doctor.

FOWLE. You were right not to bother with him.

MORGENHALL. Tactics, you see. We'd decided not to trouble with science.

FOWLE. So we had. And with Bateson . . .

MORGENHALL. No, Fowle. I must beware of your flattery. I think I might have asked Bateson . . .

FOWLE. It wouldn't have made a farthing's difference. A glance told them he was a demon.

MORGENHALL. He stood there, so big and red, with his no tie and dirty collar. I rose up to question him and suddenly it seemed as if there were no reason for us to converse. I remembered what you said about his jokes, his familiarity with your wife. I turned from him in disgust. I think that jury guessed the reason for my silence with friend Bateson.

FOWLE. I think they did.

MORGENHALL. But when it came to the speech . . .

FOWLE. The best stroke of all.

MORGENHALL. I can't agree. You no longer carry me with you.

FOWLE. Said from the heart.

MORGENHALL. I'm sure of it. But not, dare I say, altogether justified. We can't pretend, can we, Mr. Fowle, that the speech was a success?

FOWLE. It won the day.

MORGENHALL. I beg you not to be under any illusions. They found you guilty.

FOWLE. But that masterly speech . . .

MORGENHALL. I can't be hoodwinked.

FOWLE (*rising*). But you don't know . . .

MORGENHALL (*rising*). I stood up, Mr. Fowle, and it was the moment I'd waited for. Ambition had driven me to it, the moment when I was alone with what I wanted. Everyone turned to me, twelve blank faces in the jury box, eager to have the grumpy looks wiped off them. The judge was silent. The prosecutor courteously pretended to be asleep. I only had to open my mouth and pour words out. What stopped me?

16

FOWLE. What?

MORGENHALL. Fear. That's what's suggested. That's what the clerks tittered to the waitresses in the luncheon-room. Old Wilf Morgenhall was in a funk.

FOWLE. More shame on them.

MORGENHALL. But it wasn't so. (*He crosses to* c.) Nor did my mind go blank. When I stood up I knew exactly what I was going to say.

FOWLE. Then, why . . . ?

MORGENHALL. 'Not say it'—you were going to ask?

FOWLE (*turning to face* MORGENHALL). It had struck me . . .

MORGENHALL. It must have, Fowle. It must have struck many people. (*He moves up* c.) You'll forgive a reminiscence?

FOWLE (*sitting on the downstage end of the bed*). Glad of one.

MORGENHALL. The lady I happened to mention yesterday. I don't, of course, often speak of her . . .

FOWLE. She, who, in the nineteen-fourteen . . . ?

MORGENHALL. Exactly. But I lost her long before that. For years, you know, Mr. Fowle, this particular lady and I met at tea-parties, tennis, and so on. Then, one evening, I walked home with her. We stood on Vauxhall Bridge. It was a warm summer night, and silence fell. It was the moment when I should have spoken, the obvious moment. Then, something overcame me, it wasn't shyness or fear, then, but a tremendous exhaustion. I was tired out by the long wait, and when the opportunity came—all I could think of was sleep.

FOWLE. It's a relief . . .

MORGENHALL. To go home alone. To undress, clean your teeth, knock out your pipe, not to bother with failure or success.

FOWLE. So yesterday . . .

MORGENHALL. I had lived through that moment so many

times. It happened every day in my mind, day-dreaming on buses, or in the doctor's surgery. When it came, I was tired of it. The exhaustion came over me. I wanted it to be all over. I wanted to be alone in my room, in the darkness, with a soft pillow round my ears. So I failed.

FOWLE. Don't say that, sir.

MORGENHALL. Being too tired to make my day-dream public. (*He moves up* R.C.) It's a nice day. (*He moves* R. *and glances at the window.*) Summer's coming. (*He faces front.*) I think I shall retire from the Bar.

FOWLE. Don't say it, sir. After that rigorous training.

MORGENHALL. Well, there it is. I think I shall retire.

FOWLE. But, cheer up, sir. (*He rises and moves* C.) As you said, other cases, other days. Let's take this calmly, sir. (*He crosses to* MORGENHALL *and seats him on the chair.*) Let's be very lucid, as you put it in your own statement.

MORGENHALL. Other cases? I'm getting on, you know. Tuppy Morgan's back in his place. I doubt if the Dock Brief will come round again.

FOWLE. But there'll be something.

MORGENHALL. What can there be? Unless . . .?

FOWLE. Yes, sir?

MORGENHALL. There would be another brief if . . .

FOWLE. Yes?

MORGENHALL. I advised you to appeal.

FOWLE. Ah, now that, misfortunately . . . (*He turns away* L.)

MORGENHALL (*rising*). There's a different atmosphere there, up in the Appeal Court, Fowle. It's far from the rough and tumble, question and answer—(*he crosses down* L.) swear on the Bible and lie your way out of it. It's quiet up there, pure law, of course. Yes. I believe I'm cut out for the Court of Appeal. (*He moves up* C.)

FOWLE. But, you see . . .

MORGENHALL. A big, quiet Court in the early summer

afternoon. Piles of books, and when you put one down the dust and powdered leather rises and makes the ushers sneeze. The clock ticks. Three old judges in scarlet take snuff with trembling hands. You'll sit in the dock and not follow a legal word. And I'll give them all my Law and get you off on a technicality.

FOWLE. But, today . . .

MORGENHALL. Now, if I may remind your Lordships of Prickle against the Haverfordwest Justices *ex parte* Anger, reported in ninety-six *Moor's Ecclesiastical* at page a thousand and three.

[FOWLE *sits on the chair.*

Have your Lordships the report? Lord Bradwell, C.J., says, at the foot of the page, 'The guilty intention is a deep foundation-stone in the wall of our jurisprudence. So if it be that Prickle did run the bailiff through with his *poignard* taking him for a stray dog or cat, it seems there would be well raised the plea of *autrefois* mistake. But contra if he thought him to be his neighbour's cat, then, as my Brother Broadwinkle has well said in Lord Roche and Anderson, there might fall out a constructive larceny and *felo in rem.*' (*He moves to* FOWLE). Oh, Mr. Fowle, I have some of these fine cases by heart.

FOWLE. Above me, I'm afraid, you're going now.

MORGENHALL. Of course I am. These cases always bore the prisoner until they're upheld or overruled and he comes out dead or alive at the end of it all. Thank God, I kept my books. I shall open them up and say—I shall say . . .

FOWLE (*rising and crossing to* L.C.). It's no good.

MORGENHALL. What's no good?

FOWLE. It's no good appealing.

MORGENHALL. No good?

FOWLE (*sitting on the stool*). No good at all.

MORGENHALL (*moving down* c.). Mr. Fowle. I've worked hard for you.

FOWLE. That's true, sir.

MORGENHALL. And I mean to go on working.

FOWLE. It's a great comfort . . .

MORGENHALL. In the course of our close, and may I say it— yes, our happy collaboration on this little crime of yours, I've become almost fond of you.

FOWLE. Thank you, sir, but I . . . .

MORGENHALL. At first, I have to admit it, I was put off by your somewhat furtive and repulsive appearance. I saw in you a man marked by all the physical signs of confirmed criminality.

FOWLE. No oil painting?

MORGENHALL. Let's agree on that at once.

FOWLE. The wife thought so, too.

MORGENHALL. Enough of her, poor woman.

FOWLE. Oh, agreed.

MORGENHALL. My first solicitude for your well-being, let's face this, as well, had a selfish element. You were my very own case, and I didn't want to lose you.

FOWLE. Natural feelings. But still . . .

MORGENHALL. I haven't wounded you?

FOWLE. Nothing fatal, sir.

MORGENHALL. I'm glad. Because, you know, as we worked on this case, together, an affection sprang up . . .

FOWLE. Mutual.

MORGENHALL. You seem to have a real desire to help, and, if I may say so, an instinctive taste for the law.

FOWLE. A man can't go through this sort of thing without getting legal interests.

MORGENHALL. Quite so. But I did notice, just at the start, some flaws in you as a client.

FOWLE. Flaws?

MORGENHALL. You may not care to admit it. But let's be honest. After all, we don't want to look on the dreary side! but you may not be with us for very long . . .

FOWLE (*rising*). That's what I was trying to say . . .

MORGENHALL. Please, Mr. Fowle, don't interrupt, not until we've——

[FOWLE *sits on the stool.*

—cleared this out of the way. Now, didn't you, just at the beginning, put unnecessary difficulties before us?

FOWLE. Did I?

MORGENHALL. I well remember, before I got a bit of keenness into you, that you seemed about to admit your guilt.

FOWLE. Oh . . .

MORGENHALL. Just a little obstinate, wasn't it?

FOWLE. I dare say . . .

MORGENHALL. And now, when I've worked for fifty years to get the law at my fingertips, I hear you mutter, 'No appeal'.

FOWLE (*turning to* MORGENHALL). No appeal!

MORGENHALL. Mr. Fowle . . .

FOWLE (*rising*). Yesterday, you asked me to spare you pain, sir. This is going to be very hard for me.

MORGENHALL. What?

FOWLE (*moving* R.). As you say, we've worked together, and I've had the pleasure of watching the ticking over of a legal mind. If you'd call any afternoon I'd be pleased to repay the compliment by showing you my birds.

MORGENHALL. Not in this world, you must realize, unless we appeal.

FOWLE. You see—this morning I saw the governor.

MORGENHALL. You had some complaint?

FOWLE. I don't want to boast, but the truth is—he sent for me.

MORGENHALL. You went in fear . . .

FOWLE. And trembling.

MORGENHALL. And trembling.

FOWLE (*moving up* R.). But he turned out a very gentlemanly sort of individual. Ex-army, I should imagine. All the ornaments of a gentleman. (*He moves down* C.) Wife and children in a tinted photo framed on the desk, handsome oil painting of a prize pig over the mantelpiece. Healthy red face. Strong smell of scented soap . . .

MORGENHALL (*sitting on the stool*). But grow to the point . . .

FOWLE. I'm telling you. 'Well, Fowle,' he says. 'Sit down, do. I'm just finishing this letter.' (*He sits on the chair.*) So I sat and looked out of his windows. Big wide windows in the governor's office, and the view . . .

MORGENHALL. Fowle. If this anecdote has any point, be a good chap—reach it.

FOWLE. Of course it has—where was I ?

MORGENHALL. Admiring the view.

FOWLE. Panoramic, it was. Well, this governor individual, finishing his letter, lit up one of those flat type of Egyptian cigarettes. 'Well, Fowle,' he said . . .

MORGENHALL. Yes, yes. It's not necessary, Fowle, to reproduce every word of this conversation. Give us the gist, just the meat, you understand. Leave out the trimmings.

FOWLE. Trimmings there weren't. He put it quite bluntly.

MORGENHALL. What did he put ?

FOWLE. 'Well, Fowle, this may surprise you.' (*He rises and crosses to* MORGENHALL). 'But the Home Office was on the phone about you this morning, and . . .' Isn't that a government department ?

MORGENHALL. Yes, yes. And well . . . ?

FOWLE. It seems they do, in his words, come through from time to time, and just on business, of course, on that blower. And quite frankly, he admitted he was as shocked as I was. But the drill is, as he phrased it, a reprieve.

MORGENHALL. A . . . ?

FOWLE. It's all over. I'm free.

MORGENHALL. Free?

FOWLE. It seems that trial was no good at all.

MORGENHALL. No good. But why?

FOWLE (*crossing to* R.). Oh, no particular reason.

MORGENHALL (*rising and crossing to* FOWLE). There must be a reason. Nothing happens in the law without a reason.

FOWLE. You won't care to know.

MORGENHALL. Tell me.

FOWLE. You're too busy to wait.

MORGENHALL. Tell me, Mr. Fowle, why this governor, who knows nothing of the law, should have called our one and only trial together 'no good'.

FOWLE. You yourself taught me not to scatter information like bombs.

MORGENHALL. Mr. Fowle, you must answer my question. My legal career may depend on it. If I'm not to have wasted my life on useless trials.

FOWLE. You want to hear?

MORGENHALL. Certainly.

FOWLE. He may not have been serious. (*He moves above the chair.*) There was a twinkle, most likely, in his eye.

MORGENHALL. But he said . . .

FOWLE. That the barrister they chose for me was no good. 'An old crock,' in his words. No good at all. That he never said a word in my defence. So my case never got to the jury. He said the whole business was ever so null and void, but I'd better be careful in the future. (*He moves to* MORGENHALL.) Don't you see? If I'd had a barrister who asked questions and made clever speeches I'd be as dead as mutton. Your artfulness saved me.

MORGENHALL. My . . .

FOWLE. The artful way you handled it. The dumb tactics. They paid off! I'm alive!

MORGENHALL. There is that . . .

FOWLE. And so are you.

MORGENHALL. We both are . . . ?

FOWLE. I'm free.

MORGENHALL. To go back to your birds. (*He moves up* L.C., *then returns to* L. *of* FOWLE). I suppose . . .

FOWLE. Yes, Mr. Morgenhall?

MORGENHALL. It's unlikely you'll marry again?

FOWLE. Unlikely.

> [*There is a pause.* MORGENHALL *crosses above* FOWLE *to the chair and moves it down* R.

MORGENHALL. But you have the clear appearance of a criminal. I suppose it's not impossible, that you might commit some rather more trivial offence.

FOWLE. A man can't live, Mr. Morgenhall, without committing some trivial offences. Almost daily.

MORGENHALL. Then we may meet again. You may need my services . . .

FOWLE. Constantly.

MORGENHALL. The future may not be so black . . .

FOWLE. The sun's shining.

> [MORGENHALL *turns to the window, then turns again to* FOWLE.

MORGENHALL. Can we go?

FOWLE (*moving to the door*). I think the door's been open some time.

> [MORGENHALL *follows* FOWLE *to the door.* FOWLE *tries the door. It is unbolted and swings open.*

After you, Mr. Morgenhall, please.

MORGENHALL. No, no.

FOWLE. A man of your education should go first.

MORGENHALL. I think you should lead the way, Mr. Fowle, and as your legal adviser I will follow, at a discreet distance, to iron out such little tangles as you may hope to leave in your wake. Let's go.

> [MORGENHALL *whistles his fragment of tune.* FOWLE *joins in. Whistling, they leave the cell.* MORGENHALL *executing, as he leaves, the steps of a small, delighted dance.*

SLOW CURTAIN

# LORD BYRON'S LOVE LETTER
## by Tennessee Williams

# CHARACTERS

THE SPINSTER

THE OLD WOMAN

THE MATRON

THE HUSBAND

# LORD BYRON'S LOVE LETTER

SCENE—*The parlour of a faded old residence in the French Quarter of New Orleans in the late nineteenth century.*

*The shuttered doors of the room open directly upon the side-walk and the noise of the Mardi Gras festivities can be faintly distinguished. The interior is very dusky. Beside a rose-shaded lamp, the* SPINSTER, *a woman of forty, is sewing. In the opposite corner, completely motionless, the* OLD WOMAN *sits in a black silk dress. The doorbell tinkles.*

SPINSTER (*rising*). It's probably someone coming to look at the letter.

OLD WOMAN (*rising on her cane*). Give me time to get out. (*She withdraws gradually behind the curtains. One of her claw-like hands remains visible, holding a curtain slightly open so that she can watch the visitors. The* SPINSTER *opens the door and the* MATRON, *a middle-aged woman, walks into the room.*)

SPINSTER. Won't you come in?

MATRON. Thank you.

SPINSTER. You're from out of town?

MATRON. Oh, yes, we're all the way from Milwaukee. We've come for Mardi Gras, my husband and I. (*She suddenly notices a stuffed canary in its tiny pink and ivory cage.*) Oh, this poor little bird in such a tiny cage! It's much too small to keep a canary in!

SPINSTER. It isn't a live canary.

OLD WOMAN (*from behind the curtain*). No. It's stuffed.

MATRON. Oh. (*She self-consciously touches a stuffed bird on her hat.*) Winston is out there dilly-dallying on the street, afraid he'll miss the parade. The parade comes by here, don't it?

SPINSTER. Yes, unfortunately it does.

MATRON. I noticed your sign at the door. Is it true that you have one of Lord Byron's love letters?

SPINSTER. Yes.

MATRON. How very interesting! How did you get it?

SPINSTER. It was written to my grandmother, Irénée Marguerite de Poitevent.

MATRON. How very interesting! Where did she meet Lord Byron?

SPINSTER. On the steps of the Acropolis in Athens.

MATRON. How very, *very* interesting! I didn't know that Lord Byron was ever in Greece.

SPINSTER. Lord Byron spent the final years of his turbulent life in Greece.

OLD WOMAN (*still behind the curtains*). He was exiled from England!

SPINSTER. Yes, he went into voluntary exile from England.

OLD WOMAN. Because of scandalous gossip in the Regent's court.

SPINSTER. Yes, involving his half-sister!

OLD WOMAN. It was false—completely.

SPINSTER. It was never confirmed.

OLD WOMAN. He was a passionate man but not an evil man.

SPINSTER. Morals are such ambiguous matters, I think.

MATRON. Won't the lady behind the curtains come in?

SPINSTER. You'll have to excuse her. She prefers to stay out.

MATRON (*stiffly*). Oh, I see. What was Lord Byron doing in Greece, may I ask?

OLD WOMAN (*proudly*). *Fighting for Freedom!*

SPINSTER. Yes, Lord Byron went to Greece to join the forces that fought against the infidels.

OLD WOMAN. He gave his life in defence of the universal cause of freedom!

MATRON. What was that, did she say?

SPINSTER (*repeating automatically*). He gave his life in defence of the universal cause of freedom.

MATRON. Oh, how very interesting!

OLD WOMAN. Also he swam the Hellespont.

SPINSTER. Yes.

OLD WOMAN. And burned the body of the poet Shelley who was drowned in a storm on the Mediterranean with a volume of Keats in his pocket!

MATRON (*incredulously*). Pardon?

SPINSTER (*repeating*). And burned the body of the poet Shelley who was drowned in a storm on the Mediterranean with a volume of Keats in his pocket.

MATRON. Oh. How very, very interesting! Indeed, I'd like so much to have my husband hear it. Do you mind if I just step out for a moment to call him in?

SPINSTER. Please do. (*The* MATRON *steps out quickly, calling, 'Winston! Winston!'*)

OLD WOMAN (*poking her head out for a moment*). Watch them carefully! Keep a sharp eye on them!

SPINSTER. Yes. Be still. (*The* MATRON *returns with her husband who has been drinking and wears a paper cap sprinkled with confetti.*)

MATRON. Winston, remove that cap. Sit down on the sofa. These ladies are going to show us Lord Byron's love letter.

SPINSTER. Shall I proceed?

MATRON. Oh, yes. This—uh—is my husband—Mr. Tutwiler.

SPINSTER (*coldly*). How do you do.

MATRON. I am *Mrs.* Tutwiler.

SPINSTER. Of course. Please keep your seat.

MATRON (*nervously*). He's been—celebrating a little.

OLD WOMAN (*shaking the curtain that conceals her*). Ask him please to be careful with his cigar.

SPINSTER. Oh, that's all right, you may use this bowl for your ashes.

OLD WOMAN. Smoking is such an unnecessary habit!

HUSBAND. Uh!

MATRON. This lady was telling us how her Grandmother happened to meet Lord Byron. In Italy, wasn't it?

SPINSTER. No.

OLD WOMAN (*firmly*). In Greece, in Athens, on the steps of the Acropolis! We've mentioned that *twice*, I believe. Ariadne, you may read them a passage from the journal first.

SPINSTER. Yes.

OLD WOMAN. But please be careful what you choose to read! (*The* SPINSTER *has removed from the secretary a volume wrapped in tissue and tied with ribbon.*)

SPINSTER. Like many other young American girls of that day and this, my Grandmother went to Europe.

OLD WOMAN. The year before she was going to be presented to society!

MATRON. How old was she?

OLD WOMAN. Sixteen! Barely sixteen! She was very beautiful, too! Please show her the picture, show these people the picture! It's in the front of the journal. (*The* SPINSTER *removes the picture from the book and hands it to the* MATRON.)

MATRON (*taking a look*). What a lovely young girl. (*Passing it to her* HUSBAND.) Don't you think it resembles Agnes a little?

HUSBAND. Uh!

OLD WOMAN. Watch out! Ariadne, you'll have to *watch* that man. I believe he's been drinking. I *do* believe that he's been——

HUSBAND (*truculently*). Yeah ? What is she saying back there ?

MATRON (*touching his arm warningly*). Winston! Be *quiet*.

HUSBAND. Uh.

SPINSTER (*quickly*). Near the end of her tour, my Grandmother and her Aunt went to Greece, to study the classic remains of the oldest civilization.

OLD WOMAN (*correcting*). The oldest *European* civilization.

SPINSTER. It was an early morning in April of the year eighteen hundred and——

OLD WOMAN. Twenty-seven!

SPINSTER. Yes. In my Grandmother's journal she mentions——

OLD WOMAN. Read it, read it, *read* it.

MATRON. Yes, *please* read it to us.

SPINSTER. I'm trying to find the place, if you'll just be patient.

MATRON. Certainly, excuse me. (*She punches her* HUSBAND *who is nodding.*) Winston!

SPINSTER. Ah, here it is.

OLD WOMAN. Be *careful*! Remember where to *stop* at, Ariadne!

SPINSTER. Shhh! (*She adjusts her glasses and seats herself by the lamp.*) 'We set out early that morning to inspect the ruins of the Acropolis. I know I shall never forget how extraordinarily pure the atmosphere was that morning. It seemed as though the world were not very old, but very, very young, almost as though the world had been newly created. There was a taste of earliness in the air, a feeling of freshness, exhilarating my senses, exalting my spirit. How shall I tell you, dear Diary, the way the sky looked ? It was almost as though I had moistened the tip of my pen in a shallow bowl full of milk, so delicate was the blue in the dome of the heavens. The sun was barely up yet, a tentative breeze disturbed the ends of my scarf, the

17

plumes of the marvellous hat which I had bought in Paris and thrilled me with pride whenever I saw them reflected! The papers that morning, we read them over our coffee before we left the hotel, had spoken of possible war, but it seemed unlikely, unreal: nothing was real, indeed, but the spell of golden antiquity and rose-coloured romance that breathed from this fabulous city.'

OLD WOMAN. Skip that part! Get on to where she meets him!

SPINSTER. Yes. . . . (*She turns several pages and continues.*) 'Out of the tongues of ancients, the lyrical voices of many long-ago poets who dreamed of the world of ideals, who had in their hearts the pure and absolute image——'

OLD WOMAN. *Skip* that part! Slip down to where——

SPINSTER. Yes! *Here! Do* let us manage without any more *interruptions*! 'The carriage came to a halt at the foot of the hill and my Aunt, not being too well——'

OLD WOMAN. She had a sore throat that morning.

SPINSTER. '——preferred to remain with the driver while I undertook the rather steep climb on foot. As I ascended the long and crumbling flight of old stone steps——'

OLD WOMAN. Yes, yes, that's the place! (*The* SPINSTER *looks up in annoyance. The* OLD WOMAN'S *cane taps impatiently behind the curtains.*) Go *on*, Ariadne!

SPINSTER. 'I could not help observing continually above me a man who walked with a barely perceptible limp——'

OLD WOMAN (*in hushed wonder*). Yes—Lord Byron!

SPINSTER. '——and as he turned now and then to observe beneath him the lovely panorama——'

OLD WOMAN. Actually he was watching the girl behind him!

SPINSTER (*sharply*). Will you *please* let me finish! (*There is no answer from behind the curtains, and she continues to read.*) 'I was irresistibly impressed by the unusual nobility and refinement of his features!' (*She turns a page.*)

OLD WOMAN. The handsomest man that ever walked the earth! (*She emphasizes the speech with three slow but loud taps of her cane.*)

SPINSTER (*flurriedly*). 'The strength and grace of his throat, like that of a statue, the classic outlines of his profile, the sensitive lips and the slightly dilated nostrils, the dark lock of hair that fell down over his forehead in such a way that——'

OLD WOMAN (*tapping her cane rapidly*). Skip that, it goes on for pages!

SPINSTER. '. . . When he had reached the very summit of the Acropolis he spread out his arms in a great, magnificent gesture like a young god. Now, thought I to myself, Apollo has come to earth in modern dress.'

OLD WOMAN. Go on, skip that, get on to where she *meets* him!

SPINSTER. 'Fearing to interrupt his poetic trance, I slackened my pace and pretended to watch the view. I kept my look thus carefully averted until the narrowness of the steps compelled me to move close by him.'

OLD WOMAN. Of course he pretended not to see she was coming!

SPINSTER. 'Then finally I faced him.'

OLD WOMAN. Yes!

SPINSTER. 'Our eyes came together!'

OLD WOMAN. Yes! Yes! That's the part!

SPINSTER. 'A thing which I don't understand had occurred between us, a flush as of recognition swept through my whole being! Suffused my——'

OLD WOMAN. Yes . . . Yes, that's the part!

SPINSTER. ' "Pardon me," he exclaimed, "you have dropped your glove!" And indeed to my surprise I found that I had, and as he returned it to me, his fingers ever so slightly pressed the cups of my palm.'

OLD WOMAN (*hoarsely*). *Yes!* (*Her bony fingers clutch higher up on the curtain, the other hand also appears, slightly widening the aperture.*)

SPINSTER. 'Believe me, dear Diary, I became quite faint and breathless, I almost wondered if I could continue my lonely walk through the ruins. Perhaps I stumbled, perhaps I swayed a little. I leaned for a moment against the side of a column. The sun seemed terribly brilliant, it hurt my eyes. Close behind me I heard that voice again, almost it seemed I could feel his breath on my——'

OLD WOMAN. Stop *there*! That will be quite enough! (*The* SPINSTER *closes the journal.*)

MATRON. Oh, is that all?

OLD WOMAN. There's a great deal more that's not to be read to people.

MATRON. Oh.

SPINSTER. I'm sorry. I'll show you the letter.

MATRON. How nice! I'm dying to see it! Winston? *Do* sit *up*! (*He has nearly fallen asleep. The* SPINSTER *produces from the cabinet another small packet which she unfolds. It contains the letter. She hands it to the* MATRON, *who starts to open it.*)

OLD WOMAN. Watch out, watch *out*, that woman can't *open* the letter!

SPINSTER. No, no, please, you mustn't. The contents of the letter are strictly private. I'll hold it over here at a little distance so you can see the writing.

OLD WOMAN. Not too close, she's holding up her glasses! (*The* MATRON *quickly lowers her lorgnette.*)

SPINSTER. Only a short while later Byron was killed.

MATRON. How did he die?

OLD WOMAN. He was killed in action, defending the cause of freedom! (*This is uttered so strongly the* HUSBAND *starts.*)

SPINSTER. When my Grandmother received the news of Lord

Byron's death in battle, she retired from the world and remained in complete seclusion for the rest of her life.

MATRON. Tch-tch-tch! How dreadful! I think that was foolish of her. (*The cane taps furiously behind the curtains*).

SPINSTER. You don't understand. When a life is completed, it ought to be put away. It's like a sonnet. When you've written the final couplet, why go on any further? You only destroy the part that's already written!

OLD WOMAN. Read them the poem, the sonnet your Grand-mother wrote to the memory of Lord Byron.

SPINSTER. Would you be interested?

MATRON. We'd adore it—truly!

SPINSTER. It's called *Enchantment*.

MATRON (*she assumes a rapt expression*). *Aahhh!*

SPINSTER (*reciting*).

'*Un saison enchanté!* I mused, Beguiled
Seemed Time herself, her erstwhile errant ways
Briefly forgotten, she stayed here and smiled,
Caught in a net of blue and golden days.'

OLD WOMAN. Not blue and golden—gold and *azure* days!

SPINSTER.

'Caught in a net—of gold and azure days!

But I lacked wit to see how lightly shoon
Were Time and you, to vagrancy so used——'

[*The* OLD WOMAN *begins to accompany in a hoarse under-tone. Faint band music can be heard.*

'That by the touch of one October moon
From summer's tranquil spell you might be loosed!'

OLD WOMAN (*rising stridently with intense feeling above the* SPINSTER'S *voice*).

'Think you love is writ on my soul with chalk,
To be washed off by a few parting tears?

Then you know not with what slow step I walk
The barren way of those hibernal years—

My life a vanished interlude, a shell
Whose walls are your first kiss—and last farewell!'

[*The band, leading the parade, has started down the street,
growing rapidly louder. It passes by like the heedless, turbulent years. The* HUSBAND, *roused from his stupor,
lunges to the door.*

MATRON. What's that, what's that? The *parade*? (*The* HUS-
BAND *slaps the paper cap on his head and rushes for the
door.*)

HUSBAND (*at the door*). Come on, Mama, you'll miss it!

SPINSTER (*quickly*). We usually accept—you understand?—
a small sum of money, just anything that you happen to
think you can spare.

OLD WOMAN. Stop him! He's gone outside! (*The* HUSBAND
*has escaped to the street. The band blares through the door.*)

SPINSTER (*extending her hand*). Please—a dollar . . .

OLD WOMAN. *Fifty cents!*

SPINSTER. Or a *quarter!*

MATRON (*paying no attention to them*). Oh, my goodness—
*Winston!* He's *disappeared* in the crowd! Winston—
*Winston! Excuse* me! (*She rushes out onto the door sill.*)
*Winston!* Oh, my goodness gracious, he's off again!

SPINSTER (*quickly*). We usually accept a little money for the
display of the letter. Whatever you feel that you are able
to give. As a matter of fact it's all that we have to *live* on!

OLD WOMAN (*loudly*). One dollar!

SPINSTER. Fifty cents—or a quarter!

MATRON (*oblivious, at the door*). Winston! *Winston!* Heavenly
days. *Good-bye!* (*She rushes out on the street. The* SPINSTER
*follows to the door, and shields her eyes from the light as she*

*looks after the* MATRON. *A stream of confetti is tossed through the doorway into her face. Trumpets blare. She slams the door shut and bolts it.*)

SPINSTER. *Canaille! . . . Canaille!*

OLD WOMAN. Gone? Without paying? *Cheated* us? (*She parts the curtains.*)

SPINSTER. *Yes*—the *canaille*! (*She fastidiously plucks the thread of confetti from her shoulder. The* OLD WOMAN *steps from behind the curtains, rigid with anger.*)

OLD WOMAN. Ariadne, my letter! You've dropped my letter! Your Grandfather's letter is lying on the floor!

CURTAIN

# BIOGRAPHICAL NOTES

TERENCE RATTIGAN, C.B.E., dramatic author, born in London, 10 June, 1911, was educated at Harrow and Trinity College, Oxford. He is the author of *First Episode*, 1934; *French Without Tears*, 1936, which ran for over a thousand performances; *After the Dance*, 1939; *Follow My Leader* (with Anthony Maurice), 1940; *Grey Farm* (with Hector Bolitho), 1940; *Flare Path*, 1942, which ran for 670 performances; *While the Sun Shines*, 1943, which ran for 1,154 performances; *Love in Idleness*, 1944; *The Winslow Boy*, 1946; the last-named play received the Ellen Terry award for the best play produced on the London stage during 1946, and the following year won the New York Critics' award for the best foreign play produced in New York during 1947; *Playbill* (*The Browning Version* and *Harlequinade*), 1948; *Adventure Story*, 1949; *Who is Sylvia?*, 1950; *The Deep Blue Sea*, 1952; *The Sleeping Prince*, 1953; *Separate Tables*, 1954; *Variation on a Theme*, 1958; *Ross*, 1960. He is the only author who has written two plays which have exceeded 1,000 consecutive performances. During the 1939–45 War he served in the R.A.F. as an air-gunner.

CHRISTOPHER FRY, dramatic author, born in Bristol, 18 December, 1907. After six months as a schoolmaster he joined a repertory company, as an actor, at Bath; returned to his scholastic career for three years, then again returned to the stage and was for two years a member of a repertory company at Tunbridge Wells. His play *The Boy With a Cart* was produced in 1938; *The Tower* was produced at the Tewkesbury Festival, 1939. He wrote several plays for the

BBC Children's Hour, 1939–40; was producer at the Oxford Playhouse, 1940; served with the Pioneer Corps, 1940–4; and returned to the Oxford Playhouse in 1944, remaining as producer until 1946. Author of *A Phoenix Too Frequent*, Mercury, 1946; *The Lady's Not for Burning*, Arts, 1948; *Thor With Angels*, Canterbury Festival, 1948; *The Firstborn*, Edinburgh Festival, 1948; *Venus Observed*, St. James's, 1950; translated *Ring Round the Moon* (from the French of Jean Anouilh), Globe, 1950; author of *A Sleep of Prisoners*, St. Thomas's Church, Regent Street, 1950; *The Dark is Light Enough*, Aldwych, 1954; *The Lark* (translated from the French of Anouilh), Lyric, Hammersmith, 1955; *Tiger at the Gates* (translated from the French of Giraudoux), Apollo, 1955; *Duel of Angels* (translated from the French of Giraudoux), Apollo, 1958.

WOLF MANKOWITZ, novelist, playwright, journalist, film and television scriptwriter; born 7 November, 1924. Educated at East Ham Grammar School and Downing College, Cambridge (M.A.). After working for a short time as an extra-mural lecturer, he became an antique dealer, specializing in antique Wedgwood, on which he has written standard works of reference. Has contributed poetry and articles of literary and theatre criticism to numerous newspapers and magazines, and has edited two literary magazines. He went into theatrical production with Oscar Lewenstein in 1955, dissolving this partnership to start his own theatrical company in 1960. His books include *Make Me An Offer*, which was filmed in 1954, and presented as a musical play at the Theatre Royal, Stratford, 1959, and transferred to the West End; *A Kid for Two Farthings*, filmed in 1954. Author of the following plays, *The Bespoke Overcoat*, Arts Theatre, 1953 (filmed 1955); *Expresso Bongo*, Saville, 1958 (filmed 1959); *Five One-Act Plays*, 1955.

GORDON DAVIOT, dramatic author and novelist (*née* Elizabeth Mackintosh); born in Inverness, Scotland, daughter of Colin Mackintosh and his wife Josephine (Horne); educated at the Royal Academy, Inverness, and Anstey Physical Training College, Birmingham; was at one time a physical training instructress; wrote the following plays: *Richard of Bordeaux*, Arts, June 1932, and New Theatre, 1933, when the play ran for a year; *The Laughing Woman*, 1934; *Queen of Scots*, 1934: author of the novels *Kif*, *The Expensive Halo*, *The Man in the Queue*; a biography *Claverhouse*, 1937; *The Stars Bow Down*, play published in 1938, and a collection of one-act plays, 1945, etc. Also a short story writer. Died 13 February, 1952, at the age of 55.

J. B. PRIESTLEY, M.A., LL.D., D.Litt., dramatic author, novelist and essayist; born in Bradford, 13 September, 1894, and educated at Bradford and Trinity Hall, Cambridge (M.A.). He was a schoolmaster for a short time; served with the Duke of Wellington's and Devon Regiments (1914–19); and began his career as a writer, while still at Cambridge, with *Brief Diversions*. Author of the following plays: *The Good Companions* (with Edward Knoblock), 1931; *The Roundabout, Dangerous Corner*, 1932; *Laburnum Grove*, 1933; *Eden End*, 1934; *Duet in Floodlight, Cornelius*, 1935; *Bees on the Boatdeck*, 1936; *Time and the Conways, I Have Been Here Before, I'm a Stranger Here, Mystery at Greenfingers, People at Sea*, 1937; *Music at Night, When We Are Married*, 1938; *Johnson Over Jordan*, 1939. He has since written, among other plays, *The Long Mirror*, 1940; *They Came to a City*, 1943; *An Inspector Calls*, 1945; *The Linden Tree*, 1947; *Home is Tomorrow*, 1948; *Mr. Kettle and Mrs. Moon*, 1955; *The Glass Cage*, 1958. Has also written several screen plays and many successful novels and volumes of essays and autobiography.

SUSAN GLASPELL, dramatic author and novelist; born in Davenport, Iowa, 1 July, 1882. Educated at Drake University, Iowa, and University of Chicago. At one time engaged as political reporter on newspapers, and contributed short stories to several magazines. Wrote the following among other plays: *Woman's Honor, The Outside, The People, Tickless Time, Trifles,* 1916; *Close the Book,* 1918; *Bernice,* 1920; *Inheritors,* 1921; *The Verge,* 1921; *Chains of Dew,* 1922; *Alison's House,* 1930, which gained the Pulitzer prize, 1930–31. Author of a number of novels and of *The Road to the Temple,* a biography of her husband, George Cram Cook. Died 27 July, 1948.

JOHN MORTIMER, born in 1923, was educated at Harrow and Oxford University. After working as an assistant director and then as a scriptwriter in the Crown Film Unit, he became a barrister in 1948. He has written six novels, and plays for the stage, radio and television, He is married to Penelope Mortimer, novelist and critic, and lives in London. His one-act plays include a collection *Lunch-Hour* (containing *Call Me A Liar, Dock Brief, David and Broccalli, Collect Your Hand-baggage* and *Lunch-hour*); *What Shall We Tell Caroline, I Spy*; and *From One to Another.* His first full-length play *The Wrong Side of the Park* was produced in London in 1960.

TENNESSEE WILLIAMS, dramatic author; born in Columbus, Missouri, U.S.A., 26 March, 1914. Educated at High School, St. Louis, and Universities of Missouri, Washington and Indiana (B.A.). His earlier plays were in one act and four were produced in 1939, under the title *American Blues.* His full-length plays are: *The Battle of the Angels,* Boston, 1940; *The Glass Menagerie,* Chicago, 1944, and New York, 1945; *You Touched Me,* 1945; *A Streetcar Named Desire,* 1947; *Summer and Smoke,* 1948; *The Rose Tattoo,* 1950; *Camino*

*Real*, 1953; *Cat On a Hot Tin Roof*, 1955. *The Glass Menagerie* gained the New York Drama Critics' Circle Award 1944–5, and *A Streetcar Named Desire* gained both the Drama Critics' Circle Award and the Pulitzer Prize 1947–8; *Cat On a Hot Tin Roof* also gained the same two awards in 1955. Tennessee Williams has written the screen plays for *The Glass Menagerie*, *A Streetcar Named Desire*, *The Rose Tattoo*, and *Baby Doll* (1957).

# THE ENGLISH ASSOCIATION

(Founded 1906)

*President 1961/62*

### Sir Kenneth Clark, c.h., k.c.b.

*Chairman of Committee*—D. M. Low, m.a., f.r.s.l.

The object of the English Association is to promote the knowledge and appreciation of English Language and English Literature, and to uphold the standards of English writing and speech.

The Association pursues these aims by affording opportunities of co-operation amongst all those interested in English; by furthering the recognition of English as essential in education; by discussing methods of English teaching; by holding lectures, conferences, and other meetings; by publishing a journal, books, and leaflets; and by forming local branches both at home and overseas.

A leaflet with further information and a form of application for membership may be obtained from the Secretary.

## SUBSCRIPTIONS

The financial year runs from 1st January to 31st December, and an ordinary sub-scription paid at any time during the year entitles a member to the Association's magazine ENGLISH (three issues) and the Presidential Address.

The annual subscription to the Central Body is £1 1s., or, with *Essays and Studies* (New Series) and *The Year's Work in English Studies*, £2 2s., and is due on the 1st January.

Life Membership (which does not cover the two special publications *Essays and Studies* and *The Year's Work in English Studies*) is £15 15s.

The annual subscription of branch members is fixed within certain limits by the branch.

CORPORATE membership (£1 1s. or £2 2s.) is open to Colleges, Schools and Libraries and additional publications can be purchased at the reduced rate.

STUDENT membership is open on special terms to students up to the age of 23 who are interested in English Language and Literature.

Subscriptions should be sent to the Secretary, 8 Cromwell Place, London, S.W.7. (Cheques, etc., should be made in favour of the English Association.)

*The Headquarters of the Association are*
8 CROMWELL PLACE, LONDON, S.W.7.
(*Telephone:* KENSINGTON 8480)

*Organising Officer:* Mr. E. WYNNE HICKIE

*Secretary:* Mrs. E. M. FIELDING
*Auditors:* Messrs. P. D. LEAKE & Co., 84 Queen Victoria Street, E.C.4.
*Bankers:* BARCLAYS BANK Ltd., 95 Victoria Street, Westminster, S.W.1.

PRINTED IN GREAT BRITAIN
BY EBENEZER BAYLIS AND SON, LTD.
THE TRINITY PRESS, WORCESTER, AND LONDON